THE TALK AND TEXTS OF TEACHER DEVELOPMENT

The Talk and Texts of Teacher Development

Values, the Practicum, and Programmatic Change in Writing Studies

ADRIENNE JANKENS

UTAH STATE UNIVERSITY PRESS
Logan

© 2026 by University Press of Colorado

Published by Utah State University Press
An imprint of University Press of Colorado
1580 North Logan Street, Suite 660
PMB 39883
Denver, Colorado 80203-1942

All rights reserved

 The University Press of Colorado is a proud member of
Association of University Presses.

The University Press of Colorado is a cooperative publishing enterprise supported, in part, by Adams State University, Colorado School of Mines, Colorado State University, Fort Lewis College, Metropolitan State University of Denver, University of Alaska Fairbanks, University of Colorado, University of Denver, University of Northern Colorado, University of Wyoming, Utah State University, and Western Colorado University.

ISBN: 978-1-64642-786-4 (hardcover)
ISBN: 978-1-64642-788-8 (paperback)
ISBN: 978-1-64642-789-5 (ebook)
https://doi.org/10.7330/9781646427895

Library of Congress Cataloging-in-Publication Data

Cataloging-in-Publication data for this title is available online at the Library of Congress

Cover art: © Shutterstock/Ilya Bolotov

Contents

List of Illustrations   vii

Acknowledgments   ix

Introduction   3

1. Looking Back (and) to the Future: Reading Inside My Home Program   32
2. Finding Values in the Practicum Syllabus in Interviews with WPAs and Practicum Instructors   62
3. Getting to Slow Agency via Slowing Conversation in Curricular Committee Work   97
4. "But Here We Are!" Still Learning How to Teach About Language: The Practicum, a Revised Curriculum, and the Pandemic   138
5. Between Mission and Action: Restructuring Programmatic Change Through Teacher Development   183

Appendix: Semi-Structured Interview Protocol (excerpt): Interviews with WPAs and Practicum Instructors   213

Notes   215

References   217

Index   231

About the Author   243

Illustrations

Boxes

0.1. Categories of writing program values   11
1.1. Categories of readings assigned in Practicum I, 2015–2019   48
1.2. Emergent values for teacher development in rhetoric, composition, and writing studies   55
2.1. Participants' identified program values (alphabetical order)   73
2.2. Emergent values for teacher development in rhetoric, composition, and writing studies   88
3.1. Emergent values for teacher development in rhetoric, composition, and writing studies   127

Tables

1.1. Practicum I and II Calendar, 2014–2021   37
2.1. Interview participants   71
2.2. Presence of emergent values in ten practicum syllabi   89
3.1. Coding for knowledge domains   112
3.2. Experiential evidence offered in the second curricular subcommittee meeting   122

Acknowledgments

In 2006, when I was exploring doctoral programs, I wrote to the graduate director at Wayne State to introduce myself, indicating my interest in studying the preparation of teachers of writing. "We don't do that here," the director responded. After many years doing that very work at Wayne, I am happy to say it is one of the things we do best.

As I complete the journey of writing this research story, I am especially grateful for the encouragement of my colleagues and friends. Thank you to Ellen Barton for helping me identify the initial study in this project after much inventive laboring and for remarking on my resilience. Thank you to Caroline Maun for unending encouragement and professional advice and to Jeff Pruchnic, who provided access to materials and feedback on grant applications during early stages of the project. Nicole Guinot Varty, thank you for serving in the role of my favorite reader for this project (and writing partner for so many other projects). Kristi Morris, thank you for working with me through all my interviewing nerves and logistical troubleshooting and for being a supportive force. And Chris Susak, thank you for reminding me I can do more than I sometimes think and for keeping the boat steady while I work through how to manage all these professional adventures.

Thank you to the participants in the studies presented across this book, for sharing your voices and experiences so that I could tell this story. Thank you to the interview and classroom study participants who read initial chapter drafts and provided me with feedback to help shape those chapters. I am also grateful for the insightful feedback of the reviewers; your commentary was integral in helping me reinforce the core argument of the book.

My deep appreciation goes to Rachael Levay for initial encouragement as I pursued publication and to Skylar Cooper from Utah State University Press for working with me through getting the manuscript to publication. I am grateful to the staff at Utah State University Press for their enthusiastic communication and excellent work. Funds for data collection, research assistance, and writing time for the interview study were provided through a University Research Grant awarded by the Wayne State University Provost's Office. The WSU English Department's Josephine Nevins Keal Faculty Fellowship provided summer salary support for writing. Together, the WSU English Department, the Wayne State University College of Liberal Arts and Sciences, and the Wayne State University Division of Research Innovation provided funds to support the physical publication of the book.

For my parents, Jim and Jan Baker, constant supporters and cheerleaders: you have helped me make this teaching and writing life a possibility. And to Jordan, Kari, Logan, and Moses, I love you and am so blessed to be your mom. Thank you for giving me the space to work, energy for adventure, hugs for celebration, and copious laughs during tough times.

The Talk and Texts of Teacher Development

Introduction

For the first ten years I taught college-level composition classes (whether they were senior-level high school composition, AP courses, dual enrollment, at community colleges, or at universities), I did it without thinking much (*almost not at all*) about Composition as a *discipline*. I employed what innately made sense as a process pedagogy—largely the process pedagogy I had experienced as a high school and college student—along the way working with inquiry-based learning and Brian Cambourne's conditions for learning (a literacy learning framework introduced to me by my master's program mentor at Central Michigan University, John Dinan). Meaningful and rich, though not necessarily shared by the other teachers I worked with in these settings, these frameworks drove my design of lesson plans, units, and projects. Each year, I worked to be an ever-better teacher of writing and even did a couple of early-career conference presentations on using multi-genre projects in my English language arts (ELA) classes. But even as a licensed English educator, I did not think of myself as a member of any discipline. I was called to my work, engaged in my vocation of teaching high school. When I eventually enrolled in my PhD program in English, rhetoric and composition, it was with an aim to expand my *teaching*—the kind of scholar I would become still had to be developed.

This is important for me to express because it demonstrates one example of how recognition of disciplinary participation and disciplinary values, and what it means to be a compositionist or a scholar in writing studies, might come at various points, or in various ways, to those who *teach* composition courses. For some, this recognition might never come or might be a matter of writing studies being *for them, not me*. For some, it might come with a deep sense of belonging: *This work makes sense to me; it's what I love to do*. For some, this recognition might be a fraught one, as the tensions exercised at the level of disciplinary scholarship reflect personal concerns, experiences, or questions. For me, this participation felt like it came when, as a graduate student, I was invited to join an assessment committee in my program, to bring my experiences and knowledge to the table of programmatic work. In the committee's deep reading of students' reflective writing, long inquiry-based discussions, and efforts to create a feedback loop for instruction, I observed potential (and tacit) program values at play, and I began to have a voice in what our program's good work with students might look like.

Teaching composition courses and participating in the work of writing studies more broadly are about more than writing lesson plans and reading student papers, but what that *more* is is typically discovered and experienced along the way, as teachers participate in conference gatherings; as graduate students take coursework and engage in professional development; and as members of writing programs work to design, assess, and research writing, writing courses, and students' learning. For graduate students who are employed by programs to teach in support of their master's and doctoral work, the initiating vehicle for this teaching journey is often the composition teaching practicum, the course taken prior to or concurrently with graduate teaching assistants' (GTAs') first instructional assignments in a program. And it is in this course where GTAs may not only develop the subject matter knowledge of the discipline but also become initiated into local knowledges that shape the work that they do in their composition classrooms. Catherine Latterell (1996) notes the historical significance of the course, explaining that in the first half of the twentieth century, pedagogy workshops or courses were "often the only graduate-level composition courses offered in many English departments" (7). According to Sidney I. Dobrin (2005), the teaching practicum is, therefore, an enculturation "into the cultural ideologies of composition" (21). It is an integral tool for the composition program to sustain the first-year writing (FYW) course's institutional position (Addison 2005, 257) and a "site of articulation" that prepares instructors for the work they will do in a specific program

(Guerra and Bawarshi 2005, 54). When I was invited to teach one of my program's practicum courses two years after earning my PhD and sixteen years into teaching writing, I felt like I finally had something to say about what being a teacher in rhetoric, writing studies, or composition really means.[1]

But teaching composition is bottom-up just as much as it is top-down. This is evident in our research methods and methodologies, in our stories of institutional revolutions attempted and won, and in our emphasis on student voices as central to our scholarship. As writing *teachers*, we are always learning. Shari J. Stenberg's (2005) argument that a framework of *teacher development* (instead of *teacher training*) can have a change-making influence on the shape of the field is an intuitive one, and its implications may be more dramatic than we think. It is a framework that both centers this teacher development and implicates all teachers in a program in ongoing reflection and revision of teaching. Our field is grounded in the reality that its disciplinary knowledge is often made in composition classrooms, by students and teachers. A big part of what it means to teach composition in a writing program is learning not only how to roll with programmatic change but how to make changes in one's own classroom that both improve learning in that classroom context and have effects on students' and teachers' experiences in the larger university, community, and world. Therefore, all teachers in a program, including new teachers, can learn to be agents of change, even if it may feel like they are starting small. Their efforts will be especially effective and sustainable if a program has a recognized and explicit structure for this quality of teacher development, if the program has articulated its values for teacher development, and if its personnel are on board.

Defining and Locating Writing Program Values

I became interested in researching writing program values during a long-term mentoring-centered project I worked on with my colleague Joe Torok, which we describe in "Structuration and Genre: Revising Teaching Observations to Reflect Program Values" (Jankens and Torok 2023). As we explain in that article, in part, our investment in revising our program's teaching observation forms to more clearly reflect program values was the result of many office hours spent struggling with the realization that because not all of our colleagues approached conducting teaching observations with the same values in mind, GTAs regularly faced trouble or had difficult affective responses with the observation process; therefore, in administering these observations, I also regularly faced trouble and difficult affective responses from both GTAs and the faculty conducting their observations. Our revision of the teaching observation form, then, emphasized two values for teacher development that we felt were central to making sure everyone was on the same page with the teaching observation process: reciprocal interactions and written reflection (values that overlap with each other). An emphasis on reciprocity means that both those faculty conducting observations and instructors being observed articulate to each other (in writing and/or in conversation) what they learn from the observation experience, and all program personnel are engaged in reflective teacher development, not only those instructors new to a program (see also Denise Comer 2011 on this reciprocity). Written reflection, engaged by the observer in this process, is valued as an integral activity to reflective and reciprocal teacher development. We wrote these values—reciprocal interactions and written reflection—into the form to enact them.

But that rhetorical hack—merely writing them into the documents—didn't "solve" teaching observations in the local context. It has not shifted the textual presence of values deeply into shared programmatic talk. There is more emphasizing to do. The colleague who is now in charge of administering teaching observations in my program marvels at how much participants need reminders about a process that has essentially been the same for a decade. Our local search for program values for teacher development, and for how to *write* these values into the program—how to see them articulated—continues; if we explicitly share and articulate a set of values for this work, I think, it won't be a perfect (writing program) world, but it will be a coordinated one.

Recent discussions of disciplinary values (Adler-Kassner and Wardle 2015; Wardle and Downs 2018; Cole and Hassel 2021) examine not only what these values are but why and how we need to use and articulate them. Values are not always easily articulated or shared by all members of an organization, and they are difficult to research (Espedal et al. 2022, 1–2);[2] in our own field, we continue to work to find language that makes these values explicit. A primary aim of the project presented in this book has been to identify program and potential disciplinary values for teacher development. Through that work, I have found a range of ways of talking about values, both in the scholarship and in my conversations with writing program administrators (WPAs) and practicum instructors; I have also found that values are present in writing program work to varying degrees. Here, I explore a range of ways that values are described and discussed in writing studies scholarship, strategies for bringing values to the surface of writing program work, and a categorization of values from *tacit* to *articulated* that will support my analysis of talk and texts across the book.

In their chapter in Rita Malenczyk, Susan Miller-Cochran, Elizabeth Wardle, and Kathleen Blake Yancey's (2018) *Composition, Rhetoric, and Disciplinarity*, Elizabeth Wardle and Doug Downs address the ways scholars have wrestled with the field's disciplinarity. Through their examination of discourse on disciplinarity, they have identified "a number of *implicit* values and ideologies, exposing a number of our field's central values" (121–122; emphasis mine). Wardle and Downs unearth these implicit values that drive conversation and dissensus about disciplinarity: "inclusion, access, difference, interaction, localism, valuing diverse voices, and textual production" (123). They assert that these "shared values" evidence that we *"have already invented our discipline with these values as grounding principles"* (121; emphasis in original). They argue that these are values our field can build on as a means of "embracing disciplinarity" (129), and posit that, while accepting disciplinarity, we should continue to ask and answer questions about the nature of our disciplinarity, including about values (130). In a way, Wardle and Downs reveal how as we work to identify our "Why?"[3] as a discipline; even when we disagree about aspects of the nature and function of composition or writing studies, we come to understand our values.

We may also understand our values through the lens and function of adjacent frameworks, as we do through Linda Adler-Kassner and Elizabeth Wardle's (2015) discussion of threshold concepts, "concepts critical for continued learning and participation in an area or within a community of practice" (2), a term and concept borrowed from education (Meyer and Land 2006) and employed in research, teaching, and learning across contexts. In her introduction to Adler-Kassner and Wardle's *Naming What We Know*, Kathleen Blake Yancey (2015) describes the variable "use value" of threshold concepts, noting, "In one version [of this use value], threshold concepts function as boundary objects, allowing us to toggle between the beliefs of the discipline and those of individual institutions" (xix). In other words, the articulation of threshold concepts allows the discipline's beliefs or values to come to light and be put into conversation with the values of local writing programs. This note is important because it highlights the shadowiness of the values of the discipline and local writing programs as well as the functional origination of each: Writing programs do not emerge from the nebulous aura of the discipline; they emerge from the working realities of their institutions. This exigence and existence mean that writing program values grow from an in-between space, between institutional context and disciplinary ideal.

Locally, *values* may also be used interchangeably with or in conjunction with discussion of *principles*, as they are in Kelly Ritter's (2018) description of the values of the University of Illinois Urbana-Champaign (UIUC) undergraduate rhetoric program:

> To expand on what our program values—and supplement the shorthand version in the student learning objectives (SLOs)—here are some guiding principles as I would articulate them:
>
> - An academic writing course should focus on guided instruction in creating, developing, and sustaining *exigent arguments based in the principles of rhetoric*.
> - Such a course should also include instruction in *crafting and executing research proposals and projects*, including responsible and meaningful engagement with sources.
> - Lower-order concerns should be taught as needed but *always in the context of* higher-order concerns.
> - *Writing is a process* that involves peers as well as instructors, one-on-one conferences for student and teacher, and individual and group learning opportunities.
> - College writers should be guided toward understanding their work as critical to *present and future participation in the public sphere*. (Ritter 2018, 57; emphases in original)

In Ritter's expression of what the UIUC undergraduate rhetoric program values, we see articulation of values that center on the content and instruction of FYW. These values focus primarily on what students should do and understand in the course. For the purposes of understanding the set of values I seek in this project, I suggest that the relationship to teacher development is found between the lines of these *guiding principles* and *program values*: Teachers should learn how to act as guides, how to be involved in the research and writing process alongside students (57). In our examination of values and our program's teaching observation form, Torok and I report our colleagues similarly expressing the ways teacher development is bound up with student learning outcomes (Jankens and Torok 2023, 82). Reflection, and reflective writing, in our FYW course, is both a tool for developing and transferring writing knowledge and a habit of lifelong learning. So, as Joe and I note, reflection in the teaching observation process is "an important correlate" between graduate-level practicum courses and general education learning outcomes (66), and reflection on undergraduate students' learning is an important part of the reflective practice of teacher development (82; see also Miller et al. 2005, 90). This overlap of principles and values is further emphasized by participants' expression of values in the interviews I present in chapter 2.

So, the language of learning outcomes is an explicit source of information about program values, and other program documents may also implicitly or explicitly convey these values, like Joe and I demonstrate, and like Jennifer Grouling (2018) emphasizes in "Training Writing Teachers: An Assignment in Mapping Writing Program Values." Grouling explains the development of an assignment based on Bob Broad's "Dynamic Criteria Mapping," in which collaborators identify and discuss what they consider significant elements driving their evaluation of a text. In the "Values Mapping Assignment," teaching assistants (TAs) analyze their mentors' teaching materials and interview these mentors, then create visual representations of their findings. Later, they compare maps and tally representation of values to identify "the larger values of the program as a whole" (11). The assignment allows students to move beyond wholesale borrowing of their mentors' assignments, instead designing their own assignments that "fit with the program's goals" (7). In Grouling's employment of the assignment, values are defined broadly as "not only qualities that teachers wanted from writing, but also qualities they wanted from students (e.g., promptness), and course content they valued (e.g., multimodality)" (6). Coding values inductively—allowing them to "emerge organically from the TAs' interpretations"—highlights for Grouling interesting incongruities between which values are explicit and which are clearly expressed in the materials the TAs analyze (12). Grouling writes, "For example, multimodality is required in our first-year writing courses, yet TAs rarely mapped it as a value in their mentors' teaching materials, which could indicate that it is not being well-used in actual courses" (12). Discoveries like this, then, are not only ways for TAs to learn more about their mentors; they are also fuel for program-wide discussions (12).

GTAs are not the only ones who benefit from this kind of mapping. The "programmatic mapping" that happens in this location and articulation of program values may be, as Laurie A. Pinkert and Kristen R. Moore (2021) point out, analytical and metaphorical, or it may be explicitly multimodal. In either case, as these authors point out, mapping makes quite clear what may otherwise be muddy for program stakeholders (58). Not attending to the ways we articulate and communicate our programs' parts and pieces and motivations may contribute to gatekeeping via errors and miscommunications that keep students or faculty from meeting requirements (59). And, while it is important to have values in print for administrative functions and eyes, only explaining these through prose (like in syllabi or white papers, for example), might mean the "complex infrastructures" that have determined or support these requirements might be "hidden from frame" (60). Through case studies, Pinkert and Moore show the ways that programmatic mapping contributes to WPAs' knowledge-making and the development of problem-solving strategies (72–73).

This mapping might help program participants further distinguish between curriculum and pedagogy (and the values tied to these). In *Reformers, Teachers, Writers: Curricular and Pedagogical Inquiries*, Neal Lerner (2019) asserts that while as a field we largely agree on pedagogy, we do not on curriculum, despite the wide uptake of frameworks like the "WPA Outcomes Statement for First-Year Composition," the *Framework for Success in Postsecondary Writing*, Wardle and Downs's writing-about-writing curriculum, and Adler-Kassner and Wardle's identification of threshold concepts. Without emphasis on curriculum, the field's agency in change making is limited, Lerner argues: "Whatever the causes, our expertise with pedagogy and 'writing as a process' emerges as the staple of the field, and that conclusion is considered perfectly tolerable in a climate that allows 'writing as a process' to somehow define an entire discipline. But such definitions are only partial, only the shell of a discipline without substantial disciplinary content and certainly without any means to enact meaningful institutional reform" (7). Pointing to texts that claim to compile the knowledge of the discipline, Lerner highlights the ways that pedagogy remains a visible value, but a specific curriculum is not as clearly shared. Lerner argues for the "articulation of curriculum," describing curriculum as an "assertion of values" (10). In teasing out the distinctions between shared pedagogical values and shared curricular values, Lerner identifies a roadblock for writing studies:

> Such assertions [of curriculum] can be easily found in our professional statements, in our commitments to social justice, diversity, and inclusion, and in our research that shows the powerful roles that writing plays to shape/limit/make possible individual and communal agency. We work at odds with our good intentions when our design of curriculum and the curriculum itself do not reflect these values. The result is an uncomfortable relationship between who we are as a field and who we want to be, a gap that can account for the continued failure of our reform efforts. (10)

To Lerner's point, when our local curricula do not line up with the disciplinary values we have asserted in professional statements and scholarship, we have crafted our own troublesome rifts: We have set our disciplinary goal line but are maybe not all facing in the right directions to carry our local programs to it.

While I read Lerner's book late in my revision of this manuscript, I found in quoted passage a meaningful connection to the tensions between values, curriculum, and action that I experienced while I conducted research on my home program and listened to colleagues from other institutions describe their own program values. In looking at the composition teaching practicum from various perspectives—through the talk and texts of teacher development—I differentiate writing program values from other principles like threshold concepts to show how while program values may be tied to these core principles of writing (and to Lerner's point, especially writing as a process), values illuminate the ways writing program work reflects these principles (or does not).

Through my local search for values for teacher development, evidence that they might be shared across the field, and analysis of how we may best work to enact them, I have identified several categories of values, along with degrees to which they are present and made explicit in the talk and texts of teacher development, which I will briefly explain here (box 0.1).

> **BOX 0.1. CATEGORIES OF WRITING PROGRAM VALUES**
>
> **TACIT VALUES:** values that are present in program talk, texts, pedagogy, or practice, but not explicitly known
>
> **IMPLICIT VALUES:** values that are known to individuals but not articulated to others as values
>
> **EXPLICIT VALUES:** values that individuals directly express in program texts, though they may be idiosyncratically presented
>
> **EMERGENT VALUES:** values that are shared between some writing program personnel and present in some program texts, to a weight and degree that suggests they might be articulated as program values
>
> **ARTICULATED VALUES:** known and shared values that circulate in the talk and texts of writing programs

Values often begin in the domain of the tacit and may have a positive or negative valence. That is, a program's tacit values may be evident in challenging or problematic ways as much as in progressive and unifying ways. For example, Andrea Dardello (2019) describes the bullying she experienced as a result of the conflict between her novel coaching approach to teaching writing and the traditional pedagogical values held by influential faculty in her department. While coaching approaches were highly valued at her institution, the department's tacit commitment to the "Western patriarchal view that reinforces objectivity, the teacher as sole knower, and the divorce of emotion from the subject being taught" manifested in administrative actions that ultimately quashed Dardello's project (111–112). These values—beyond being at odds with much of the progressive rhetoric of the field—expressed to Dardello in conversations with faculty who were "not comfortable with the course design," ultimately function as challenging to productive programmatic action (111). On the other hand, tacit values might unite program actors in their approaches to work. For example, in our analysis of a group interview with four instructors serving in support roles during the transition to remote learning in 2020, Nicole Guinot Varty and I find the group "worked from a tacit perspective on mentoring during this challenging moment: we should support teachers; we should use expert teachers to support other teachers" (Jankens and Guinot Varty 2025, 148). While we argue that the articulation of explicit values would have led to even more productive teacher development outcomes during this time, the tacit values driving the support team served to unify their aims, if not their results (148).

Implicit values (values that are present in program talk or texts without explicit attention as values) and explicit values (values that are stated but perhaps idiosyncratically), are most evident, I think, at the individual level. For example, in a syllabus for a graduate course on composition theory I taught in 2020, I put only texts by women composition scholars on our reading list, to center the work of women and marginalized scholars. I did not articulate this value to my graduate students, however, as I took a more subversive approach to those curricular choices (choices that today I explicitly articulate to students). Explicit values, on the other hand, are those we can point to in course artifacts. In my present first-year writing syllabus, I state the value of peer and teacher feedback to our classroom assessment ecology (and this language has been included in our program's common syllabus for FYW as an example, so it likely appears in many other teachers' syllabi as well). After describing our "complete/incomplete" grading system, I explain in this passage in the syllabus that

> if an assignment is marked as "incomplete," I will provide feedback in Canvas explaining what you need to do to complete the assignment, and you may revise and resubmit the assignment based on the timeline I provide. As Asao B. Inoue (2021) writes in *Above the Well*, "Both writer (student) and readers (teacher and peers) are vital in assessing whatever they produce because we must dialogue, have a give and take . . . We can only make sense of the writer's work when we understand how it is read by others and ourselves in the classroom context" (41). Peer and teacher feedback, and your own reflection and revision, are significant to your work in this class.

This language I developed, and that draws on Inoue's description, makes explicit to my students and colleagues that feedback, talking with each other about our writing, reflection, and revision are the central activities I value as the teacher of the class, and they bear out in the activities of the course. In my discussions with WPAs and practicum instructors in chapter 2, these program personnel identify implicit and explicit values in their own syllabi and programs: Sometimes the language of a syllabus presents a value explicitly; sometimes the inclusion of particular activities in a course implies a value.

Emergent values, like those I identify in chapter 1, are present across program talk and/or texts, though they may not have been identified, yet, as shared program values. Michelle LaFrance's (2019) description of the "ruling relations" that organize the ways that work happens in workplaces is helpful for explaining emergent values:

> Ruling relations make themselves visible when we see over time and space how the work of one person (or a small group of people) bears similarities to the work of others in other programs, classrooms, or locations. When we see writing teachers or writing programs, for instance, share vocabulary, philosophies of writing, and similar sorts of assignments or when those we interview independently tell the same stories, reflect on the same moments, discuss the same issues, or offer a shared sense of purpose, ruling relations are coming into visibility. (32)

When we look intently for these workplace practices, we may be able to identify locations where shared approaches emerge. In this project, I seek out these similarities as they relate to writing program values broadly and values for teacher development, specifically. These values function as ruling relations whether they are explicitly known by writing program participants or not, and they do so in tension with other contextual realities, group norms, positionalities, and pressures.

Finally, articulated values in the writing program context are those values (for teacher development, for writing instruction, for writing program administration, etc.) that are actualized in the work of the program—the ideas and motivations that can be identified in the concrete actions, documents, and policies of the program and that are present in the talk of program actors. Articulated values are stated, shared, and acted upon. On the Antiracist Language and Literacy Practices Research Team I have been a part of since 2020, to articulate our values we created a living "values and practices" document that we continue to revisit and revise as a grounding touchstone for our research team's work. In the document, we outline our dedication to equity, inclusivity, and change, and tie each of these to action. For example, about equity, we write,

> First and foremost, our research agenda is driven by the following goals related to **equity**: (1) ensuring all students' language and literacy practices are acknowledged, valued, and welcomed in university classrooms, and (2) identifying and interrogating white supremacist literacy and language systems inherent to institutions of higher learning and current configurations of "academic English" as the language of higher learning. With these goals in mind, we work to identify the language attitudes and practices of WSU students and faculty, understand and assess the impact of antiracist language and literacy practices, and foster more equitable teaching and assessment practices across the disciplines. For our collaborative work as a team, *equity* means sharing both the responsibility and merit of research and publication. Equity also means intentional collegiality, not only between members of the team, but between research team members and the community participants with whom we engage. (Antiracist Language and Literacy Practices Research Team 2022)

In these lines, we articulate our commitment to equity; this articulation is met with research design and collaborative writing practices that put this value into action. As a living document, the "values and practices" statement supports the engagement of new team members and shapes the work we take on each academic year.

The work of writing programs is expansive, and it can be powerful to know how to explain why we do the variety of work we do in classrooms, in conference rooms, in writing centers, in practica, and in committees. I prepare an argument in this book that making these values explicit and articulating them in program talk are powerful steps for program personnel (especially GTAs and the faculty engaged in their professionalization) and for the discipline at large, as we proceed toward more determination of what holds us together and how we will accomplish our disciplinary ideals. I demonstrate the need for this articulation through studies tied to a core site of teacher development: the composition teaching practicum. Focusing on the practicum allows me to dig deeply into one site where values, curriculum, and pedagogy come together.

Why Focus on Teacher Development?

In *Professing and Pedagogy: Learning the Teaching of English,* Stenberg (2005) argues for the field to take on a notion of teacher development over and above one of "teacher training." Teacher development, Stenberg argues, frames the learning of teaching as a "lifelong process" (133). When our first contact with new teachers in writing programs positions their initial experiences as part of this process, we also carry out the idea that all teachers are "knowers" (135). For Stenberg, this framing of teachers as knowers has the power to reshape what it means for our field to enact a disciplinarity—the field is built from our pedagogical knowledge-making. Teaching is not private, Stenberg asserts, but rather should be made "public for reflection and revision" (135). It is a collaborative act, and one that should happen across disciplinary lines (135). We need to make this teacher development framework clear to new teachers in our programs upon first contact, including making it known that there is a triad at work, a "dialogue between new teacher, experienced teacher, and the field, with all three open to revision" (134). As I will describe in this introduction, the project I lay out in this book takes teacher development as its focus for understanding program values; it also, however, takes up a methodological framework that, in part, demonstrates teacher development in action, particularly through Stenberg's emphasis n on teaching being made "public for reflection and revision," as I write through my own learning as a teacher-scholar.

In this brief discussion of literature on teacher development and the practicum, I assert why this project necessarily explores teacher development through discussions about values. As Kristine Hansen (2018), describing the role of a sole supervisor of new composition instructors, writes, "One person (sometimes two or more) with disciplinary expertise and professional status is expected to constantly make writing teachers out of dozens of people who have had little or no opportunity to study the discipline of Writing and Rhetoric prior to teaching" (136). This bald-faced way of putting the job emphasizes the kind of magic that is expected to happen in a pre-semester orientation or semester-long practicum course. The reality of this expectation is likely what, in a more positive way, lends itself to the kinds of teaching and learning strategies developed by practicum instructors, and the theoretical orientations that will most effectively lead to the magic outcome of semi-professionalized writing instructors emerging from the practicum. Orientations of teacher development over teacher training (Stenberg 2005) and classroom projects like peer-to-peer teaching, reflective writing, and observing mentor teachers (as described in scholarship on the practicum and as employed by the practicum instructors I interview in chapter 2) remove the top-down, filling-empty-vessels imperative of this structure by naming the work as something else. It is not banking (ala Freire); it is a collaborative cultivation, as each teacher (practicum instructor included) brings their experiences in the classroom and their conceptions of literacy (Brewer 2020a) to bear on the lessons of the practicum course itself.

Scholarship on the practicum has well-addressed the challenge of how to bring GTAs to composition theory—or composition theory to GTAs—through the course. As noted at the top of this introduction, the practicum often serves more as the point of initiation for GTAs into the discipline as much as it prepares them to work as teachers in the local site. To avoid inculcation, and instead take up the collaborative knowledge-making central to our field, practicum instructors must design ways for GTAs to interact with theoretical concepts and disciplinary content. Often, studies of GTAs' experiences lead to arguments for specific content in the teaching practicum (e.g., Ebest 2002, 2005; Winslow 2005). For example, Aimee Mapes and Susan Miller-Cochran (2019) pose threshold concepts of writing as central to the course, using the examples from a pre-semester orientation and activities in the practicum course at University of Arizona to show the ways that this approach addresses "two primary challenges GTAs face when assigned to teach writing classes for the first time: lack of disciplinary knowledge in writing studies and lack of a theoretical construct for teaching writing" (219). The shared vocabulary provided by the threshold concepts allows GTAs and mentors to construct pedagogical content knowledge for teaching in the local context (222). In this book, I look both in and around the practicum course to understand the ways that program (and even disciplinary) values, specifically, might better (or also) function as core to this training, to help GTAs understand why they are working as they do. That is, if we can agree on what these values are.

To be clear, I am not advocating for skipping past disciplinary knowledge or threshold concepts of writing in our teacher development and to some more wiggly conception of values. The development of disciplinary knowledge happens for the individual teacher over time, as they engage with scholarship and work through their own classroom practice (often in reverse). While, as I noted in my opening remarks, I was a conscientious and caring writing teacher in my vocation, I experienced an a-disciplinary apprenticeship to the work, dancing on the outskirts of writing studies even as I taught courses, completed my first graduate degree, and applied for doctoral programs so that I could more confidently, appropriately, and sustainably teach college writing as a career. However, like Hansen (2018) warns, "Because we haven't protected our profession's boundaries for insisting on qualified teachers with adequate disciplinary knowledge, the boundaries we should have set are often now out of our control" (155). Hansen is not only concerned for the workaday lives of WPAs who oversee hiring and training teachers for their writing programs but also and especially for the students who work through our courses. To best serve them, to best prepare them for their future classes and for civic engagement, Hansen says, we need "a truly professional class of teachers whose judgment is grounded in deep, broad disciplinary knowledge before they undertake this important work" (155).

And to be an effective instructor within a specific site, a "truly professional class of teachers" needs to understand the specific pedagogies and necessary processes structuring teaching in that program; beyond this, they need to know why these pedagogies and processes function as they do in that program. Ideally, they *do* function, and ideally, they function because program personnel share core values that drive this coordinated work. While we may expect to see program values manifest in discussions of pedagogy or in pedagogical materials themselves, analysis of local sites might show otherwise. Indeed, In chapter 3, I demonstrate how when nodes of material relations like intentional access of institutional history and curiosity about teachers' experiences are not explored, curricular recommendations begin to take a shape curiously different from previous iterations of the practicum course.

The work of teacher development in writing programs serves as a rich site for studying the evidence and articulation of values because it is both a site where GTAs are introduced to the work of the field, through their teaching assignments and a site where multiple, complex writing program activities converge to demonstrate to graduate students what is valued *in practice*. Thus, the practicum, as the core location of this teacher development, can be a kind of proving ground for which local or disciplinary writing studies values "stick." More pointedly, Dobrin (2005) calls the practicum a "site of control" for composition studies (23), a means by which programs "maintain control over what can and should be taught not just in FYC classes but also in any other classes students then teach" (25). However, as Dobrin notes, and Amy Cicchino (2020) reiterates, the teaching practicum has not widely been a site of theorization for the field at large, though composition and writing studies scholars have often published on their work in local programs. Much of this scholarship, even that which theorizes more broadly, focuses on the experience of graduate students in the practicum course (e.g., Ebest 2002; Restaino 2012; Grouling 2015), or on the impact of the practicum on GTAs' subsequent teaching (e.g., Winslow 2005; Reid et al. 2012), or offers examples of and rationale for the practicum syllabus (e.g., Guerra and Bawarshi 2005; Odom et al. 2005). While these are stories that are also included in this book, I work, in addition, to consider the picture these narratives weave together.

Looking at Teacher Development Through a Responsive IE Framework

I started teaching our program's second practicum course, which I will call Practicum II in this book, in the winter of 2016, my fifth year working at Wayne State, with the specific charge to help GTAs begin to explore online teaching and our various intermediate composition (IC) courses. This assignment changed each year in response to program needs and has been significantly different each of the four times I have taught it. I began teaching our first pedagogical practicum course, which I will refer to as Practicum I, in 2019 and taught it again in fall 2021, the semester I conducted the interviews I present in chapter 2, and in fall 2023, when I had completed the first draft of the book for review. Writing program administration was something I had a peripheral relationship with in my role administering our program's teaching observations for five years (see Jankens and Torok 2023), in my roles on several assessment and curricular committees and task forces, and in what seemed to be an unofficial role as a kind of contemporary program historian, simply because I could hold everyone's projects and experiences and working lives in the files of my brain. It seemed understood that I would likely take on the role of WPA post-tenure, but I was not tasked with that role before reaching the tenure milestone. I was grateful for my chair's support and protection in my pre-tenure role, for the chance to focus on my research, and, especially, for the chance to learn about the role of WPA, and, more specifically, about how to reconcile program values and teacher development through my research. In effect, I got to research the role and landscape before inhabiting it. I got to think through both what I hoped to do and what obstacles and challenges might face me in that work.

The methodology necessary for this project came to light as I worked through the material of each of the studies of this book, from 2020 to 2022, as we grappled with teaching and administering writing instruction during the COVID-19 pandemic and its related protocols and struggles. My experiences with practicum instruction and some administration of teacher development in my home program shaped my research questions and analysis. Participation in any institutional site is context driven and laden with subjectivity; LaFrance (2019) explains, "As such, an individual's social alliances, experiences, and sensibilities play a defining role in how that individual negotiates everyday institutional settings and sites of writing (such as classrooms, programs, or departments)" (37). This influence of context on me, as program actor and researcher, will be highly evident in the chapters in this book; it is also brightly presented in the experiences of participants in my studies: practicum instructors, committee members, and practicum students. I have worked to be as attentive as possible to these contextual influences articulated by participants or emergent in my analysis of their contributions. This is my effort to attend to standpoint, the dynamic social context that shapes discourse and action in my studies and from which I view and interpret this discourse and action (LaFrance 2019, 36–37). In participating in and examining the sites I consider in this project, my perspective—indeed a sometimes (re)visionary one—is made explicit and sometimes problematizes the work. This is part of the "inward journey" described by feminist scholars Jacqueline Jones Royster and Gesa E. Kirsch (2012, 85), wherein the researcher attends to "how they process, imagine, and work with materials." As I read and reread the artifacts from a historical program archive, the work of a committee, transcripts from class sessions and interviews, a collection of student work, and practicum syllabi, they become a part of my own story as a researcher (85).

My conversations with practicum instructors and analysis of practicum syllabi (chapter 2) required me to look up from my position as a peer—an instructor in the same course at another university—but also to acknowledge that I was not yet in the WPA position presently or recently held by my participants. I had much to learn from our conversations and found, as the interviews began, an irrefutable enthusiasm for talking with other people who had worked through the decisions I had made in organizing and teaching the practicum. It is an energy that comes through in the ways we affirm and encourage each other in the Zoom calls that allowed us to spend time together during the pandemic. In conducting teacher research on my own practicum course (chapter 4), I embodied, as an instructor, many of the same urgencies and struggles as GTAs in my class, teaching a new curriculum and teaching online during the pandemic. But I had to balance these urgencies and struggles with the necessities of acting from my position of teacherly authority, and then as a classroom researcher, to provide an honest, if subjective, picture of what we worked through in the course. This required me to take careful notes, record sessions, read, reread, and member-check the ways I constructed the story of that class so that my standpoint of researcher and graduate advisor did not cloud the teacherly parts of me that faced similar challenges to GTAs that term. In my study of our local program history and curricular revision (chapters 1 and 3), identifying this standpoint was the most difficult. I wrestled with emotional reactions to my initial readings of a committee's work revising the practicum syllabus: as a longtime practicum instructor, and as someone not serving on that committee, I had no contemporary voice to insert into the site of inquiry.

While the committee spent time reviewing documents that I and other former practicum instructors had created, I was in part a specter of semesters gone by, in part the assistant professor who set up an audio recorder at the beginning of meetings instead of attending because (it was thought) her physical presence might have kept committee members from sharing their real thoughts about the course. This wrestling is what led me to understand my guiding methodology, one that I call *responsive institutional ethnography*, or *responsive IE*.

As I define it, the responsive IE framework I employ is inquiry based, focused on a local problem, and produces action. It is responsive in that it attends to listening, reflection, and revision (as presented in strategic contemplation and the work of teacher development), and it is IE because it takes up the coordination between texts, processes, people, and more ephemeral concepts (like values and change) in the writing program workplace, a workplace that functions within the pressures and politics of the larger university. I might have taken up a solely IE project (the initial impetus for the work, an examination of committee discussions and recommendations, might have allowed that) but the pull of my role as a practicum instructor and program actor made the work inherently different for me, as I was invested in not only the results of the work for my scholarship but also the program-based work I would need to do with the results. As I describe in chapters 1 and 3, the very concrete local problem that engaged my attention at the start of this project was that a curricular subcommittee was tasked with making recommendations for a common syllabus for our teaching practicum, and, as a longtime instructor of the course not on the committee, I was curious with what knowledge and purpose they would do that work, what values for teacher development they would center in their recommendations. The action that emerged from this initial curiosity was that I wanted to make sure that teacher development in my home program (indeed, in any writing program) is structured via a shared set of values for this work, because, as described earlier, the practicum initiates teachers into working for a specific program and even into the discipline. The broadest question I asked was, Where are program values in this writing program work? To get at that, I asked more focused questions that began with these: What do I see when I work to read my writing program's artifacts for program values? What do I hear when I talk with other practicum instructors about values and values-driven work? What happens when I try to structure (or sometimes shoehorn) values-driven work into my practicum course?

LaFrance's (2019) description of three phases of her work as an institutional ethnographer certainly provided an inroad into the project for me. The first includes the identification of a problematic (52), a problem, its context, and the people and conversations working through and around and because of it (39). LaFrance clarifies: "A 'problematic' is not necessarily a 'problem,' such as the issue of low pay per course for contingent faculty. A problematic may begin with such a problem, but it then recognizes and accounts for the situated, complex, and interconnected relations among people, their experiences, and their practices related to that problem" (39). The "problem" under discussion across this book is the need to provide new graduate instructors with immediate and ongoing preparation for teaching FYW. The problematic I explore includes the following: the changing nature of the practicum courses in my home program; the diversity of approaches to and values for constructing teaching practica across the field; the ways that various instructors have approached the curriculum of the course; the work of administration to compose white papers on GTA training and gather GTA perspectives on the practicum via informal focus group sessions; and the committee structure of the program, which brings together non-tenure track (NTT) faculty and graduate students to design recommendations for a common syllabus.

The second phase of IE includes gathering data, including official documents and personal accounts (LaFrance 2019, 53). I work specifically in my local site to preserve institutional memory through the collection and analysis of documents related to teacher development and the stories of participants in our local teacher development. I began gathering materials for this project in January 2020 and conducted my last interview in November 2021. This collection included historical program documents related to our teaching practicum courses (syllabi, white papers, and focus group notes), transcripts of committee meetings and committee documents, and transcripts of class discussions in a teaching practicum course. Most of this qualitative research and artifact gathering was done online and remotely during the COVID-19 pandemic, though, to me, one gift of the study presented in chapter 3 is that I was able to capture face-to-face recordings of committee discussions about the practicum syllabus in the weeks before our campus shifted to remote learning. As I composed each chapter, I worked to capture the processes and experiences that stem from program decisions or lead to concrete programmatic outcomes.

The third aspect of IE relevant to this project is "an ongoing and recursive development of an analytic framework" (LaFrance 2019, 54). In my project, this ongoing and recursive development happened as I reflected on and read across the data for all three studies. Across this project, I look at how individual players draw on and work through their experiences in talking about the work of teaching writing and designing teacher development in writing programs, to help these identities, expertise, and labor come to light. The positions and relative power of these individuals are worn on their sleeves; they are aware of these and bring them into conversations. The immediate contexts in which these articulations happen (in Zoom-based interviews, in committee meetings, and in an online practicum course) and the broader contexts in which these discussions are situated (collaborating, teaching, and administering in writing programs, during the time of the pandemic and significant cultural action related to race and equity in the United States) impact the content and circulation of ideas. While I attend to my local site, both as longtime participant and researcher, I also investigate the ways other WPAs and practicum instructors see (or do not see) program values manifest in their sites of teacher development. Therefore, a strictly framed institutional ethnographic approach would not work; I needed to amend it to be able to see and listen both inside and outside of my home program, which a responsive IE approach would allow me to do.

As noted, this project also works to enact Stenberg's (2005) framework of teacher development in that it, in part, publicly presents reflections on teaching, with revision as a primary aim of this reflection—an important part of what makes this work responsive. Stenberg's description of teacherly reflection as core to teacher development was one I tacitly understood and employed during the work of composing this book. It was in composing the first draft of the final chapter that I recognized that my writing work, and its production of revised teaching work, was a kind of demonstration of the reflection and revision that Stenberg asserts is central not only to a framework of teacher development but also to what makes teaching into knowledge making in our discipline. Throughout the project, I reflect on my role as a practicum instructor, the decisions I made in constructing practicum syllabi and in classroom conversations, and the revisions I would make to classroom and curriculum talk because of these reflections. I describe this work as demonstrative of a teacher development framework not because the project takes teacher development as a central topic but because the research work of the project has an impact on me, as a practicum instructor—it changes me, as a teacher. These personal teacherly changes and the teaching problems, decisions, and revisions of participants in my studies are made public in these pages (Stenberg 2005, 135).

Finally, I employ strategic contemplation (Royster and Kirsch 2012) to engage reflection not only at the individual level (mine, as a researcher and practicum instructor) or program level (especially my home program, as

I unearth implicit values for teacher development) but also to engage the values-focused concerns of WPAs and practicum instructors across the field. In strategic contemplation, the researcher spends time listening to the subjects (present and past) with whom they engage, reflecting on what they hear from these voices, in texts, and how they engage with these voices and text in a particular time and place. Often employed with archival research, strategic contemplation allows the researcher to find the resonances between past and present, between understanding oneself and learning the text. Royster and Kirsch describe the researcher being "willing to stop and think multidirectionally, from the outside in and the inside out, not just about the subject of the study but about themselves as the agents in the process" (86). I do use strategic contemplation in this way, as I examine recent historical program documents associated with my program's practicum courses, with the relative distance and space provided by a handful of years and paradigmatic changes provided by the pandemic. But I also employ strategic contemplation in this project as a necessary method for slowing down the responsive nature of WPA research and teacher development, of being both program actor and researcher at once. Royster and Kirsch emphasize this iterative and chrono-circular deliberation: "Our view is that contemplative practices need to be seriously engaged and strategically incorporated over the course of the work in order for researchers to function optimally as critical and creative thinkers" (86). In a simple way, the natural elements of time and writing process were conducive to this methodology, as I worked inductively from study artifacts to craft the analytical frameworks and processes driving each chapter and then wrote the implications and conclusions of those chapters. Less simple was the work of intentional reflection, as I talked about the project, shared drafts with participants, and stepped back from the whole to consider the complex insights stretching across each study. Recursively working between listening, analysis, and reflection, I methodically practiced this strategic contemplation as I read program artifacts and attended to the talk of participants in my studies; as Cheryl Glenn (2018) clarifies, "Strategic contemplations are not mystical; they are authentic encounters of creatively working together toward that greater good" (120).

As an insider analyzing discussions and documents from my own writing program, as I do in chapter 3, stepping back and acknowledging my feelings became crucial to being able to work through the process. As I describe in that chapter, when institutional knowledge seemed to be disregarded or simply unknown, when instructors' experiences were minimally acknowledged but not engaged, or when I didn't agree with the outcome of the conversations I was reviewing, I felt frustrated and dismayed, especially since I was researching the curriculum revision process in real time, and because my teaching work would be directly impacted by the decisions of the committee I was studying. But, a responsive stance was integral here, because, whether I was researching the committee's work or not, whether this was any other daily problem-solving task that members of my writing program might engage in together, I was going to have feelings about it—maybe relief, irritation, ambivalence, or who knows, even joy—so being able to acknowledge those feelings, consider alternative viewpoints, inquire into absent but important voices, and work through the process would all be important. That is to say that practicing a responsible responsivity—both in research and in the daily work of writing program administration—is necessary. Somewhere between the "slow agency" recommended by Laura Micciche (2011) for WPAs' reflective practice and action and the "urgent agency" described by Stephen Monroe (2021), when WPAs and program personnel must make quick-thinking and -acting decisions based on always-changing circumstances and even emergencies, responsive IE would function as both a research and administrative orientation. As a research method, responsive IE allows me to look at and listen to the artifacts from my studies with a creative and critical distance (Royster and Kirsch 2012, 86). As a work orientation, this responsive IE can prepare me for action.

Contributions

In the introduction to their recent collection *Transformations: Change Work Across Writing Programs, Pedagogies, and Practices*, Kirsti Cole and Holly Hassel (2021) gesture to the articulation of program values, writing, "We must articulate what that [change] work is and how we can do that work just as well as we articulate our changing pedagogies" (4). While they do not use the term *values* here, Cole and Hassel call for this articulation of work in a discussion of attention to labor and to "offer models for faculty who hope to build new programs or revise existing ones" (4). This "hope" is, I assert, a values-driven one. In closing their introduction, Cole and Hassel more directly call for an articulation of values, especially in light of the changes brought to writing programs and institutions of higher learning because of the COVID-19 pandemic, saying, "It will be more important than ever that we articulate these values to ourselves, our colleagues, and our discipline as we face unprecedented and swift calls for change" (15). The chapters of their edited collection convey perspectives inclusive of the array of writing program personnel working in this vein and the myriad projects they attend to, including advocacy for underserved members of the university and community, instructor labor conditions, and the often hidden or unnoticed work of writing program personnel. These are stories and studies that indeed serve as models of change work in action.

While I emphasize teacher development and values-based change as the center of writing program work in this book, this is not a project proclaiming the centrality of teaching to the work of writing studies. We teach writing, we teach graduate students how to teach writing, and we are teachers of writing at the same time that we are scholars of what writing is and does. Rather, this project presents the ways that the values of this complex and energized field manifest in the primary location where teacher development is exercised—the composition teaching practicum—and the talk and texts that support and direct that course. The overarching argument of the book is that we must build programmatic values into the administrative talk, texts, and processes that structure teacher development and then assess our work with these values by listening to the experiences of teachers. That articulation of values, activated through the design of teacher development and assessed through sites of teacher development, bolsters writing programs as they work to instigate and sustain change, especially social-justice-oriented change. This, then, brings the two—teacher development and programmatic change—inextricably together.

In *The Talk and Texts of Teacher Development: Values, the Practicum, and Programmatic Change in Writing Studies*, I foreground these two ambitions (teacher development and programmatic change) as both core to writing program work and as viably bound up with each other. The question of writing program and writing studies values served as the impetus for the studies presented in the book: I wanted to understand what program values where driving decisions about our program's teaching practicum, how other practicum instructors and WPAs saw their program values present in practicum syllabi and the wider work of the course, and what happened when I integrated texts tied to implicit program values into our practicum. These inquiries resulted in practical applications for making values explicit in the composition teaching practicum and other teacher development settings. This approach empowers all teachers in a writing program to effect lasting change within the classroom, program, university, and wider community.

This project adds to recently published scholarship exploring the focus of the practicum course (Brewer, *Conceptions of Literacy*, 2020), the positionality and experience of GTAs in writing programs (Macauley et al., *Standing at the Threshold*, 2021), and the perennial work of the field to identify its core values and disciplinary identity (Malenczyk et al., *Composition, Rhetoric, and Disciplinarity*, 2018). The project aims to understand the work of teacher development from the perspective of programmatic structures and their ties to disciplinary energies. As such, the focus of individual chapters necessarily moves between examining teacher development in a local context (the composition program at an urban R1 university) and examining values in teacher development from a more expansive qualitative viewpoint (through interviews with WPAs and examination of teaching practicum syllabi from across writing programs and through consideration of recent scholarly discussions of values-based action in writing studies).

This discussion will be especially valuable to instructors new to teaching the practicum and instructors weary from teaching the practicum. I can certainly relate to both audiences. As a practicum instructor, I have become used to an almost annual exercise in wholesale revision, our needs for the course changing every year. GTA feedback on our program's Practicum I has kept that course shifting in a way that, as my colleague Nicole Guinot Varty described it in a pandemic-era Zoom call, has had us working like softball players, always in ready position, used to swings and misses. Over the last decade of leading teacher development in our program, it would have been easy many times for us to fall into fatigue and, frankly, sorrow about teaching the course—something like what Lu Ellen Huntley (2005) describes in "Finding Myself Lost in the Composition Practicum Course," and concluding, or hoping, "I probably will not teach the practicum course again" (299). However, going up to bat every semester has made me somewhat of an experiential expert in ready, responsive teacher development—Nicole and I describe some of this work in our chapter in *WPAing in a Pandemic and Beyond: Revision, Innovation, and Advocacy* (Jankens and Guinot Varty 2025). Like the WPAs and practicum instructors I interview in chapter 2, I hold a persistent assurance about the work of the practicum and the possibilities the course holds as a site for change.

Outline of the Book

I recognize that this project treads a line between the local and empirical. In attending to the local, I seize responsivity in moments where teacher development is happening outside of traditional semester and classroom boundaries: I engage a study of committee work and artifacts in a semester that ends up abbreviated due to the stay-at-home order in the spring of 2020; I provide an account of working to implement readings on social justice, antiracist teaching, and linguistic justice in an online practicum class during the third semester of the pandemic. These are moments where our best-laid plans for teacher development shift to *making things work*, and I strive to listen to what happens in and around that work to discover where values for teacher development manifest in action. In my turn to the field, then, in discussions with WPAs and classroom instructors from other institutions, I analyze texts and talk in depth, rather than aiming for breadth—this deep listening is crucial. This responsive examination of the people, texts, ideas, process, and values that coordinate the work of the composition teaching practicum offers a practice that is intuitive, practical, and productive.

    The chapters of this book first focus on identifying emergent shared values for teacher development, both within my home program and across programs. Then, I examine whether and how these values manifest in curricular planning, and I look pointedly at integrating values-based action in my own practicum course. I begin my work in chapter 1 by reading inside my local writing program via an examination of a small archive of historical program documents related to the composition teaching practicum. It is a study incited by the concurrent work of a curricular subcommittee who would be making recommendations for a common syllabus for the practicum. The local program history that I compose, which prepares me to engage with curriculum committee artifacts later in chapter 3, emphasizes multiple perspectives on the practicum course between 2014 and 2019. Through the presentation of several themes that emphasize these varied perspectives and programmatic tensions, I work toward the identification of emergent program values for teacher development, values that are evident across historical artifacts but not always explicit in program talk and texts. Therefore, this history highlights the institutional (program) knowledge and values-focused talk available for my program's curriculum committee's uptake in their work making recommendations for a common syllabus for the teaching practicum.

    While I was learning a lot about the practicum in my own program as I explored this recent program history, I also wanted to understand practicum courses in other writing program contexts. The work of chapter 2 answers two central questions: *How are teacher development values articulated from the standpoint of the WPA?* and *Do these values match with those represented in practicum syllabi?* My intention in investigating these expressions of values is twofold: to work toward an understanding of the ways that values manifest in local program work—specifically the work of the practicum—and to provide conversational examples to writing programs working to reconcile any gaps between what they say they value and what happens in practice. In this chapter, I present findings from interviews with four WPAs and practicum instructors from writing programs at universities with graduate programs in writing studies. Recounting themes from my conversations with participants, I present examples of congruence or disjunction between program values and values at work in the practicum. I also demonstrate the practicum as a site wherein program change often originates. Through looking at practicum syllabi from a larger set of programs, I propose that perhaps the emergent values for teacher development that I can see historically at work in my home program do indeed hold water in the field, providing a clarity of vision for this core work of our discipline.

In chapter 3, I return to examining teacher development in my home program as I read transcripts from curricular subcommittee meetings about making recommendations for the common syllabus of our program's teaching practicum course. I consider the implications of the committee's resulting work, both on the practicum itself and on future committee work. Using a triad of knowledges to organize my reading of the committee transcripts, I consider the ways that intuition, institutional knowledge, and experiential knowledge manifest in committee talk. I especially consider the ways that committee talk might be deepened and slowed down to better consider institutional and experiential knowledge, necessities for tuning in to the ways that shared program values might influence or shape curricular recommendations. Further, in my analysis, I show how three of the emergent values for teacher development I identified in chapter 1 are evident in the committee's work, but I raise questions about the ways that disciplinary frameworks and the local imperative of writing instruction factor into the committee's recommendations. This chapter provides one narrative of the development of a practicum curriculum, drawing its impetus from narratives like Juan C. Guerra and Anis Bawarshi's (2005) description of their work revising an orientation and practicum sequence for new GTAs. It contributes to scholarship outlining the important service work of NTT faculty and graduate students in composition programs, as well as responds to Latterell's (1996) identification of a disciplinary challenge to make writing pedagogy "part of the regular conversations of many people in a department" (22). Placing my description as a response to Micciche's (2011) "slow agency" and Stephen Monroe's (2021) "urgent agency," I demonstrate how the study—as part of the larger project of the book—explores the administration of teacher development from both within and standing under (Ratcliffe 2005, 28) the circulating discourses of program actors, program texts, and scholarship.

Taking my initial findings (and frustrations) to heart, I worked in my own practicum course to integrate what I understood as implicit program values and inquired about GTAs' experiences in the course as a result. In chapter 4, I tell the story of my winter 2021 Practicum II course, focusing on our class discussions about assigned readings on social justice, antiracist teaching, and linguistic justice, and the degree to which these texts might be integrated into GTAs' work with students in our program's IC course. This teacher research study emphasizes students' voices, using dialogue from transcripts as a central vehicle for conveying the tensions GTAs feel between their investment in working with students on critical language awareness and linguistic diversity, the material demands of teaching IC, and their relative authority in their dual roles as both teachers and graduate students. Unlike other narratives of GTAs' experiences in the practicum, which capture their experiences prior to or during their first semester of teaching (e.g., Restaino 2012; Brewer 2020a), I present the experiences of GTAs in their fourth semester as doctoral students, in a second practicum course. This contextual distinction allows us to see the differences between the ways new and more advanced GTAs in a program might reflect on and operationalize curricular inquiries and changes. Further, capturing these experiences in an online practicum course, during our third "pandemic semester" and a continued season of searching for racial justice in our country, provides a picture of teacher development work during a culturally urgent and innovative time.

In the overall project I present in this book, while I attend to local examples of teacher development (in my home program and in the examples described to me by my interview participants), I listen to these examples as they pulse with values-laden energy and yet sometimes evince quiet sighs of exasperation and exhaustion, especially during the pandemic. In these examples of what it means to structure teacher development with vision and values in mind—even when these are implicit, tacit, or unspoken—I can hear echoes about labor, agency, and possibility that begin to synthesize into a meaningful next chorus. So it is that my project ends in this final chapter with a conversation with writing studies scholarship on writing program labor, change work in the discipline—and designing for this work—and on GTAs as change makers, to emphasize both how these essential program actors can be empowered through sites of teacher development to engage in values-based change making *and* how, through a clearer articulation of values, they may also be bolstered by a sense of sustainable, actionable hope. Drawing from the conclusions of each chapter, I demonstrate revisions to the texts and instruction of my practicum course that aim to engage GTAs, practicum instructors, and other program personnel in the articulated, coordinating, and coordinated values-centered talk of teacher development and programmatic change.

Concluding Thoughts

In the span of time I conducted the studies of this book, the world was hit with the COVID-19 pandemic, our communities' devastated screams for justice seemed to finally begin to breach the too-long soundproof walls of white supremacy surrounding our schools, my local program shifted to wholly remote teaching and learning for a year, and we struggled with how to reconcile these larger contexts with what we were doing in our classroom (never mind the pervasive challenge of too many unprepared teachers teaching—or failing to teach—online, in life situations that made learning to teach online an impossibility of time and capacity) (see also Jankens and Guinot Varty 2025).

As I searched for shared values for teacher development, I learned also about how the ways we talk about our work in teacher development can make the articulation or manifestation of values more or less possible for writing program actors. Thus, across the chapters in this book, I trace two threads: the search for values for teacher development and the larger work of writing programs, and a developing understanding of both how we talk about this work and how we can talk about it better. Being able to better articulate our values for teacher development, the role teacher development plays in our local sites, and the ways that teacher development takes shape can better connect this central writing program activity to the values of the field at large, and therefore better equip teachers doing this work with ways to talk about and enact values-driven change in their classrooms and programs.

In all, I recognize the challenge of what I work to do in parts of this book and what I ask participants in my interview study in chapter 2 to do. Articulating a program's values at any one moment in time is akin to the challenge of capturing a snapshot of a writing program's identity; as Ritter (2018) notes, this work requires "being mindful of how important such declarations of identity and intent can be" (48). Indeed, my colleague Joe Torok and I felt this challenge, analyzing the values implicit in our own writing program's teaching observation form, and acknowledging these values to be both tacit and aspirational (Jankens and Torok 2023).

In this project, I take something I think I can pin down (teacher development in writing programs), consider it in light of the ever-present activity of programmatic change, and use those common goals within and across programs to seek something too often less apparent: the explicit values of writing programs. Recognizing teacher development as core to the field—as itself one of the core values of the field—I hope this exploration illuminates and validates other values, helping us identify interconnections between the strategies we implement and sustain for the growth of our programs and their personnel. LaFrance (2019) asks about the work of sites of writing, "How does our work take shape?" (23), and I add these questions: How can we better attend to program values—and program values for teacher development—in this work? And how can we use articulation of those values to support the change work we hope to do?

1
Looking Back (and) to the Future

Reading Inside My Home Program

In the movie *Back to the Future* (Zemeckis 1985), Marty and Dr. Emmett Brown consider the power required to generate the amount of electricity they need to create the conditions for Marty to return to 1985. What's needed, says Dr. Brown, is "a bolt of lightning." But there's a problem: "Unfortunately, you never know when or where it's ever gonna strike." Marty holds a "Save the Clock Tower" flyer from 1985. The flyer describes the historical moment of the lightning strike that damaged the clock tower in the 1955. Marty hands the flyer to Doc: "We do now." The scene—like so many others in the film—demonstrates the interplay of past and present in the construction of knowledge. If we look even at the short histories of our writing programs, we see that the events and discussions and challenges of writing program administration replay themselves. Attendance issues at teaching workshops may be a perennial challenge. Instructors who had a hard time finishing one semester may be the same instructors whose students require intervention from administrators the next semester. The practicum schedule and syllabus may be ambitious and unwieldy no matter who is teaching the course. Responses to these problems may have been already attempted in the recent past: Who catalogued these attempts and their results? Who holds the knowledge about what might and might not work in their experience? Where in program history can we find the information that

https://doi.org/10.7330/9781646427895.c001

can help us zero in on solutions to our present challenges? How can we learn a responsible responsivity to the challenges of teacher development, a primary writing program function? Are there clues in this program history that tell us something about what we value in teacher development, even as we struggle to align our practices with these values?

Shirley K. Rose (2016) notes that while writing program histories are local, they "help to establish the broader disciplinary, social, and cultural contexts in which individual programs undergo change" (287). That is, these specific accounts of the changes that take place in writing programs tell us something about the broader context shaping programmatic work. In this book, for example, the history and accounts of the work of my home program tell us something about the struggles of teacher development during times of crisis. For example, as Nicole Guinot Varty and I (Jankens and Varty 2025) explore in "Navigating 'A More Tense Area': A Response Team's Approaches to Conversations About Online Teaching During the Shift to Remote Instruction," there may be a need to prepare teachers to teach online when they may have to but don't want to, or may want to but are facing other pressures (like a pandemic) that require significant emotional energy. This book's story about teacher development fits into a longer narrative about the changing labor market in academia and about the pressures faced by a growing body of NTT faculty. And, as Rose (2016) points out, the availability of multiple program histories is important for painting a more accurate picture of the field at any time, as the institutional pressures and circumstances may change from locale to locale. Even in the COVID-19 pandemic, for example, when many of our campuses remained closed to in-person instruction and work from March 2020 through the subsequent semester, other writing programs worked largely in person in fall 2020; instructors and WPAs at those campuses remember a quite different teaching and teacher development experience from those who worked asynchronously and remotely from each other. Within programs, these histories are significant as well; Rose explains, "Knowing how and why specific practices such as curricular models, administrative structures, and policies were originally designed can help current participants in the program recognize how the program has developed and carried out its mission in the past, and to understand as well why current practices that might seem problematic were initially put in place" (288). Indeed, this motivation is what initially led me to dig into the recent program history of teacher development in my home program: As changes to the practicum needed to be made for multiple reasons, explored in this chapter, I wondered whether and how this recent history would be consulted by those writing program personnel making recommendations for these changes. I worried it might not be.

I begin my research on program values for teacher development in this chapter by reading inside my local program, examining an archive of program documents related to the composition teaching practicum over the short historical period that most especially influenced the development of a recommended common syllabus for that practicum and the research work I undertook for the book. Then, I recount my analysis of these historical program documents from 2014–2019 and the teacher development values that emerge from this analysis. The local program history I compile and analyze reveals both a hearty structure and emergent values for teacher development alongside challenging idiosyncrasies across teaching cohorts and practicum syllabi and instructors. I argue that these idiosyncrasies can be reconciled through foregrounding and making explicit values for teacher development, instead of letting these remain implicit or in the background of our work. This description of teacher development in my local context and of emergent program values then forecasts and fuels the work of the following chapters.

Local Histories and Sustainable Change

The first step for my research was to read back in time, to consider the history that led my program to revise the curriculum for the practicum. A coordinated program archive did not exist for me, but I was able to compile one through requesting files I knew existed. The institutional memory of my brain—a brain that had worked in my program for ten years—kicked off the project. I held contextual knowledge about teacher development in my program that positioned me to effectively begin this historical work, because I had previously taught the practicum and administered the teaching observation process for several years (Rose 2016, 291). However, this institutional memory needed validation from the historical program documents I collected. As I recount in this section and the next, scholarship on local histories and on program archives demonstrates the necessity of knowing these local histories—of a *shared knowing* of these histories—for the development of sustainable programmatic change.

When formal archives of a writing program do not exist, writing program historians turn to informal records, searching "among former directors' papers, teachers' records, and staff files in closets, bookshelves, file cabinets, and cupboards in program offices" (Rose 2016, 293). These "papers in piles" found in WPAs' offices are not themselves archives, Rose (1999) points out in her chapter "Preserving Our Histories of Institutional Change," but they can be drawn from and cultivated into true program archives, valuable not only within our own programs but to researchers from other sites (109). Rose (2016) asserts that WPAs are therefore positioned to design and contribute substantively to program archives (294), which can then support their ability to draw on "credible evidence" for making arguments to program stakeholders (297). When a WPA takes on the role of archivist, Rose (1999) notes, the WPA must become attune to selecting the appropriate documents and crafting a sustainable management system (113–114).

Sustainability means not only that projects potentially exceed the individual's tenure as a WPA but also that the memory of these projects is sustained beyond the individual. Laura J. Davies (2013), acknowledging the often too-short accounting of program initiatives, urges writing program administrators to work to understand the long-term implications of this work, not just "creation stories" (82). As Davies points out, this "long-view" approach is in line with Laura Micciche's (2011) argument for WPAs' uptake of "slow agency" in their decision making. To construct a twenty-five-year history of the Syracuse University writing program's teacher evaluation system, Davies compiled an archive of administrative documents, such that the archive would "tell a multi-voiced history"; these documents were complemented by a set of hour-long interviews with program personnel (83). Davies traces debates about and revisions to the program's teacher portfolio evaluation system—a history that includes the voices of teaching assistants, instructors, and administrators. Davies uses this constructed history, then, to demonstrate the ways that the system performed principles that centered reflective teaching and responsiveness to change (104).

Accounts of the histories of specific courses or program initiatives can be found across the literature on writing program administration, including in works by Ritter (2018), Rolf Norgaard (2017), and others cited in this book. The short history presented in this chapter adds to these accounts, and to see it fully, this history can be read as complemented by the work of the other chapters of the book.

Reading Inside My Writing Program

In describing their collaborative work revising the orientation and practicum attached to the teaching of an already-rigorous and thoughtfully designed FYC course, Guerra and Bawarshi (2005) conceptualize the practicum as a "site of articulation" that prepares TAs for their local teaching work and "confirms and reproduces disciplinary theories about the study and teaching of writing" (54). The many descriptions of the emphases of practicum courses in our field's scholarship demonstrate, however, the variability of which disciplinary theories and which studies of the teaching of writing is emphasized. As evident in many of the examples included in this chapter, the theories and practices highlighted in a practicum are typically dependent on the instructor teaching the course. This does not mean, however, that there is not—or should not be—a shared set of values across composition faculty about how teacher development should be framed in a program; it does mean that, like in any community of practice, the ways that individual actors express and choose to emphasize values is highly contextual.

As part of my research for this chapter, I reviewed several white papers composed by our composition program's administrative team. The white papers attend to the purpose and timing of our Practicum I and Practicum II courses (table 1.1), issues in those courses, and administration-driven changes proposed for those courses. I include details from those white papers across the sections that follow, but first I foreground a tension that emerges when I read across these papers: Administrative and faculty cohort values for teacher training and teacher development may not align with graduate students' values for the same. The closing acknowledgment in a 2018 white paper that "recent feedback from a [Practicum II] focus group suggests that at least some GTA MA students may view the six-credit commitment to practica courses as onerous" is one such indicator (Wayne State University Composition Program 2018, 4). This tension is a sentiment that echoes across programs, a story told in accounts by scholars who write about GTA resistance (e.g., Ebest 2002, 2005; Grouling 2015). More recently, Emily Jo Schwaller (2022) contends that GTA resistance can be productively reframed as "acts of well-being" (113); however, documents I read for this study do not provide enough detail to include discussion about GTAs' experiences in my home program's practicum in this vein.

STUDY CONTEXT

The composition program I work in is housed in an English department that is home to several graduate and undergraduate programs: a doctoral program with a concentration in rhetoric and writing studies and one in literature, culture, and media; a master's program (with concentrations in creative writing and technical and professional writing); and undergraduate majors (English) and minors (creative writing, professional writing, film and media studies,

TABLE 1.1. Practicum I and II calendar, 2014–2021

Fall 2014 Practicum I, 1st-semester GTAs	Winter 2015
Fall 2015 Practicum I, 1st-semester GTAs	Winter 2016 Practicum II, 2nd-semester GTAs
Fall 2016 Practicum I, 1st-semester GTAs	Winter 2017 Practicum II, 2nd-semester GTAs
Fall 2017 Practicum I, 1st-semester GTAs	Winter 2018 Practicum II, 2nd-semester GTAs
Fall 2018 Practicum I, 1st-semester GTAs	Winter 2019
Fall 2019 Practicum I, 1st-semester GTAs Practicum II, 3rd-semester GTAs	Winter 2020
Fall 2020 Practicum I, 1st-semester GTAs	Winter 2021 Practicum II, 4th-semester GTAs

Note: Practicum II was first taught in winter 2012 and was temporarily eliminated as a course offering in winter 2015 (Pruchnic and Susak 2015b, 2) and shifted from winter to fall in 2019. I begin this calendar in 2014 to align it with the time period I examine in this chapter.

and interdisciplinary minors). The department's most recent self-study reports the composition program serving over 6,000 undergraduate students per year. Important for this book is the makeup of the graduate teaching force and faculty in rhetoric, composition, and writing studies. The department funds doctoral and (sometimes) master's-level GTAs across English studies concentrations via their instruction of general education composition courses. Most GTAs teach general education composition courses across the duration of their funding, though occasionally advanced GTAs have the opportunity to teach undergraduate courses in their areas of study (e.g., courses in women's literature or film). Though recent changes in available teachables for full-time faculty across the department have led to some noncomposition faculty teaching general education composition courses, the program's courses are primarily staffed by faculty with master's and doctoral degrees in rhetoric, composition, and writing studies, with several NTT faculty having received their doctoral degrees from our program in the last ten to fifteen years. Cohorts of NTT faculty were hired in 2011 and 2013, with a low level of NTT turnover resulting in a handful of replacement hires in the time since then. In contrast, a high level of tenure line losses due to relocation and retirement, without the college's granting of replacement lines, has led to a small cohort of graduate faculty.

NTT and tenure-line faculty work closely together with the director of composition as the Composition Committee to make administrative decisions, conduct assessment, design curricula, and facilitate teacher development. The increased "commitment on behalf of the lecturer cohort" acknowledged at the end of a "White Paper on GTA Training" amounted to each NTT faculty member conducting "around three [teaching] observations per year" (Pruchnic and Susak 2015c, 5). Building up to the study described in this chapter, the NTT faculty cohort significantly led and facilitated aspects of teacher development from 2014 to 2019, including the pre-semester orientations for new and returning faculty, teaching the practica, administering and facilitating teaching observations, building teaching-focused mentoring relationships, facilitating teaching workshops and teaching circles, and designing curricula.

So, while I revise this chapter in the spring and summer of 2023, the composition faculty is composed of a largely long-sustained group of personnel. However, some aspects of the program are presently undergoing significant changes, particularly due to the need to respond to the effects of the COVID-19 pandemic on the ways that first-year students enter the university and the ways that our university's students' lives have become even more complex, as they balance full-time employment and school, caregiving for family members, and economic and wellness challenges. For example, the program is in the process of significantly revising common syllabi in place since 2015 for general education courses, to explicitly attend to antiracist writing instruction and to continue to support student success and retention in these courses. The online teaching experiment forced on almost all American universities during the pandemic has urged our program to return almost wholly to in-person instruction, rather than to embrace teacher development in online courses; there are just some things that only work as well as the will and attention of the people involved (see Jankens and Guinot Varty 2025).

And while some staples of our teacher development—like teaching workshops, a pre-semester orientation, and teaching observations—are perennially present and experience micro-revisions from time to time (see Jankens and Torok 2023 for an example), the pedagogical practicum courses have experienced variable approaches since their first iterations. Reading into the history of the practicum courses shows their consistently changing nature. As described in the "White Paper on GTA Training," the first iteration of the practicum course was in place in 2006 (Pruchnic and Susak 2015c). Previously, the program required a central pedagogy course. One iteration, "Teaching Expository Writing," overlapped with graduate students' work tutoring or teaching in a "Writing Workshop" (Brereton 1981, 20). Another was a seminar, "The Teaching of Writing," that engaged students in critical discussions about the teaching of writing (Marback 1995), a course that still functions as part of our doctoral-level requirements. For many years, GTAs received their primary training for teaching the FYW course via their work as tutors in the writing center (Pruchnic and Susak 2015c). The first practicum course was initiated as part of a grant supporting a "Digital Literacy Initiative"; Jeff Rice, who taught in our program at the time, alludes to the impetus for this initiative in his chapter in Dobrin's (2005) *Don't Call It That*, when he writes, "I propose that composition studies reevaluate its practica to better reflect the writing done in new media" (Rice 2005, 279). As the authors of a white paper on our program's practicum note, while its central focus and function changed, the practicum persisted across time and "quickly became a robust training site for the general training of instructors in pedagogical methods relevant to teaching ENG 1020 at Wayne State" (Pruchnic and Susak 2015c, 1). The nature of the course's structure or service has changed in part, over time, due to the following systemic pressures, which are rehearsed across three white papers on GTA training composed during this historical period:

- A flux in the amount of credit hours borne by the practicum course and an accompanying flux in formal training outside of the practicum (i.e., in the writing center) (see also Wallis and Jankens 2017).
- A change in teaching load for new GTAs (increased across time), including teaching during their first semester of funding (see also Wallis and Jankens 2017).
- The need for GTAs to teach outside of the FYW course, both because of a decrease in full-time rhetoric and composition faculty and because of the change in intensity of course offerings due to university "student success" efforts, specifically advisors encouraging students to enroll in basic writing (ENG 1010) and FYW (ENG 1020) in the fall, and intermediate composition (ENG 3010) or technical communication (ENG 3050) in the winter of their first year, with completion of general education composition courses being a key marker of students' ability to complete their undergraduate degrees within six years. This need coincided with a "desire" for graduate students not in rhetoric and composition to "simplify their teaching experience and pedagogical training outside their subject area" (Pruchnic and Susak 2015c). That is, graduate students studying literature and film often preferred to focus attention on their areas of research, not on learning how to teach new composition courses.

Indeed, yet another change in the amount of credit hours borne by the practicum course was at least one impetus for a curriculum subcommittee's charge in winter 2020 to make recommendations for a common syllabus for Practicum I. To better allow graduate students to take the "right" amount of courses to meet with their funded coursework, eight credits per semester, practicum courses in the department (both in composition and in literature) were more mathematically serviceable as two-credit courses than as three credit courses. Creating a common syllabus for the course at two credits was a practical necessity a composition curriculum committee could undertake. However, there were also more cultural reasons for designing a common syllabus: striking differences in the approaches taken by various practicum instructors (myself included) had led to integral differences in the ways that GTAs experienced the practicum courses; more significant, pushback from GTAs regarding some aspects of the course led to a need for a kind of programmatic stamp of approval on the course's curriculum, a need to be able to say, "Well, this is how we do things." In office discussions in 2019, around the time I began to craft the study described in this chapter and the next, Ellen Barton, my colleague and mentor, suggested that idiosyncrasy might emerge as a significant driving theme in this study. This motif presented itself again in her marginal note on a very early draft of this chapter's themes. As I have continued to work through the studies of this book, idiosyncrasy indeed continues to show up, and I continue to work to understand why. How do potentially competing forces like *shared* values and visions and *individual* agendas and approaches to teaching come together in the problem solving of writing programs?

While teacher development in our program has been cited as "urgent" for many years (Pruchnic and Susak 2015b, 3), and while there has long been an explicit mentoring program within the composition program in our department (Wallis and Jankens 2017), we have, as of yet, no explicitly articulated "program" for teacher development. Instead, the program is comprised of a responsive set of teacher development practices that are revised from year to year. Thus, stepping outside of both my own experiences teaching the course and the circle of decision makers to instead research the history, discourse, and values inherent in the practicum courses and the program's *talk about* the practicum courses, allows me to understand the bigger picture of how these courses fit into teacher development in our program, how teacher development is situated as one of the core outcomes of our program, and how teacher development functions as a shared value in the field.

ASSEMBLING ARTIFACTS FOR ANALYSIS

The just-described fluctuations in the nature of the practicum, along with my own experiences working in the program since 2011, allowed me to identify a window of time for examining historical program documents related to the course. Specifically, I identified 2014–2019 as a meaningful window for several reasons. First, the beginning of this window aligns with the timeline presented in the "White Paper on Composition Practica," noting 2014 marking a change in first-year GTAs' teaching assignments from a 0/1 load (no courses taught during their first fall semester of coursework, and one course taught during their second semester) to a 1/1 load (Pruchnic and Susak 2015b, 3), meaning GTAs would no longer enjoy a semester of training for teaching prior to serving as instructors of record for a course.[1] Second, and more important, in 2015 NTT lecturers in the program began teaching the practicum courses; instruction had previously been restricted to tenure-line faculty. This change opened up functional administration of the course beyond a sole WPA or graduate faculty member. Third, a revised common syllabus for our FYW course was piloted in fall 2015 (that syllabus would remain in use until winter 2023). Finally, fall 2019 was the last time I taught the course prior to the committee's work developing a common syllabus; it was also our last semester before the myriad changes brought to writing instruction and teacher development by the COVID-19 pandemic, but I did not know that yet when I began this study. These dates, thus, bookended a time in the program where multiple faculty members responsively worked to adapt and instruct the practicum courses. While I was familiar with many of the parts and pieces of this work during this period, looking at the artifacts all together, and with some critical distance, would allow me to see evidence of shared program values for teacher development, not just my own.

The artifacts I gathered for my analysis of historical program documents included the following:

- seven ENG 6001 (Pedagogical Practicum I) and 6004 (Pedagogical Practicum II) syllabi;
- four white papers drafted by the director of composition and assistant director of composition regarding the practicum courses in composition, in 2015 and 2018;
- notes from focus groups with GTAs enrolled in practicum courses (conducted by the assistant director of composition in 2017, 2018, and 2019).

I obtained written permission from the director of composition and the chair of the English department to use those documents in my reporting and analysis.

FROM THEMATIC CONTENT ANALYSIS TO EMERGENT VALUES

To begin to identify emergent values for teacher development from historical program documents, I read each set of artifacts (syllabi, white papers, and focus group notes), looking for connections across documents in each set, and I recorded my notes for each set. To identify these connections, I hand-coded documents, working through a process of open coding and then correlating codes across documents. Then, I composed a synthesis of the coded notes into themes (e.g., Merriam 2009). As I continued to read across the themes and the original documents, this relatively simple conventional content analysis (Hsieh and Shannon 2005) made way for my identification of emergent values for teacher development: potential implicit or explicit values for this specific work of teacher development, drawn from evidence in the historical practices and perspectives of those administrators, faculty, and graduate students involved in the process. This identification of emergent values for teacher development was an intuitive next step beyond the cataloging of content themes. As Johnny Saldaña (2016) notes, values codes may be constructed during coding (132); in the case of this study, I identified emergent values based on, to again reference Saldaña, the "importance" attributed to specific approaches for teacher development, either implicitly by their presence, or explicitly, as expressed by program participants (131). These emergent values are hypotheses about what shared values are held by members of my home program (and potentially other writing programs) regarding teacher development in composition and writing studies. Once I identified potential emergent values in my initial coding processes, I reread materials to test them in the historical program documents; several persisted and remain in the discussions that follow.

Historical Program Document Themes

In this section, I present my synthesis of my notes on syllabi, white papers, and focus group notes to describe themes evident across these three sets of documents, providing a rich picture of the practices and pressures of the Practicum I course—and some detail of our variable Practicum II course—including commentary on orientation, teaching circles, assigned course readings, preparation for online teaching, and the role of senior GTA mentors in the course. These practices and pressures exist across curricular choices, structural components, and the roles of individuals and groups of personnel. In crafting this picture, then, I am able to see ways that the practicum course does and does not have an identifiable set of characteristics, the ways it may or may not be shaped by shared values for teacher development.

WHAT HAPPENS BEFORE THE PRACTICUM STARTS

While teacher development during GTAs' first semester in our department has responsively developed to support the change in initial teaching load over the last decade or so, time devoted to pre-semester orientation has largely stayed the same. New instructors receive a morning orientation in which they meet department administrators and writing program personnel and are provided with contextual information about the general education courses they will be teaching. While returning instructors spend the afternoon in sessions focused on the courses they teach across the sequence, new instructors receive a walk-through of the common syllabus for FYW (ENG 1020) and work with the practicum instructor to build their syllabi and discuss strategies for the first week of classes. During the orientation, they meet with faculty and senior GTA mentors and learn where their offices are and how to access the mail room and copiers. At our university, new GTAs from across departments also participate in a university-level orientation where they receive briefings on policies and resources. Pre-pandemic, they also participated in a micro-teaching session, receiving feedback on a short teaching demonstration from an experienced faculty member and their new GTA peers; for GTAs in many other departments, this micro-teaching session was their only teaching preparation during the week.

However, despite often receiving more group preparation than GTAs in other departments at Wayne State, GTAs in our department report in focus groups that they desire more advanced preparation, though *when* to offer this is not as clear. The winter 2018 focus group notes included GTAs' reflections on the two-semester practicum sequence and include the following: "Optional mid-summer: meet to talk about teaching; get documents. Suggestion: Comp Camp (week long orientation!) was expecting to get more orientation." Indeed, in summer 2018, one NTT colleague held a one-day "Comp Camp" in June, an event that has returned post-pandemic. The fall 2018 cohort focus group notes include a comment that because of this opportunity, they "were set up to get close as a cohort so quickly," but the notes also include some disagreement about whether the Comp Camp was too short, too early in the summer, or even appropriate for summer, when GTAs and faculty are off contract.

Echoing the need for continued or ongoing preparation, a program white paper mentions a suggestion made for a "required half-day 'mini-orientation' for classes assigned to new GTA instructors" (Wayne State University

Composition Program 2018). This requirement was tested in December 2020, as I prepared to work with fourth-semester GTAs in winter 2021 in our Practicum II course, supporting their contemporaneous teaching of our IC course for the first time (an experience I describe in chapter 4). Because, based on the university calendar, the practicum would begin officially meeting the day after some GTAs taught their first sessions of IC, it was imperative that we offered a short orientation before the semester started. Our remote teaching that year required a combination of synchronous and asynchronous sessions; because we had to hold a synchronous orientation session before the practicum started in January, I could not require it as part of the grade for the course, but students were tasked with watching any orientation videos they had not viewed yet by the end of the first week of class in January. All of that detail is included here to demonstrate the labor considerations and university policies that make training opportunities like a "mini-orientation" challenging to implement. To address this, in winter 2022 our director of composition strategized a series of teaching workshops centered on instruction in our technical communication courses; GTAs who would be teaching the technical communication courses in the summer and beyond were required to attend these workshops to meet the workshop requirement in their job descriptions.

Lauren Obermark, Elisabeth Brewer, and Kay Halasek (2015) identify the challenge of appropriate teacher preparation in the opening of their article on professional development: "Despite the prevalence and history of graduate teaching assistants (TAs) teaching writing courses at many universities, the field continues to struggle with how to prepare them meaningfully for the teaching they will do in their immediate future as TAs and for the responsibilities they will take on as they move forward in their careers" (32). In this statement, Obermark et al. capture our local struggle—one that will be reiterated later in this book—that there is so much to do in a pre-semester orientation and so little time to do it. They also describe how those primarily responsible for teacher development in writing programs (practicum instructors and WPAs) have to not only consider what GTAs will need to do next week but what they will need to be prepared to do as they enter the job market, move to new positions, and even lead programs of their own. The authors' solution is a collaborative, ongoing, and distributed approach to professional development, an approach that takes this work beyond the purview of a single administrative overseer (like the practicum instructor or WPA) (34).

In contrast with Obermark et al.'s argument that teacher training should occur cross-institutionally, in our local context, cross-site training for teachers has actually shrunk over time. While possibilities for cross-institutional training on our campus are available via resources like the Office for Teaching and Learning, the library, and the Humanities Center, each in different scope and kind, students must avail themselves of these resources on their own initiative. So, while GTAs may experience varied levels and aspects of a multifaceted approach to mentoring and professional development, their collective experiences with the required orientation can leave lasting impressions. GTAs' focus group feedback on our orientation raises questions about the scope of this pre-semester workshop opportunity. What do GTAs need to know to begin their first week? What do they need to figure out along the way, like anyone in any job? How do we most effectively structure this initial and ongoing teacher development?

DIVERGENT PERSPECTIVES ABOUT TEACHING CIRCLES

Teaching circles are small groups of like-minded teachers who gather regularly to reflect on and discuss their teaching experiences in light of particular themes or problems; Laurel Black and Mary Ann Cessna (2003) describe the varied ways membership of teaching circles may be composed (e.g., within departments or across disciplines) and how participants can feel a sense of "shared ownership" in the activities of the group. As described in "Collaborative Development: Reflective Mentoring for GTAs," a chapter Jule Wallis and I (2017) wrote about our mentoring program, we integrated teaching circles for new GTAs in 2014 alongside changes in GTAs' teaching load. That semester, instead of building community and learning about the FYW course while they worked as writing center tutors during their first semester, GTAs would be teaching upon entering the program, with only a couple of days of orientation before the first day of classes. Our solution to this problem was to coordinate frequent teaching circle meetings that brought together new GTAs, experienced GTAs, and NTT faculty teaching composition courses. In these teaching circle discussions, participants worked through practical matters of FYW, social aspects of the department, and fears and concerns about teaching. The teaching circles therefore provided an opportunity for collaborative, reflective learning among teachers of various levels of experience, outside of the structure and formality of a graduate course (the practicum) (Wallis and Jankens 2017, 170).

The 2015 "White Paper on GTA Training" includes a proposal for deeper integration of teaching circles after they had been part of our teacher development plan for a few semesters. The authors of the white paper write,

> We propose that bi-weekly teaching circles become explicitly mandatory for GTAs in their first fall and winter semesters, but be more organically

integrated into the practica (perhaps by actually taking place during the final hour of the practica's scheduled times on specified dates, if logistically possible). We also propose that attending teaching circles be a mandatory activity for GTAs teaching a new class and/or teaching online for the first time, which would expand their impact beyond the first-year cohort. (Pruchnic and Susak 2015c, 3)

These proposals were indeed put into effect in the semesters following the composition of the white paper. In my winter semester Practicum II courses, we ended class an hour early every other week, and GTAs would head either back to the faculty lounge in the department or over to a local pub to gather with senior GTA mentors and NTT mentors to discuss experiences and problems with teaching. In other semesters, I met biweekly with small groups of experienced GTAs in a department conference room to discuss their experiences teaching our IC course for the first time.

While instructors and administrators have emphasized the value of teaching circles for teacher development, notes from focus groups with GTAs, especially, evidence divergent GTA perspectives on what does and doesn't work with teaching circles. While we had tried integrating the teaching circles into the class period on a biweekly basis in winter 2018 to make the requirement fit better within the temporal confines of the class, this amendment did not appease dissatisfaction. Instead, some GTAs in winter 2018 asked whether teaching circles could be additional to class, because class content was shortened. The cohort overall disagreed about whether teaching circles should be "totally open" or focused on specific inquiries. While GTAs appreciated meeting people in the department outside of their cohort, the partially social function of the teaching circles made their purpose "less clear": "Maybe they could come to class and we could ask questions." One student noted that they "resent" teaching circles; another mentioned, simply, "I was tired." The fall 2018 cohort only had a few thoughts on teaching circles in their focus group session: They did not know they had to attend the teaching circles, so they did not go. The fall 2019 cohort expressed, however, that they felt the required teaching circles were a "keep" and not a "cut" for the course.

The "decrease in contact hours available for GTA training" noted in the "White Paper on GTA Training" has potentially, more subversively, continued, as teaching circle requirements have shifted over time. The deep integration of teaching circles proposed in that white paper has, indeed, changed in response to focus groups with GTAs. As I revise this chapter in 2023, teaching circles, dormant during the pandemic, have not returned to active practice, perhaps in part because of the department's slow return to in-person activities and ever-present Zoom fatigue, or perhaps because the reflective practice of teaching circles is being engaged in other third spaces of department mentoring (e.g., teaching workshops, instructor observations) (Wallis and Jankens 2017, 164).

WHICH COMPOSITION THEORY AND PRACTICE TEXTS ARE EMPHASIZED

The historical documents I collected show that both instructors and GTAs value a balance of theoretical and practical readings about composition pedagogy, which acknowledges the diverse makeup of GTAs taking the practicum and their varied teaching experiences. But I wondered as I reviewed the materials whether there were divergent perspectives on *which* kinds of theoretical and practical texts were emphasized by each practicum instructor; I knew from teaching the class that I did not teach all the same texts as my NTT predecessors, as we took turns teaching the course between 2015 and 2019.

GTAs expressed strong perspectives about assigned readings in their focus groups sessions. In fall 2018, the focus group notes include a comment that a "Non-rhet comp student said he could have used a firmer grasp on theory in a discipline he knows nothing about." Fall 2018 notes also include a suggestion for units structured around specific themes in pedagogical theory and practice to help establish a sense of "coherency." The notes from the fall 2019 focus group include a desire for readings that support "best practices for teaching 1020 (along with just enough theory)" and a suggestion that the reading list be reviewed for what could be cut; the notes with Practicum II students that semester include a suggestion that readings pertaining to K–12 instruction be cut.

While I have limited access to the details of each course (e.g., I am not accessing readings that are unlisted in the syllabus but shared via email or the course learning management system [LMS]), those readings listed in the syllabi for Practicum I nevertheless reflect the shifting weight of attention to readings each year, suggesting one way in which the course might lack a coherent identity and benefit from the recommendation of a common syllabus. Identifiable readings across the syllabi for Practicum I fell into several categories: texts on teacher development; texts used in the local FYW course; texts on composition theory, composition studies, or literacy; texts on composition pedagogy broadly or teaching FYW, specifically; and disciplinary frameworks or position statements (box 1.1).

> **BOX 1.1. CATEGORIES OF READINGS ASSIGNED IN PRACTICUM I, 2015–2019**
>
> **TEXTS ON TEACHER DEVELOPMENT**
>
> 2014: *What the Best College Teachers Do* (Bain); McKeachie's *Teaching Tips*; *Clueless in Academe*
>
> 2015: none
>
> 2016: Brookfield, *The Skillful Teacher*
>
> 2017: Brookfield, *The Skillful Teacher*; Palmer, *The Courage to Teach* [optional]; Tobin, "Teaching with a Fake ID"; "Conquering the Imposter Syndrome"; "Writing a Statement of Teaching Philosophy for the Academic Job Search"
>
> 2018: Brookfield, *The Skillful Teacher*; Palmer, *The Courage to Teach* [optional]; Tobin, "Teaching with a Fake ID"; Reilly, "The Peaceable Classroom"; "Writing a Statement of Teaching Philosophy for the Academic Job Search"
>
> 2019: Reid, "On Learning to Teach"; Stenberg, "The Teacher as Learner"
>
> **TEXTS USED IN THE LOCAL FYW COURSE**
>
> 2014: none
>
> 2015: Carroll, "Backpacks vs. Briefcases"
>
> 2016: Carroll, "Backpacks vs. Briefcases"
>
> 2017: none
>
> 2018: none
>
> 2019: Ball and Loewe, *Bad Ideas About Writing*; Greene and Lidinsky, *From Inquiry to Academic Writing*; Carroll, "Backpacks vs. Briefcases"; Hanlon, "College Students Aren't Cuddly Bunnies"; Lessner and Craig, "Finding Your Way In"; McKinney Maddalena, "I Need You to Say 'I'"; Postman and Weingartner, "What's Worth Knowing"; Macrorie, "I-Search"
>
> **TEXTS ON COMPOSITION THEORY, COMPOSITION STUDIES, LITERACY STUDIES**
>
> 2014: Harris, Harris, Harris; and Silva, Morrow, Neville, and North
>
> 2015: Ritter, *Exploring Composition Studies*
>
> 2016: Ritter, *Exploring Composition Studies*
>
> 2017: Bergman and Zepernick, "Disciplinarity and Transfer"
>
> 2018: Bergman and Zepernick, "Disciplinarity and Transfer"; Wardle, "Mutt Genres"; Seitz, "Who Can Afford Critical Consciousness?"; Fleischer, on teacher research methods; Shor; Freire; hooks; Cooper; Adler-Kassner, Majewski, and Koshnic-threshold concepts; Bartholomae and Elbow, conversation; Shipka; Yancey; Lindquist; Stenberg
>
> 2019: Adler-Kassner and Wardle, *Naming What We Know*; Cambourne, "Toward an Educationally Relevant Theory of Literacy Learning"; Elbow, "Revising by Reading Aloud"; Ritchie, "Beginning Writers"; White, "The Scoring of Writing Portfolios"
>
> **TEXTS ON COMPOSITION PEDAGOGY OR TEACHING FIRST-YEAR WRITING**
>
> 2014: none
>
> 2015: Good and Warshauer, *In Our Own Voice: Graduate Students Teaching Writing*; "Reciprocal Teaching for Reading Comprehension"; "Forging Rhetorical Subjects: Problem-Based Learning in the Writing Classroom"

> 2016: none
>
> 2017: Hewett, *Reading to Learn and Writing to Teach*; "First-Year Writing: What Good Does it Do?"; Baker, "Get it Off My Stack"; "Responding to Student Writing: Teachers' Philosophies and Practices"; Hillocks Jr., "Teaching Argument for Critical Thinking and Writing"
>
> 2018: Hewett, *Reading to Learn and Writing to Teach*; Graff, "Rhetorical Analysis"; *Understanding Rhetoric*, excerpt; "Responding to Student Writing: Teachers' Philosophies and Practices"
>
> 2019: Hewett, *Reading to Learn and Writing to Teach*; Yancey, *Reflection in the Writing Classroom*
>
> DISCIPLINARY FRAMEWORKS AND POSITION STATEMENTS
>
> 2014: none
>
> 2015: *Framework for Success in Postsecondary Writing*; "WPA Outcomes Statement for First-Year Composition"
>
> 2016: none
>
> 2017: *Framework for Success in Postsecondary Writing*
>
> 2018: none
>
> 2019: none

Note: I had access to syllabi and not course wikis, websites, or LMS sites for this study. Fall 2014's weekly readings were posted on a course website.

The idiosyncratic nature of practicum reading assignments is apparent in this summary of assigned readings listed in the historical syllabus set. Less apparent is the motivation for these differences: Are they mere idiosyncrasy, reflecting the preferences and scholarly leanings of individual instructors, or responsive decisions based on reflection on teaching experiences, or top-down directed revisions, based on changing program priorities? Look, for example, at the sudden deep leaning into attention to the texts assigned in the FYW course in 2019, when I taught the practicum. I assigned practicum students to read all the texts we would use in FYW so that we could discuss and work with them in the practicum; this expectation of work with FYW assigned texts was not present in the practicum syllabi before that year, however, suggesting that other matters were prioritized in those practicum courses. But it is not clear from looking just at the syllabi what drove me to make that change. Was it driven by my own past experiences having taught Practicum II, regularly hearing GTAs' wishes for more immediate practical work in Practicum I, and thus a central value of hands-on work with FYW materials? Was it because of my previous role as mentoring coordinator and my access to review transcripts of focus group sessions with GTAs, and therefore a value of letting student (GTA) voices drive curricular change? Without those values being made explicit, the syllabus can only tell so much.

Seeing this dramatic shift (and the other shifts between each year's reading lists) suggests to me something like what LaFrance (2019) illuminates when she writes, "We often represent pedagogy as a series of generalized and conceptual moves that organize our own work and the work of others; my own work reveals instead that pedagogy, in a local sense, is often more process than concept, more individualized than generalized, and more closely imbricated with materiality than we typically acknowledge in our field's discourses" (51). That my reading assignments in fall 2019 vary significantly from my predecessors' assignments suggests an individual motivation was at play (even if it was one drawn from my experiential evidence teaching FYW and mentoring GTAs); undocumented, the values driving that pedagogical decision remain inaccessible for other teachers of the course.

The *Framework for Success in Postsecondary Writing* (Council of Writing Program Administrators et al. 2011) and the "WPA Outcomes Statement for First-Year Composition" (Council of Writing Program Administrators 2014) make a brief appearance in the curriculum for Practicum I, but attention (per assigned readings in the course) seems to have shifted in more recent years to either composition theory broadly or the very local teaching of FYW, and not the concrete or specific tie to disciplinary frameworks and outcomes. Despite their minimal presence, I retain mention of these here and in the following sections because their absence raises as much of a question to me as their presence, one I will return to across the book.

PREPARATION FOR FACILITATING CHALLENGING DISCUSSIONS

While instructors integrate readings, discussions, and assignments about challenging but necessary teaching topics, the focus group notes suggest a need for practicum faculty to be prepared to facilitate conversations about these challenging teaching topics and disagreements between students in the course. This tension is in line with what Clare Russell (2020) writes about in her case studies of practicum instructors' curricular decision-making, where the instructors either dropped topics when they became challenging and moved on, or simply did not treat specific topics deeply enough. Russell uses the term *curricular tokenism* primarily to explore several absences or limitations in the curricula of composition practica:

1. disproportionally limiting coverage of the same topics and scholars;

2. continually using the same few scholars to represent a theory or branch of study;
3. designing assignments that do not encourage the translation of marginalized theory into classroom practice (56).

Russell tells the story of Cora, a first-time practicum instructor who reflected that she would remove Vershawn Ashanti Young's (2010) "Should Writers Use They Own English?" from her assigned readings for the course because "her graduate students 'seemed to like it but didn't know what to do with it'" (Russell 2020, 61). Russell notes that she includes this story to demonstrate how practicum instructors might "perpetuate curricular tokenism unconsciously," including texts by marginalized and minoritized authors in the syllabus that they do not fully work through with students (61). As a counterpoint to this story, Russell includes short narratives of other practicum instructors working through discussions and even collaborative action with students based on their reading of texts by diverse authors. Particularly because the practicum is a location to "dismantle" harmful language ideologies and for directing how GTAs perceive and work with "linguistically diverse students," says Russell, it is important that deep attention is given to these texts and topics (64).

As Russell outlines in her project, and as is evident in both historical program documents and the studies in the chapters to follow, positioning active work with assigned readings in the short time available in the practicum course—balancing discussion of readings with other practical discussions GTAs require—is a perennial challenge. A comment in the fall 2018 focus group notes states, "Readings were an afterthought in class." Separately, the fall 2018 notes include a desire for attention to context-specific needs: "We never talked about how to address the needs of WSU students. We did know basic demographic data but didn't talk about how to address that diversity in our own classrooms." This cohort also wanted more time and attention spent on discussion of "trigger warnings." The notes state, "'Ok for 20 minutes we're going to talk about trigger warnings' wasn't useful."

LEARNING ABOUT "TEACHING WITH TECHNOLOGY"

While myriad other teaching topics are evidently competing for time in the practicum, "teaching with technology" continues to be a necessary, yet backgrounded, focus of the course, though there is at least some disagreement about its emphasis in the focus group notes. The practicum's initial 2006 purpose, to prepare teachers for teaching with technology, was taken up later in my first Practicum II course (as promised in the "White Paper on GTA Composition Practica" [Pruchnic and Susak 2015b]) and then shifted, by me, into my fall 2019 Practicum I course. I was initially tasked by our director of composition with providing GTAs some foundational practice with using our learning management systems and designing online modules in the event that they *might* teach online. However, the value of preparation for online instruction, even as supplementary to their face-to-face instruction in FYW, was evident to me after years of teaching both online and in person: A significant amount of our interaction with students was happening in the LMS and in email, not face-to-face.

In the focus group notes from winter 2018, GTAs express a variety of responses to this instruction and practice in using online instructional approaches. For example, the notes include this sentiment about the assignment to create an online teaching video, "Not useful bc I won't ever teach online," to which other group members apparently responded, "You might teach online"—"you could create a video on a snow day." The fall 2019 notes do not include any commentary on this practice with online teaching.

As one instructor I interviewed about our program's transition to remote teaching at the beginning of the COVID-19 pandemic noted, teaching writing means teaching both online and in person, preparing instructional materials for students to engage with synchronously and asynchronously, no matter the primary mode of the class. Beth Hewett (2015b), in *Reading to Learn and Writing to Teach*, which we read for that fall 2019 practicum, emphasizes this in her assertion that universities need to understand where analog and digital technologies are most effective in their local contexts to support students' learning (6). Jessie Borgman and Casey McArdle (2019), introducing their book on strategies for online writing instruction, point out that because students are already working in digital spaces on their own time, these spaces are ready and available for uptake in the writing classroom (11). Without diving into the mounds of scholarship on the necessity of working with students on multimodal composing and composing in digital spaces (composing that they are already doing outside of school), I will simply reaffirm that this acknowledgment of the reality of composing and where we compose is a threshold concept necessarily explored with the diverse graduate students in our practicum courses (Mapes and Miller-Cochran 2019).

THE ROLE OF SENIOR GTAS IN THE PRACTICUM

It is common for senior GTAs in a program to take a role in mentoring new GTAs in their teaching and departmental life. Wanda Martin and Charles Paine

(2002) describe an orientation to teaching FYW almost exclusively facilitated by experienced GTAs (226) and a structured mentoring experience between new and senior GTAs (228). Martin and Paine cite heavy GTA involvement in leading orientation as the reason that other GTAs find value in the sessions (228). GTAs' involvement continually leads to programmatic innovations, they note (229). In our program, senior GTAs have regularly taken on roles in leading orientation sessions, including workshops on teaching specific courses and mentoring Q and A sessions; many years, senior GTAs have been invited to give presentations to practicum students, and GTAs on our mentoring committee meet individually and in teaching circles with new instructors. While the pandemic put some of these practices on pause, senior GTAs remain valuable assigned points of contact for new instructors. While a determined mentoring structure might seem "antithetical to the spirit of the mentoring relationship," as Martin and Paine (228) and others note, this structure ensures that new GTAs have a "reliable" source of support (229). However, resistance to GTAs' involvement in training new instructors is also a common thread in writing programs, one Irwin Weiser (2002), in his description of the program at Purdue in the 1980s and '90s, attributes to shifts in graduate student enrollment, the availability of faculty mentors, and the "ambivalent attitudes" of administrators regarding GTAs serving as mentors (43). However, as Weiser details, despite potential challenges with perceived agency and authority in these mentoring relationships between GTAs, organizing teacher development and mentoring to include strong participation and leadership from GTAs helps to move these structures from the individual level to the programmatic level (47).

Despite a history of senior GTA involvement in mentoring and teacher development in our program (Wallis and Jankens 2017, 164), an organized program or practicum-based structure does not always ensure interpersonal success in mentoring pairs. On one end of the mentoring program, mentors attended committee meetings to discuss and plan mentoring events and to troubleshoot challenges; on the other end, new GTAs received assignments in the practicum to help them engage with their mentors and observe their teaching. The focus group notes suggest evidence of a large-scale coordination problem with senior GTA mentors as well as tensions about the role senior GTAs could or should play in teacher development. This is heavily evident in the fall 2018 focus group notes, in which students offered what amounted to one-third of the total focus group commentary on this single topic. Only two students in the fall 2018 cohort felt their mentors were helpful; one student felt a burden placed on them to reach out first in the relationship; one student felt "intimidated" and did not reach out to their mentor; one didn't feel they needed a mentor; an assignment for new GTAs to observe their mentors' teaching did not come to fruition because of poor contact between mentors and mentees. One suggestion to improve this mentor/mentee relationship from the fall 2018 notes is that senior GTA mentors should be in the practicum sessions with new GTAs.

Considering the program's attention to structured meetings between mentors and mentees at the pre-semester orientation and structured practicum assignments working to facilitate this relationship, as well as the support of a mentoring committee, the problems described by GTAs in focus group notes may have been interpersonal (and thus hard to externally facilitate), or structural in ways we could not perceive or control as a program (see also Jankens and Torok 2023, 67). One tension seems clear: As a program, we value senior GTAs' involvement in mentoring and teacher development, but GTAs do not always feel or experience the benefit of our intentions.

Discussion: Emergent Values for Teacher Development in Practicum Syllabi from 2014 to 2019

Though it bends and changes in response to systemic pressures like credit hour changes, the historical program documents described in the preceding section and scholarship describing teacher development in our program (i.e., Wallis and Jankens 2017; Jankens and Torok 2023; Jankens and Guinot Varty 2025) show that it is hearty and ultimately structured and designed to support GTAs' degree completion and marketability. The "White Paper on GTA Composition Practica" suggests that the *structure* of teacher training in the program is designed to support the long game of funded dissertation completion (Pruchnic and Susak 2015b, 4); the "White Paper on GTA Training" suggests the *quality* of teacher training and teaching assignments is to support the marketability of graduates (3). Focus group notes reference GTAs' varied perspectives on the practicum courses' roles in shaping professional development. The winter 2018 artifact includes this note: "Curriculum is structured as everyone will go into Rhet/Comp as a career. Disagreement-I think it's one more thing I can do, have some Rhet/Comp." The white papers acknowledge this sentiment, noting, for example, a tendency of GTAs who are not interested in teaching composition in their future work choosing to only teach the FYW course rather than branching out into learning how to teach other composition courses (3).

Overall, instructor and program-held values for teacher development and graduate student values for teacher development do not wholly align, though there are points of intersection. As I read historical program documents, I noted potential emergent values based on the set of Practicum I syllabi from 2014 to 2019. Some of these emergent values gathered strength as I read the other historical documents; some further strengthened when I examined the curricular subcommittee's discussions about the practicum (outlined in chapter 3). This set of emergent values (see box 1.2) described in the following subsections functions as a set of priorities and expectations for the ways we structure and engage teacher development. They are often shared implicit or explicit guidelines we follow as facilitators of teacher development that allow for teachers to meet the first value—becoming enculturated in the "Wayne way" of teaching writing—as well as guidelines that could facilitate GTAs' transitions into teaching in new contexts.

BOX 1.2. EMERGENT VALUES FOR TEACHER DEVELOPMENT IN RHETORIC, COMPOSITION, AND WRITING STUDIES

EV1: The practicum should emphasize local commitments to and strategies for teaching composition courses.

EV2: (New) composition teachers need opportunities to hear and learn from experienced and expert teachers.

EV3: Teaching composition is, materially and ideologically, a shared enterprise (composition teachers regularly share materials and strategies and co-construct knowledge).

EV4: Composition teachers need to be familiar with disciplinary frameworks.

EV5: Composition teachers should learn from written reflection on teaching.

Some of the emergent values I initially included in the following list fell off after I conducted these analyses; if they were not presented in the other historical program documents or did not appear in the committee's conversations about the practicum, they were maybe mere idiosyncrasies. In chapter 2, I look at whether they carry weight in other writing programs; in chapter 3, I account for the ways these values were or were not taken up by the curriculum subcommittee in their discussions about a common syllabus for the practicum. Here, I provide evidence for each emergent value for teacher development, and, at times, evidence of resistance to these values, drawing from the historical program documents.

EMERGENT VALUE 1: THE PRACTICUM SHOULD EMPHASIZE LOCAL COMMITMENTS TO AND STRATEGIES FOR TEACHING COMPOSITION COURSES.

Explicit or not in the syllabi, there is an effort to support GTAs' enculturation in a "Wayne way" of teaching writing—at minimum, an acceptance of the function of the common syllabus for FYW. Reference to the "Wayne way" of teaching writing is explicit in the Practicum I (ENG 6001) syllabi from fall 2014 to fall 2018, implicit in the fall 2019 syllabus's emphasis on reading texts used in FYW. It is also evident in attention to instruction in teaching the common syllabus for FYW, rather than a primary emphasis on the discipline or composition theory. The "White Paper on GTA Training" notes that "the return of 6004 would allow the focus of ENG 6001 to be restricted to instruction of teaching in ENG 1020 and for responding to issues and concerns that arise in real-time as instructors teach that course for the first time" (Pruchnic and Susak 2015c, 2). This emphasis on the local curriculum in Practicum I (ENG 6001) and on the reintroduction of Practicum II (ENG 6004) to enhance and continue GTA training might have also alleviated concerns in the director of composition's office about instructors diverging from curricular requirements, which led to the revision of general education composition curricula and the integration of required assignment sequences in 2015 (Pruchnic and Susak 2015a, 7).

The notes on the focus group sessions with GTAs include, again, a variety of perspectives on this "Wayne" emphasis in the practica. For example, referencing the Practicum II assignment in winter 2018 to construct a unit plan in response to the outcomes of the common syllabus, these notes are included: "2nd semester could be a focus that we are interested in—you can design your own syllabus. Not just tailored to common syllabus; it should be what we want the assignments to be." In addition to the preference stated by some GTAs to teach "what we want," other notes, like one from the fall 2018 cohort, indicate that an "overall review of pedagogical concepts could have been helpful-specifically what the WSU curriculum used and why," suggesting that an explanation of the pedagogical research driving the common syllabus was desired. (However, a review of the course schedule for that fall 2018 Practicum I suggests that both theoretical and pedagogical research was assigned for reading in the course; for example, GTAs read texts by Jody Shipka and Kathleen Blake Yancey on multimodal composing prior to teaching an infographic assignment.) Additionally, the fall 2018 notes indicate that students wanted increased practical preparation for each day of teaching, especially early in the course. While fall 2018 students wanted "more grade norming sessions," fall 2019 students wanted fewer.

EMERGENT VALUE 2: (NEW) COMPOSITION TEACHERS NEED OPPORTUNITIES TO HEAR AND LEARN FROM EXPERIENCED AND EXPERT TEACHERS.

Practicum instructors value providing contact time between new GTAs and experienced and expert teachers in the local context, as evident in the schedules for the practicum sections, which include regular guest presentations from both senior GTAs and NTT faculty in the program. These guest presentations have been important moments for introductions to and interactions with mentors; however, there are suggestions from GTAs in the focus group notes (in fall 2019, for example) that fewer guest presenters might also be useful. Also important, is the role that peers within the practicum play in mentoring each other. The fall 2019 cohort reported this as a strength. This was less so in the winter 2018 section, where the focus group notes reveal the tension between classmates. The integration of teaching circles and work with senior GTAs shows that instructors and the program recognize that peer relationships are important teacher supports; as outlined in the earlier sections, the focus group notes evidence that this is a hit-or-miss phenomenon.

As Joe Torok and I (2023) have described, new GTAs' interactions with faculty members conducting their observations have also, sometimes, been a source of tension. While the program has structured observations as opportunities for reciprocal, reflective mentoring (see also Comer 2011), Joe and I have argued that without these values explicitly documented in program discourse (like in the teaching observation forms themselves), we miss out on an important grounding touchstone that can align GTAs' experiences with program visions. Nevertheless, the program has worked to structure multiple interactions between new GTAs and experienced teachers of composition.

EMERGENT VALUE 3: TEACHING COMPOSITION IS, MATERIALLY AND IDEOLOGICALLY, A SHARED ENTERPRISE (COMPOSITION TEACHERS REGULARLY SHARE MATERIALS AND STRATEGIES AND CO-CONSTRUCT KNOWLEDGE).

That composition teachers regularly share materials and strategies and co-construct knowledge is evidenced in the ways that practicum instructors share syllabi, the invitation for NTT faculty and GTAs to give guest presentations in the practicum, the development of resource sites, and the collaboration of a committee of teachers (who have taught the FYW course) on making recommendations for the curriculum. From curriculum development to daily practice to assessment to research, teaching and teacher development in the program primarily functions, or is designed to function, as a shared endeavor.

This value becomes clearer the more I read into the details of each practicum syllabus. While the program expresses a value in a "Wayne way" of teaching writing, readings assigned in the practicum show that instructors also value connecting GTAs with the knowledge of the field. Several years' lists demonstrate robust attention to reading texts on composition theory, composition studies, and literacy studies, which is sometimes balanced out with more practical published examples of strategies for teaching FYW in various contexts. In this way, we can see the ways that knowledge about composition pedagogy is constructed across the work of the field, not only within individual classrooms. This value is also demonstrated in the ways that collaboration and peer-to-peer sharing are built into practicum assignments: teaching demonstrations, peer feedback on teaching portfolios, observations of peers' teaching, group design of lesson plans, and even grade norming highlight that teaching is shared work, whether theoretically, practically, or both.

EMERGENT VALUE 4: COMPOSITION TEACHERS NEED TO BE FAMILIAR WITH DISCIPLINARY FRAMEWORKS AND POSITION STATEMENTS.

Two iterations of the practicum courses used the *Framework for Success in Postsecondary Writing*, and students in the 2015 section of Practicum I worked explicitly with the WPA Outcomes. Instructors also organized GTAs' study of and practice with teaching from educational, literacy learning, and professional development frameworks. Students in my sections of the practicum courses frequently worked with Brian Cambourne's conditions for learning in planning instruction. I had been introduced to this framework in my master's program and had found it useful for planning and scaffolding students' work in the composition course. In the 2018 Practicum I syllabus, the instructor also explains that GTAs' experience across the semester in the practicum is one they will reflect on via Cathy Fleischer's Framework of Professional Development for Teacher-Writers (Fleischer 2004). The fledgling presence of disciplinary and scholarly frameworks is important for me to include here because while these frameworks are historically used in the course, they are not consistently used. There seems to be some agreement about the need to engage first-year GTAs with professional frameworks but not which frameworks. While not as strong an emergent value as the others, this one tentatively holds on; yet another disciplinary framework will appear in chapter 3, in the committee's recommendations for the syllabus.

EMERGENT VALUE 5: COMPOSITION TEACHERS SHOULD LEARN FROM WRITTEN REFLECTION ON TEACHING.
This value becomes more evident over time in the syllabi set, partially due to the expertise of the instructors teaching the course, instructors who have researched and long-implemented reflection and reflective writing in composition courses. Focus group notes suggest at times, though, that there is "too much" reflection and that students might prefer what they see as more practical conversations to written reflection; the fall 2018 notes express, "We could have focused more on teaching and day to day prep than reflections" and that students wanted to be always preparing for what they had to teach next rather than to "reflect some more every week."

Examining the syllabi for Practicum I shows that reflection and written reflection are always present in the course in some form: keeping a weekly reflection journal, writing personal applications of professional development experiences, reflecting on teaching demonstrations given in class, composing essay-length reflections on significant learning encounters with students, and others. Without analysis of GTAs' written reflections, it is hard to know whether these are working to support teacher development in the way we hope, but whether or not written reflection seems to be working in the courses, conversational reflection is laden with tension. The winter 2018 focus group notes describe students' frustration with feeling like "everyone judges" each other in practicum discussions; "I think people should feel comfortable working through ideas and not be attacked [by classmates]," a GTA expressed. The fall 2018 focus group notes include this comment: "'Class has an identity crisis'—is it a therapy session, theory course, or a practical day-to-day how to teach comp at WSU course?" This group struggled with the manifestation of emotion in class sessions. The fall 2019 notes do not include mention of reflection (written or conversational) at all, though I used the same reflection assignments in that semester that I had in previous semesters, when I taught Practicum II.

The Benefit of Identifying Values in a Program's History

As I noted at the front of this chapter, a question of idiosyncrasy loomed the semester I gathered and first reviewed these documents related to the composition teaching practica in our program. In Practicum I, different instructors had each brought their own purposes and preferences to teaching a course that, essentially, prepared students to do the same thing each year from its initiation in 2006: teach our FYW course. In Practicum II, shifts in our local context had led to the course necessarily emphasizing slightly different outcomes and thus different approaches in each of its five iterations from 2012 to 2018. In looking at just the available materials from 2014–2019, the five years leading up to the semester a curricular subcommittee was preparing to make recommendations for a common syllabus for Practicum I, I hoped to discern whether there was something more than idiosyncrasy, however. I hoped to see what values for teacher development were, actually, consistent across these sections of the practicum courses and even present in the perspectives shared in white papers and GTA focus groups. While each of the five emergent values I have identified is present with some level of tension, their presence across time and teacher development sites provided me with the beginnings of a foundation from which to read the committee's recommendations. While the committee's output would necessarily, again, be different and distinct from what had been done before, because they would be called to help us shift the practicum course into a two-credit scenario, shared values could provide a level of consistency across time in the enactment of teacher development in our program. I hoped, as I read their work, that I would see the members of the committee drawing from these emergent values as they worked through their tasks, as shared touchstones to sustain the role and presence of teacher development as a core part of our program.

Conclusion

I first read these historical program documents in winter 2020, the semester a curriculum subcommittee talked through making recommendations for a common syllabus for Practicum I, to prepare for that course's shift to two credits (chapter 3). I was able to identify several themes through this reading that highlighted issues or tensions the committee would likely need to address at some point in their conversations: how the pre-semester orientation would complement the work of the practicum, the benefits and drawbacks of integrating teaching circles into the course, what readings to assign, how the instructor needs to prepare for holding discussions, preparation for teaching online, and the role of senior GTAs in the course. Reading across course syllabi, program white papers, and notes from focus groups with GTAs, I was also able to assess the presence of emergent program values for teacher development as well as the tensions that exist within sites of teacher development. This analysis of historical program documents also functioned for me as a look into the institutional knowledge and the program values potentially at hand for the curriculum committee's consideration. Re-seeing this program history outside of my own experience was imperative for structuring the ways I could look, with a research perspective, at the work the committee would undertake. It was an orientation I hoped they would also take when crafting their recommendations.

And I hoped to be able to understand values for teacher development not only outside of my own experience but outside of my home program as well. I wanted to learn more about the ways other practicum instructors described their program values, broadly, and values for teacher development, specifically. When I looked at practicum syllabi from other programs and talked to their writing program administrators, would I find similar moments of congruence and dissonance like I do in our own program? Could I identify any of our program's values for teacher development as shared values across writing studies? These are questions that guide my work in the next chapter, as I step outside of my program.

2
Finding Values in the Practicum Syllabus in Interviews with WPAs and Practicum Instructors

In chapter 1, I considered the recent history of my home program's composition teaching practicum through a compilation of artifacts that allowed me to see teacher development through the eyes of our practicum instructors, administration, and GTAs. In that study, I was able to see both that a coherent set of values of teacher development was emerging in the program over time and that alongside several shared values existed idiosyncratic curricular decisions and divergent GTA perspectives on the design of the practicum course and its attendant support structures for teacher development. To only look at my home program, however, merely adds another local account to the piles of local accounts of teacher development and writing program administration we have been gathering as a field for decades, leaving us in want of empirical evidence (e.g., Dobrin 2005; Cicchino 2020). Despite the bounty of local narratives, in scholarship on writing program administration we see that WPAs face institutional pressures that, while locally experienced, track across institutions. Similarly, in scholarship on teacher development, we can see how this essential work responds to intensely local demands as much as it draws on disciplinary values and ideals for preparing teachers of writing. The study in this chapter highlights both of these influences in an effort to further reveal potential shared values for teacher development in the discipline as well as

https://doi.org/10.7330/9781646427895.c002

examples of how these values are articulated in practicum syllabi by WPAs and practicum instructors from four universities on the east coast and across the Midwest. Following my study of historical program documents in chapter 1, this chapter's study has me listening outside of my home institution and across programs as I try to understand the degree to which there are shared values for teacher development in writing studies across training sites, and the degree to which these values are articulated in our talk about the practicum and practicum syllabi.

Realistically, teaching the practicum is just one small part of a WPA's multi-faceted annual work. While the common work of a WPA includes "scheduling classes, training teaching assistants, developing and assessing curriculum, observing and evaluating faculty, and maybe arbitrating student complaints about instructors and grades," this work is regularly punctuated with emotional events, for example, a need to respond to conflict or tragedy and the personal challenges that affect any of us while we navigate work as half of life (Costello and Babb 2020, 4). Black WPAs experience the additional labor of ever-considering race work as part of their position (e.g., Kynard 2019; Inoue 2019b; Perryman-Clark and Craig 2019). Accordingly, Adler-Kassner (2016) points out that seemingly mundane decisions about program work actually reflect priorities and more complex choices about resources, time, or personnel (461) and suggests that WPAs need to operate via "strategies underscored by principle" (471). The stakes of this strategic decision-making are high: Engaging in data-driven research, the WPA works toward the development of evidence-based programs (Donahue 2016) and sustaining the writing program's position within the institution (Anson and Brown 1999; Hesse 2012). So, the WPA's work is responsive to present local demands and anticipatory of local futures, while the program itself functions as a satellite of the larger discipline.

In this chapter, I examine the articulation of program values across institutions. Interviewing WPAs and analyzing practicum syllabi from several programs, I develop themes that strengthen the discussion of emergent values begun in chapter 1. This study further cements these emergent values as shared values for teacher development in the discipline; it also highlights that there are sometimes distinctions between a WPA's or practicum instructor's values and program values. Further, while disciplinary statements like the Conference on College Composition and Communication (CCCC) "CCCC Statement on Preparing Teachers of College Writing" are available to guide WPAs in structuring teacher development, explicit attention to frameworks like this, including the degree to which disciplinary statements bear on discussions within the practicum, varies within and between programs. This variance is present even if the essential principle upon which writing programs base their overall approach to curriculum and instruction—that is, to Lerner's (2019) point, "writing as a process"—has been long shared across the field (7). Cole and Hassel (2021) assert that the values of the field are long held and, despite myriad institutional changes, "haven't really changed" (15). Cole and Hassel articulate the general value of the discipline: "We strive to support literacy development for our students, in ways that meet their needs, that are sustainable and responsive, and that help students name and achieve their educational goals" (15). I am convinced, though, that if we dig into our values by talking about what they are and how we see them manifest in particular writing program sites, we can learn more about how we enact them and how to enact them better. In addition to capturing examples of the pedagogical practices of the practicum, the study in this chapter aims to capture some of the values-driven "talk" about teacher development in the practicum (and the imprint of these values in course syllabi), to understand whether we share any of this language from site to site, from program to program, and what we can learn from this articulation. Reflecting on the emergent values for teacher development I identified in chapter 1, I wondered whether I could say anything about Wardle and Downs's (2018) call for further "accounting" of the field's values, specifically as they related to teacher development (130). As noted in the introduction, in their examination of scholarly discussions about composition's disciplinarity, Wardle and Downs identify several "shared values" that unite the disciplinary work of our field: "inclusion, access, difference, interaction, localism, valuing diverse voices, and textual production" (123). They posit that while accepting disciplinarity, we should continue to ask and answer questions about the nature of our disciplinarity, including about values (130). In this chapter, to take up Wardle and Downs's question "What values are central to our field?" in light of teacher development, after identifying themes in what participants had to say about program values and practicum syllabi, I read for the emergent values I identified in chapter 1. I then add to this conversation my application of the emergent values for teacher development to a collection of ten practicum syllabi from graduate programs in rhetoric and composition or writing studies. The evidence of this chapter allows me to assert with more surety that there *are* shared values for teacher development that are interwoven with the core values of the discipline as articulated by Wardle and Downs and noted earlier; each of these values emerge in material and nuanced ways through examining the sites of teacher development. Further, the work of this chapter suggests that while the WPA-as-practicum-instructor might, at times, operate like a tired, midlevel manager, their attention to these values in sites of teacher development allows these program personnel to act as conjurers of micro-evolutionary program changes.

Practicum Syllabus as Values-Driven Artifact

As described in the introduction to this book, the practicum is just one stop along the career long path of teacher development. GTAs with previous experiences teaching in K–12 or college classrooms or working in writing centers will recontextualize this prior knowledge in the site of their new program. For new GTAs with no teaching experience, the influence of mentors (Grouling 2018) and their conceptions of literacy and previous school experiences (Brewer 2020a) come to bear on how they approach the practicum. This influx of previous experiences to the practicum course is balanced out by the ways the course, by its structure, serves as a "point of control" (Dobrin 2005, 23), a means by which programs "maintain control over what can and should be taught not just in FYW classes but also in any other classes students then teach" (25). Whether the work GTAs will do concurrently with or subsequent to their time in the practicum is tightly controlled or merely encouraged in particular ways is one of the core distinctions between programs. The practicum is nevertheless a professionalizing site, preparing teachers for the local program and, ideally, for a professional life beyond (Yancey 2002; Miller et al. 2005).

The syllabus of any given practicum course is primed, then, to be a site for a writing program to make its values explicit. The syllabus is a meaningful writing program document for the study presented in this chapter because it serves multiple functions: it helps instructors organize and plan for teaching a course; it helps instructors communicate expectations to students; it helps students conduct planning and self-assessment for their work; it aids WPAs in assessing whether individual courses meet program standards; it aids these administrators in assessing student learning. The syllabus of a practicum course, whether it is designed by a sole instructor or WPA, or is developed in conversation with multiple program personnel, may be a program text that not only dictates the work of instructors and students in a course during a single semester but also directs their larger perception of teacher development practices and purposes. As Shari J. Stenberg and Amy Lee note (2002), the syllabus of the course demonstrates to graduate student instructors "what kind of [teacher-]students they are expected to *be*" (332; emphasis in original). However, as LaFrance (2019) points out, if the language and values of a text like the syllabus are not taken up by users in the institutional circuit, it does not have this directive power (44); instead, the language and contents of a syllabus may have a limited impact on the ways GTAs experience or perceive teacher development, let alone program values.

William Germano and Kit Nicholls (2020) further emphasize the ways that specific syllabus language may reveal or conceal what students will experience and learn in a course, sometimes prioritizing the genre as a kind of legal document (8–9). In this sense, the practicum syllabus might be demonstrative only of a checklist of to-dos GTAs must accomplish before earning their credits and moving on to the next step of their graduate education. Institutional policy and legalese may squeeze out the character and heart of the syllabus document. Germano and Nicholls write, "The teacher's contribution to the syllabus can seem as if it's crowded out by administrative fine print, so that it's easy to look at a syllabus and think that the three Rs are readings, regulations, and recourse. We're not teachers if we're salespeople servicing customers. The syllabus isn't the warranty on a Toyota" (10). They provide further caution about the ways that instructors might implicitly (and improperly) write their roles into the language of a syllabus: "We're not lay therapists or auxiliary police, either. We're teachers" (10). But the syllabus is a "contested space," the authors write, its rhetorical effect and import undeniable in the present tensions of higher education (10). We teachers are reminded that we are on alert, by their description: The syllabus is a place where faculty may assert their values, but there are competing agendas sharing that space (10). Germano and Nicholls caution us to consider these competing agendas and their impact on how the syllabus will be taken up by students:

> Is it too much, too little, too complicated, too filled with arrows that point the student to side roads? Could you read your own syllabus and make a reasonable guess as to what the course wants to accomplish, as opposed to what your department's course catalogue says that the course studies or describes? Could you recognize what the course challenges students to do? And how exactly would you, the teacher who wrote that syllabus, follow through on your own expectations for students? (3)

Though program values for teacher development may be identifiable in other program texts, like I demonstrate in chapter 1, the syllabus for the composition teaching practicum is certainly the central representative text for the ways that program values manifest in teacher development. While other program documents, including curricular documents for the courses GTAs will teach, provide clues to the kinds of teacher development they will require, the syllabus of the practicum itself is worth looking at to identify how a program conveys its intentions for teacher development. As Germano and Nicholls put it, "Anyone who's ever taken a class knows that the real real of a class isn't going to be in a course description. It's going to be in the syllabus" (21). So, what do practicum syllabi tell us about what kinds of teachers will emerge from a particular program? What can we understand about our field's investment in cultivating teachers in particular ways, with particular values? I begin to explore these questions in this chapter.

Studying Practicum Syllabi and Talking with Their Designers

To contextualize my program research on values for teacher development within the larger field, I had to thoughtfully turn outward. As several recent studies have dealt with the first-semester practicum (e.g., Restaino 2012; Brewer 2020a), with the wider range of teacher development (Cicchino 2020), and with doctoral training more broadly (Driscoll et al. 2020), I needed to carefully distinguish my goals from those studies. For example, while I worked through this study, Amy Cicchino had recently published the results of a survey of writing pedagogy education (WPE) for GTAs in thirty-eight doctoral programs in rhetoric and composition. Cicchino's results focus on kinds of training done in orientations, practicum courses, and workshops, and other sites of this education. In coding responses, Cicchino looks, in part, at what participants' goals were for WPE and what they hoped to change (90). She reports coding 130 phrases into ten categories: "composition theory; practices tied to teaching writing; rhetorical theory; local program, curriculum, or policies; curriculum/course development; development of teacherly ethos/identity; development of student-writers; mentorship; time/timing; and technology" (90). My more narrow goal, on the other hand, was to look at the ways that program values manifest in the site of the teaching practicum, and the syllabus specifically, which coincides with Cicchino's study in only some aspects, namely, the ways that teaching and learning happens in the practicum, as I outline in the sections that follow. Cicchino and I clearly share an audience, however, and there is certainly overlap in what my participants identify as values and the categories of goals or priorities for change just listed. In her conclusion, she emphasizes the need for WPAs to reflect on their programs' WPE. Cicchino writes, "Based on these data, it seems reasonable to suggest that WPAs should engage in a recursive process of reflecting on the goals for their

GTA preparation, they should align these goals to contemporary scholarship, and they should conduct regular assessment" (102).

I wholly appreciate Cicchino's recommendation for this triad of reflection, alignment, and assessment, and add to it, in this chapter, a fourth recommendation: alignment with program values. In my study, talking with WPAs about the ways that their program values manifested in the practicum syllabus would provide a helpful parallel to my look at the curriculum committee's work (chapter 3) and my own attempts to inscribe values into the syllabus via the reading list for the course (chapter 4). Analyzing practicum syllabi would provide me with a sense of how these values look across programs. I share my specific interest in the presence of program values in documents with my friend and disciplinary colleague Jennifer Grouling—our discussions fall within the larger parameters of the work of writing studies scholars who look at the ways disciplinary values manifest within the pressures of specific institutional contexts (e.g., Poblete 2014; Perryman-Clark 2018). I build on our discussions of this phenomenon in this chapter by emphasizing values for teacher development, specifically, that support my broad presentation of that activity as central—not supplementary—to not only my own program but also the work of the field.

DATA COLLECTION AND ANALYSIS

The study presented in this chapter uses textual analysis of semi-structured interviews with WPAs and teaching practicum syllabi to understand how disciplinary values are articulated by program personnel and manifest in writing program documents.[1] Data collection and analysis occurred in stages. First, I contacted fifty-five potential participants via institutional email to request syllabi and interviews. These participants were identified using the department or program websites of relevant institutions, universities granting MA or PhD degrees in writing studies or rhetoric and composition or graduate level concentrations in these degrees. I selected this pool using a similar rationale as Cicchino (2020), cited earlier, the assumption that these programs would "have faculty specializing in rhetoric and composition, and, thus, their WPE is more likely to be informed by recent scholarship" (89). However, unlike Cicchino, who focused on doctoral programs in rhetoric and composition, I also included programs with MAs and PhD *concentrations* in rhetoric and composition and writing studies, because teacher development for graduate students teaching FYW also happens in these programs. I identified potential participants' institutional email addresses using their program or department websites and sent them an introductory email with a description of the study, a request for syllabi to be sent in response to the email, and an invitation to participate in an interview. Once participants agreed to interviews, I conducted background research on the writing programs and WPA-specific work of these participants for context (Blakeslee and Fleischer 2019, 154). I read the documents they shared with me, and prepared an interview script for semi-structured interviews, adaptable to each interview occasion (Merriam 2009; Driscoll 2011; Creswell and Creswell 2018; Blakeslee and Fleischer 2019). Hour-long interviews were conducted online using Zoom and were recorded for transcription.

Prior to each interview, I reviewed the syllabus and schedule materials the participant had shared with me and integrated specific questions about these materials and their courses into the interview protocol (appendix). Because I would have the opportunity to read and analyze each participant's practicum syllabus before and after the interview, I designed the interview protocol to allow me to integrate relationship-building and discussion about each participants' approach to the class into the hour-long call. Specifically, I wanted to ask questions that would allow me to understand participants' decisions in their dual roles as administrators and practicum instructors, as well as to encourage them to articulate their program values and expound on the ways they saw these evident in the text itself. I hoped the discussions would allow me to see ways that the official texts (i.e., syllabi) aligned with participants' articulations and would allow us to see as a cooperative pair whether discussion about the artifact in this way would help uncover any room for (re)alignment.

Using Zoom interviews allowed participation from WPAs to whom I could not feasibly travel and whose availability would have been otherwise limited during the busy fall semester, never mind the pandemic-related research travel limitations imposed by many universities at the time. During the interview, I used the screen-sharing feature in Zoom to highlight specific passages in the syllabus or schedule to the participant, contextualizing my questions. Our working together with the document in the screen-share allowed participants to also show me portions of the document, in response, if they chose to. This feature of Zoom allowed the course artifacts to function as a material touchstone in the interview conversations, a feature not supported in phone interviews (Gray et al. 2020, 1294). This shared review of the syllabus provided not just a means of collaborative textual analysis but also a window into the motivations participants brought with them to teaching the practicum. Germano and Nicholls (2020) note,

> The syllabus as we traditionally know it may read as if it's all about what *will* happen in the next sixteen weeks, but to a great extent it's really about

what the teacher has experienced as recently as last year and as long ago as graduate school. A teacher crafts a syllabus based on the teacher's own prior experience as a student, in conversation with peers, as a result of the bruises and exaltations last time teaching the course, or some combination of all three. (5)

Thus, in addition to inquiring about instructors' intentions in designing the practicum and how these intentions were accompanied by particular values for teacher development or writing program values writ large, we sometimes ventured into the ways these participants' own teacher development—especially previous experiences teaching FYW or the practicum—shaped their decisions, design, and values.

Following the interviews, I used Otter.ai to run and check transcriptions. I then read each transcription to write a summary of the conversation and worked through collaborative open coding with a graduate research assistant, Kristi Morris, to identify distinct expressions of values and to develop analytical themes. Then, through conversation and collaborative coding, we applied the emergent values for teacher development identified in chapter 1 to the entire (modest) collection of practicum syllabi from across programs, including our own. I used this set of analyses to begin to draw conclusions about the manifestation of potential disciplinary values for teacher development.

I made the decision early on in my data collection process to allow my interview sample to remain small. Of the fifty-five WPAs I contacted for syllabi and interviews, only six initially responded at all: four of these supplied syllabi and agreed to interviews, and I describe these conversations in the text that follows; one supplied a syllabus; one offered to participate but did not ultimately respond to my follow-up scheduling email. I attribute this participation level both to the timing of my study (I was recruiting in summer for fall interviews, during what would be the fourth "pandemic semester," in ever more uncertain times for WPAs and everyone else) and to what I have seen in multiple studies I have conducted with small teams over the last few years as an ever decreasing bandwidth for even those who strongly advocate for research engagement to participate as research subjects. Significantly, I was also limited by timing and made decisions about data collection based on the boundaries of the grant-funding timeline I had for working with Kristi, as well as managing this work alongside the other studies of this book.

TABLE 2.1. Interview participants

Participant	Institution Type	Location
Amanda	Public research university	East Coast
Michelle	Public research university	Midwest
Stephanie	Public research university	East South Central
Toni	Public research university	Upper Midwest

PARTICIPANTS

Four present or recent-past WPAs and practicum instructors participated in hour-long Zoom interviews in fall 2021. Additionally, from August 2021 to February 2022, I received syllabi from five additional present or recent-past WPAs or practicum instructors, representing graduate programs in rhetoric and composition or writing studies across regions (programs on the Pacific Coast and in the Southwest are not represented in this study, though invited).

In an effort to preserve the anonymity of the colleagues I interviewed, I summarize here their similarities and the distinct differences in their experiences, to provide a sense of the range of perspectives shared in these interviews. Details specific to their individual experiences may emerge in the discussions that follow; however, for the sake of anonymity, I have worked to leave out any potential identifying information (for example, discussion of participants' research or particularities about their schools). These colleagues are represented by pseudonyms, and I have shared the draft of this chapter with them for review and discussion.

Amanda, Michelle, Stephanie, and Toni represent programs in rhetoric and composition in public research universities that are all a bit bigger than my home program. At the time of the interviews, one was pre-tenure, the others associate professors; three were presently serving as WPAs and one had just completed several years in the role. One was teaching the practicum for the first time. Three taught the practicum during the pandemic, in either fall 2020, fall 2021, or both; one taught it for the last time in 2019. The two participants teaching the practicum in fall 2021 did so in person; three participants had previous experience teaching the course online. Their practicum courses include both MA and PhD students, often with more MA students than PhD students—an opposite weight of my home program's enrollment, which sometimes funds MA students but mostly PhD students. Because of the focus of my interviews and my efforts to provide participants with anonymity, I did not inquire during the interview about other aspects of their identity that might position them as minoritized or marginalized in any ways, though I recognize asking for that information might have more fully contextualized some of the decisions or experiences these participants describe. However, even without capturing more nuanced demographic information in interviews, I found that the apparent demographic similarities between these participants and me (at least in terms of gender and age) made it a compelling sample for me: Through interviewing, I had the chance to learn from four early-tenure and pre-tenure women whose work I admired.

Finding Common Ground in Interviews About Practicum Syllabi and Program Values

I prepared for each interview by reviewing the practicum syllabus and schedule the participant had shared with me to understand how it was organized and to prepare specific questions about program values or components of the class. For example, reviewing Stephanie's materials before our interview, I knew I wanted to ask her about how she developed the reading list for the course, because each week was labeled with a discrete thematic focus and included a set of several readings from diverse authors. Discussion about this reading list could help elicit an articulation of program values broadly or for teacher development specifically. The four interviews I conducted took place, for me, in my dining room, my laptop and notes spread out across the table, a safe distance on some days from my youngest son, Moses, who was five then, watching a show in the TV room, when he was home sick or on a class quarantine from school. For my participants, the interviews took place in their offices or living rooms. Zoom had become a social and research necessity and a familiar parlor for meeting and greeting friends, colleagues, and new contacts, and a gift for eliminating most of the restrictions of geography. The day of my first interview, a large storm cell progressed across metro Detroit and toward my town; I paced the house, concerned about losing power, worried about fumbling through the interviews. Mostly, the sense of distance (and panic) evaporated for me once we began talking, except for the occasional interruptions on either end, like when Moses came into the room to talk to me and Toni about the boat he was building out of stuff in our recycling bin.

Here, I present topical themes that cut across two or more interviews, including participants' articulation of program values, before looking at the ways that values for teacher development, more narrowly, are present across the ten practicum syllabi I examined. These themes emphasize tensions related to the ways that practicum instructors work to integrate their own values into the work of the course and the ways that these individual values and program values sometimes align and sometimes "push back" against each other (to use Michelle's phrase) in the site of the practicum. More broadly, the topical themes provide context for whether and how these values can be seen at work in local programs.

(ATTEMPTS AT) ARTICULATING VALUES (BOX 2.1)

> **BOX 2.1. PARTICIPANTS' IDENTIFIED PROGRAM VALUES (ALPHABETICAL ORDER)**
> Antiracism
> Attention to faculty and graduate student working conditions
> Care
> Community-engaged learning
> Compassion
> Critical reading
> Equitable approaches toward language
> Equity
> Expanding the definition of writing
> Inclusive excellence
> Inquiry-based research
> Instructor autonomy
> Language difference
> More expansive notions of rhetoric
> Multimodality
> Racial justice
> Research
> Revision
> Rhetoric
> Rhetorical flexibility
> Understanding genre
> Writing about writing
> Writing process

After asking each participant how their semester was going, I asked, "What, would you say, are the core values of your writing program?" I wanted to know both what explicit values participants' programs might have articulated and which values these WPAs and practicum instructors might be directly bringing to their work in teacher development, and I wanted to begin with this question to see what values were at the forefront of participants' minds. For some participants, like Amanda, it was a familiar conversation, one they had been engaged in in their programs and departments. The terms that each of these instructors initially presented were also familiar—a mix of values for what should be taught in FYW and for how writing programs should be administered, values that were historically evident and values emerging more recently in their local sites: *antiracism, equity, inclusive excellence, multimodality, expanding the definition of writing, writing process, writing about writing, revision, rhetoric, research, valuing language difference, the importance of understanding genre,* and *instructor autonomy*.

As our conversations unfolded, more values rose to the surface, along with admissions from participants that these additional values may not be as explicit in the practicum syllabus as they could be, or that they were values participants hoped to be more explicitly introducing as they navigated their roles. For example, as Amanda admitted in our discussion, she wasn't sure these values were "clear in the document itself," though there were scheduled topics for each practicum meeting that she highlighted as evidence of the values she articulated. These less explicit values described by participants included *more expansive notions of rhetoric, rhetorical flexibility, equitable approaches toward language, community-engaged learning, inquiry-based research, critical reading, attention to faculty and graduate student working conditions, compassion, care,* and *racial justice*. Sometimes, participants' individual values—not program values—were emphasized in moments in the syllabus, and, like Michelle noted, it may be "a little tricky" for GTAs to know whether what they are doing is an investment of the practicum instructor / WPA or of the program. Overall, the challenges participants sometimes had in talking about values (or reported their instructors having) reflect the categorization of values outlined in the introduction: some are implicit, some explicit, some shared across programs, and some individual.

Our discussions revealed several locations for program values within the practicum syllabus. These values were typically not present in the front matter of the syllabi in learning outcomes and course descriptions that GTAs review to get a sense of the purpose of the practicum but rather expressed implicitly across the document:

- Values like reflection are evident and practiced in assignments like teaching portfolios and peer feedback.
- Values may also be present in the custom textbooks GTAs use, crafted specifically for local FYW classes; these direct manifestations are present in print and drive classroom activity.

- Values may also be present in program policies; Michelle gave the example of her program revising their absence policy to better support students.

In these cases, program values are present but dispersed across the materiality of the class. Other, more implicit values might be more like a presence of an idea—as Michelle put it—present in program culture, if not in the syllabus or other printed material of the practicum. In the course of our conversation, Michelle remarked that she has worked hard to make sure program values are explicit and that TAs seem to be able to articulate those values, often better than long-term faculty, who "seem confused by talking about it that way." Michelle and I didn't talk about why this confusion might occur. It may be that these faculty need more definition of what makes an idea a value, what makes it a driving force of one's teaching or administrative work. It may be that this corporate speak is both familiar and unfamiliar to our academic context; values appear in the lofty talk of upper administration, but faculty may be incredulous of what might be perceived as hollow rhetoric; may not participate in the conversations, classes, and workshops where these values are discussed; or may simply not be accustomed to values discourse. Whatever the case, Michelle's remark reinforced the value of integrating values-focused talk in program work so that not only the discourse but also the values themselves become familiar and actionable.

Each conversation took on its own life, but at the end of the interviews, I pointedly returned to our focus on the ways program values manifest in the practicum syllabus. This summative moment provided a chance for assessment, wherein participants spoke to the degree they feel these values are present in the course and known to GTAs—the degree to which these values are articulated. For example, when I asked Toni to describe where she saw program values evident in the document and whether there were other values she saw present there, she said that one of the goals of the practicum is to introduce students to the fact that there is scholarship on writing, that there is evidence of best practices and long-held debates about how best to teach writing. Readings are therefore discussed in the weeks before GTAs work on practical assignments, like making videos on course topics, so that they have scholarly support in crafting these materials. In terms of writing as a process and genre being present as values in the syllabus, Toni described how she has students reflect on the materials in their teaching portfolio, what the genres in their portfolio look like, how to use feedback to revise and develop their materials. She thought these values were well integrated into the syllabus.

When I asked Amanda if there was anything else she would like to add about program values or the documents we looked at, she noted the difficulty of concretizing program values in a practicum syllabus, a document (and class) that is necessarily changing in increments over time. She said, "There are probably some touchstones here though, to keep, but I just think as a program evolves, this course's syllabus and materials, and approach have to evolve along with it so that students can kind of get what they need out of it." I asked Amanda to give me an example of something that would be included in the practicum syllabus if she were teaching it in the upcoming semester. She mentioned "This Ain't Another Statement! This Is a DEMAND for Black Linguistic Justice!" (Conference on College Composition and Communication 2020) and other work on antiracist writing instruction. Amanda's reflection emphasizes the ways that the practicum must be, to a degree, both static and dynamic: possessing structural soundness in place to support GTAs learning how to teach the curriculum but socially responsive to help them teach actual students in the present cultural context. Further, her reflection suggests that explicit, articulated values for teacher development can maintain the structural soundness of the practicum while also being dynamic.

While I asked about program values in at least two specific moments in each interview, discussion of these values emerged at various points across each conversation. There was congruence in these stated values in some instances between one conversation and another; however, participants mainly expressed values unique to them or their programs in the interviews, representative of the localization of the field (Wardle and Downs 2018, 127). One talking point that emerged across all four interviews was WPA labor. While one participant, Amanda, identified attention to instructor and graduate student labor, more generally, as a program value, the fact that WPA labor came up in each conversation is not surprising, as teaching the practicum is only one of the overlapping workplace contexts WPAs attend to each week.

THE PRACTICUM AS (JUST ONE) LOCATION FOR PROFESSIONALIZATION

The interviews emphasize the importance of the opportunity to professionalize graduate students in writing studies via the practicum. Its potential and necessity as a site of professionalization are evident in situations like what Amanda described at her campus, where administration regularly demands more sections of composition and sees the hiring of the appropriate adjunct instructors as a simple solution ("as if there are a million writing studies adjuncts waiting for me to snap them up and put them in a classroom," Amanda commented). For Amanda, this problem led her to collaborative attention to working conditions for faculty and graduate students, one of the values highlighted earlier. In addition to the problem of mounting work hours and course overloads, it is neither preferable to only offer instructors adjunct positions in their specialty areas, limiting their teaching options, nor to staff composition courses with unprepared nonspecialists (Conference on College Composition and Communication 2015). The practicum can be, then, a site where the distinction of what it means to be assigned to teach composition and what it means to be a composition professional is made clear to students (and to other stakeholders).

Kristi and I identified discussion of *professionalization* as an explicit term in three of the four interview transcripts; in the fourth transcript, the idea appears just slightly differently as discussion of joining a teaching community. What is meant by professionalizing in each of the contexts I explored with participants becomes clear in several moments of these conversations; sometimes, it is directly tied to teaching in the local context and sometimes to joining the discipline. While professionalizing does not happen wholly in the bounds of the practicum (see Hansen for a critique of professionalizing in the discipline), the course is certainly a key location in the process (Yancey 2002). Interview participants emphasize connections with mentor teachers and with disciplinary frameworks and position statements as two key strategies for professionalization in the practicum; branching out from their own teaching, being paired with mentors, and discussing disciplinary statements connect GTAs with other members of the program and field and help them understand core arguments about teaching writing.

GTAs must also become part of the local "teaching community," as Michelle's syllabus emphasized. Thus, immersion and observation are also key professionalizing strategies. Sometimes new GTAs are teamed with mentor teachers, and they practice teaching in mentor teachers' classrooms. Amanda's program's scaffolded teaching (observation, co-teaching, solo teaching) is intended to help students feel "supported" as they shift from reading about teaching writing to teaching their own classes. Michelle has students analyze their mentors' teaching materials before adapting them for their own teaching preparation. In Stephanie's practicum, students are assigned to observe their mentor teachers' classrooms and their peers' classrooms.

Supporting GTAs' authority as teachers is also a significant part of this professionalization. From early on in Toni's practicum course, students reflect on what they know about good teaching and "identify their own expertise." As they begin teaching the course, both students and Toni are concerned that students "present themselves with as much authority as possible." Providing GTAs with checklists for making sure their use of technology is organized, for example, helps them get a strong start in their own classrooms. She explained that is also able to anticipate classroom concerns that GTAs may not be prepared to think about; these may be minor logistical issues, or they may be serious cultural challenges, like facing undergraduate students' xenophobia. Toni does not provide all of this problem-solving advice herself, however. Her practicum course, in part, engages students in giving each other feedback on their instructional videos and class activities. Toni remarked that the act of giving feedback and collaborative problem-solving is "such a hard skill to develop" and that as a practicum instructor, providing space for practicing this is "the most important thing [she] can do." This practice comes along with stakes for the whole teaching community: The instructional videos Toni's students make are shared with the rest of the program; therefore, the feedback and discussion in class integrally support their creation.

The complexity of problem solving and advice giving is captured in Toni's description of the things she attends to when she does teaching observations for GTAs in her practicum:

> With brand new teachers, in the first observation, a lot of my conversation we have is a lot of practical stuff—things that I know that if they don't resolve now will become bigger problems. Just basic stuff, you know, really. And I try to offer really practical advice, like, if you give the homework at the end of the class, no one is listening. At the beginning, just really basic stuff that can really set them up and their students up for really understanding the purpose of the class, etc. I would say, a lot of what I do is giving them an idea of what they don't know that they're doing. Obviously, like all of us, we don't know we have these habits or these things that we're doing that might be shutting students down. We might not really be listening. We might be interrupting students when they speak. We might not be repeating what they say or validating anything they say. We might be asking really closed questions instead of open questions that have real flexibility in their answers. So, I've occasionally, with more experienced teachers, who are more confident, sometimes they don't know this, but they're ignoring certain kinds of students. And so I'll point that out to them. And, obviously, I spend time telling them what they're doing well, too. Like, this is really strong. I can hear you from the back of the classroom, this kind of stuff. Your students were really participating well, so that means that they feel engaged.

I include this long quote from Toni's description both because I love writing about teaching observations and talking about how we engage during these observations, and because her description highlights the inextricability of teacher development in the practicum from FYW students' learning experiences. The description highlights the performance of composition pedagogy: knowing when to talk and when to listen, asking the right kinds of questions, even how to vocally perform. In her asynchronous observations during online teaching in the pandemic, while the object of her observation attention was qualitatively different, Toni was still able to regularly provide students with feedback on the organization of their courses and to use examples from individual GTAs' courses for discussion in the practicum.

Participants noted that what GTAs experience in the practicum is a bit different from in their other classes. GTAs from across English studies might be familiar with the feedback structures embedded in the course; however, their other graduate courses may not include weekly assigned deliverables in the same way the practicum does, a structure that often mirrors the schedule of FYW. This practicum helps GTAs learn how to plan and how to adapt, how to set expectations and how to be flexible. As Amanda pointed out, many GTAs are in their programs to obtain their degrees, not, primarily, to teach composition courses, so part of the practicum's work is to help them see how all of these pieces of their experience can function together, acknowledging their labor conditions.

TEACHING THE PRACTICUM DURING THE PANDEMIC

I talked with interview participants during fall 2021, when we were still working our way through what it meant to prepare teachers of writing and to support writing program projects during a pandemic. I did not ask participants a specific question about teaching the practicum during the pandemic, but because we were still all very much working through that long season and multiple unknowns at the time of these interviews, it is not surprising to me that in each conversation there were references to the way teacher development was changed during this time. These mentions emerged both in discussions about how we prepared GTAs to use technology for teaching and in how we helped them develop a balance between being clear about their expectations for student learning and demonstrating grace and compassion to students under stress and in distress. Teaching the practicum during this time allowed instructors to model particular aspects of professionalism and allowed program values to manifest in sometimes new ways.

As noted in the descriptions of Toni's students making instructional videos, some attention to technology was simply a matter of course. Because GTAs needed to make instructional videos to share new information with their undergraduate students, class time in the practicum needed to support this activity, and feedback needed to be built in via peer commentary and teaching observations. As acknowledged by Ellen Carillo (2021), changes in classroom assessment practices, while serving more socially just ends also came during the pandemic more as a practical (and compassionate) matter of course (3). The shift to online instruction during the pandemic led Michelle to try complete/incomplete grading for weekly assignments, even though she refrained from using it for the major project of the semester (the portfolio) because of the weight that assignment holds for ensuring teachers are ready to teach classes in subsequent semesters. I asked Michelle if she thought graduate students were receptive to that grading style and she said yes, as it had become part of the program culture and was being used in their other classes.

This compassion, along with a serious measure of grace, appears in practicum syllabi balanced with transparency about classroom expectations. I asked Amanda about course policies that seem like they would be the same kinds of policies in an FYW syllabus (i.e., a "crisis pass" and "free absence"). Amanda explained that she includes those policies to help graduate students "feel what it means to be a student who" needs to take up those opportunities. She also noted the common assumption that graduate students are not like undergraduate students, and reflected, "I don't actually know that I think that's entirely true." Because GTAs come to the practicum from different areas of English studies, Amanda asserted the importance of being clear with GTAs about what is expected of them in the practicum, in order for them to each "find their own space in it." Amanda's assertion highlighted the importance of program values not only being dynamic but also capacious, such that the diversity of instructors in a program can find their pedagogical and scholarly foothold as they work to support those values.

I asked Michelle to describe how she developed a section on expectations for GTAs' participation in the program's teaching community. She noted challenges she has experienced, as a WPA, helping GTAs understand the distinction between the requirements of their jobs as teachers for the program and their responsibilities as students in the practicum and what the parameters of assessment are for each role. She noted that some of the language of the expectations section of her syllabus comes from those experiences: how much time students will spend on their work for the class, and how they should treat each other (especially when they disagree).

The expression of policies allows for practicum instructors to model approaches to teaching writing courses. Stephanie's syllabus includes policies related to flexibility and to boundary setting (especially regarding when she will respond to emails). She explained she is trying to model these practices for students and described revising a plagiarism statement to better address students as colleagues. Stephanie's instruction of graduate-level courses, including the practicum, includes scaffolded writing assignments and feedback to support students' development of larger projects. She also noted flexibility and cutting readings or shortening reflections when she notices students getting burned out. Modeling this decision making can then support GTAs in making similar decisions in their teaching, complementing the modeling of methods selection, assessment, presentation, and reflection that practicum instructors must necessarily do (Miller et al. 2005, 89).

PLANNING READINGS FOR THE PRACTICUM

Selecting weekly themes and readings for the practicum syllabus is a tremendous organizational and curricular challenge (Trubek 2005), and it is a task that we practicum instructors think matters a lot to the success of the course. As I demonstrate in the next two chapters, most of our planning attention for the practicum could go into selecting readings. Decisions about course readings do not only impact practicum discussions; Michelle and I briefly discussed how readings both directly support GTAs' immediate teaching and indirectly support the decisions they will make in their teaching in future semesters. With individual or program values in mind, alongside additional logistical needs for teacher development, practicum instructors need to make rhetorical and practical decisions about course texts. Amanda described the challenge:

> You know, there's so much good scholarship in the field about how to teach writing ... coming at that from so many different angles, that really makes constructing a syllabus like this really difficult in good ways, because you're sort of like, Oh, no, there's so much that we could pack in—so much that I always want to cover, and I'm always having to whittle back from this giant list of—you know, if we ideally have, like, a whole year, we could do work on this then.

Amanda's wish for a whole year for the practicum feels very familiar. If you have not taught the practicum yet, perhaps you have felt it in teaching FYW, as you continually make revisions to the time and space granted to specific activities with the aim of supporting student success. As pedagogical values rise to the surface in teacher development settings, and as we are able to articulate them for ourselves, we continue to work to align classroom activities, assigned readings, and projects with these values.

As I noted in chapter 1, program personnel might approach the creation of a syllabus—even the reading list for the syllabus—quite differently, based on their individual values or perceived program concerns. When Stephanie shared a highly organized and thick reading schedule with me, I couldn't wait to ask her about her planning strategy. Turning to the schedule of the syllabus, I asked Stephanie to explain her organizing logic for determining the themes for each week's work. She noted that part of this logic is tied to what GTAs need to teach; for example, they read about multimodal composing to prepare to work with their own students on a video project, and they read about language ideologies, "Students' Right to Their Own Language" (Conference on College Composition and Communication 1974), and other related topics in the practicum before they read those texts with their own students. Practicum students also read about research writing toward the end of the semester before they teach research writing in the second course of the composition sequence. Stephanie also described including readings about remediation, response, inclusivity, and histories of pedagogies but struggling with what sometimes feels like a "hodgepodge" of readings that is hard to sequence. Some of the organization she tried "just didn't feel good," she said. She described wanting to develop a "throughline" of scholarship on antiracist pedagogy and explained her experience trying to combine readings on trauma-informed pedagogy and access but thinking these topics would be better separated in the future.

Stephanie described her iterative work incorporating more scholars of color into the reading list, to be more "intentional" about the authors students would be reading. She also described being conscious about how much she is asking students to read, sometimes giving them choices between texts and using jigsaw discussions, in which each participant in the discussion is responsible for presenting a part of the assigned reading, to facilitate work with texts in class. I reflected on the challenge of finding time in a two-credit class to work through recommended readings while still wanting to advance particular values through the class; Stephanie related experiences with not having enough time to discuss texts in class because of other activities. She reflected on shifting the focus and timing of other assignments in her course to make more time for discussion, and I responded that it feels like the constant tension of a practicum seems to be never having enough time to get everything done. Invited to add final thoughts about the program values or syllabus, Stephanie explained the challenges of scheduling some topics for the course and choosing a piece to end the semester with. She described wanting to emphasize and model to her students how teachers are always growing and learning. Stephanie noted that for her next course, she was going to start planning the syllabus sooner and would spend more time reading work by Indigenous scholars, because she wants to avoid tokenizing any scholars or work in her syllabus.

While across the syllabi these instructors shared with me there is tremendous diversity in reading assignments, there are also some important consistencies. *Naming What We Know* (Adler-Kassner and Wardle 2015) appears on two of these participants' syllabi, *Bad Ideas About Writing* (Ball and Loewe 2017) on three, position statements from CCCC on three. I mention these texts because they are texts that, themselves, forward specific values, by wrestling with conversations central to the field and in the classroom. Amanda commented, specifically, that the books are "useful introductions to the field and concepts in the field." Texts like these, which capture the larger conversation and shared foundation of the field, are complemented, then, by the selection of texts in which practicum instructors assert their individual values, shaping what GTAs will come to understand about what it means to do the work of teaching writing.

LIFE CYCLES OF PROGRAM CHANGE

As Cole and Hassel (2021) present in the introduction to their edited collection *Transformations: Change Work Across Writing Programs, Pedagogies, and Practices*, writing programs are constantly responsive to change and are, themselves, always changing. Change is unavoidable, they remind us, and change work is often led by NTT faculty and graduate students, workers who "are doing good work" that no one is making them do (4). My interviews with WPAs and practicum instructors highlight ways that the practicum itself must be responsive to change, as well as both the ways that these instructors serve as change makers and whether and how they position GTAs to practice this work. Understanding the life cycles of change in a local context—learning how and in what timelines change can be implemented—is a crucial part of engaging this values-based action.

Amanda described how she has seen micro-evolutionary changes in her program since she last taught the practicum. Specific ideas and priorities connected to reading, research, and rhetorical flexibility had "come into sharper focus," and the practicum syllabus would need to continue to evolve with those. Amanda gave an example of the wider program's work on antiracist teaching needing to be more strongly integrated into the practicum. Her description showed the constant flux between practicum and program at large, reflecting, again, the need for program values to be dynamic and capacious.

Early in my interview with Stephanie, she commented that she was "overwhelmed" by what she had to do and wanted to for her program. When we returned to talking through her goals and the pressures she senses, her earlier comment made sense. Without a formal program assessment in place, Stephanie could make some choices about where to put her attention. Especially important to her was the work her program had been doing raising awareness of antiracist pedagogy and language difference, and she hoped the Institute of Race, Rhetoric, and Literacy's forthcoming recommendations for working with these topics would be helpful.[2] While Stephanie would like the program to have a more systematic plan for racial justice work, she acknowledged that it "keeps getting pushed to the backburner." She shared that she planned to rewrite the program's mission statement and craft a five-year plan to share with a committee. In Stephanie's program, the practicum instructor has a lot of instructional agency that they then pass on to GTAs. Stephanie explained that whoever teaches the practicum determines the curriculum that first-year GTAs teach in the introductory writing course; these GTAs then develop their own curriculum for the second course in the sequence, which they teach in the winter.

In my interview with Michelle, I shared that I find her program's structure and work to be aspirational and that I wanted our program to be doing similar things in teacher development, like successfully organizing opportunities for new GTAs to observe other teachers teaching and finding an institutional pathway to returning to a full semester of preparation prior to teaching. I asked her if there is buy-in across the teaching cohort for work in things like trauma-informed pedagogy and contract grading, the topics of recent professional development workshops. Michelle acknowledged that because much program work had been virtual in the past year, it was hard to tell, but she felt there had been buy-in from graduate students and contract faculty, with a smaller group of contract faculty perhaps more invested.

Michelle noted, though, that the official FYW curriculum sometimes proves slightly obstructive to these goals and offered the example of the emphasis on "persuasion" in the first course syllabus as at odds with her interest in focusing on rhetoric more broadly. Michelle noted that she has more influence in this regard over the GTAs than over faculty who have been teaching the course for twenty or thirty years. She also noted that some faculty do not feel they have time for professional development or might be concerned that they need to take the terms in the syllabus in a narrow way. This example of a sharp distinction between individual values and program values represents not only a tension in local values but also between the local and the discipline: Where the discipline has turned to examination of *rhetorics* instead of a singular, Western approach to rhetoric, local instructors long teaching only Aristotelian appeals are dug into that instructional approach.

We talked about helping GTAs negotiate new ideas in the practicum. I asked Michelle if her students work through different perspectives in class discussion or whether they are generally on the same page about the ideas presented in the readings and about how to approach teaching FYW. Michelle responded that "it depends on the year and the class," as well as the influence that mentor teachers have over their teaching; sometimes, she said, GTAs will learn and work through ideas in the practicum, but their materials primarily reflect the investments of their mentor teachers. Michelle described a desire to "push back" against what is inscribed in program texts and related a practicum conversation where she asked students to consider how new course materials "fit in with but also resist" current program goals. In this conversation, Michelle provided insight to students on the long process of changing course outcomes and goals. She described what often makes changing perceptions of curriculum requirements difficult: "These things get passed down . . . like, you can with your graduate students, encourage them to approach teaching the class in a certain way, but outside of that, you know there's some lore that's pushing against it." I asked Michelle how long she thought that life cycle of change is in her program. Noting that she had been in the position for a few years and may be for a few more, she said that if she could not make the changes she hoped for in the next couple of years, she felt like she still had time.

In these examples, participants displayed an awareness of the interpersonal, material, and temporal elements that need to align for them to instigate programmatic change, including resistance from or disconnects with senior instructors and instructors from across English studies backgrounds; teaching the practicum online, as many of us did during the pandemic; contending with institutional pressure to hire more adjunct instructors; and other elements. Rather than waiting for the stars to align, these participants also related the reflection they have been doing to prepare for this work. These (anticipated) timelines reflect a reality of context described by Glenn (2018), in which she describes the little progress made in the material conditions of writing program administration, particularly for feminist WPAs:

> [Nan] Johnson's point is the crucial one: What difference do feminist principles actually make within such an academic-administrative arrangement? Many of the essential, ideal qualities of a feminist WPA are impossible to employ when taking an administrative position, whether the WPA is experienced or not, tenured or not. Each administrative position is contained by or contains its own scene. No one can enter the scene fully prepared; there is always on-the-job training as one learns the ins and outs, the backstories and histories of any scene. (112)

The local pressures faced by the WPAs and practicum instructors I spoke to—demands for adjunct instructors, the influence of longtime instructors, and so on—may both drive and hinder values-based program changes.

WHAT STUDENTS WALK OUT OF THE PRACTICUM BEST UNDERSTANDING ABOUT THE FIELD

For many GTAs, the composition teaching practicum is their primary exposure to composition pedagogy and to the field, an introduction that tells them whether the work of teaching writing is work they want to do or work they just may feel they have to do to secure gainful employment. It may be a gateway to deeper work in writing studies; it may be a useful semester-long laboratory in composition teaching; it may be fifteen weeks of training they simply endure.

When the conversation permitted, I asked participants what they thought students walk out of their classes understanding best about the work of writing studies. Amanda replied that students realize they are not teaching "in a vacuum" and that "there is scholarship to support the practices" used "in the classroom." Similarly, Toni said she thinks they understand "there's a lot of good ways to do teaching. And there's a lot of views about how to do teaching." She explained they understand writing as a process and that giving feedback is about more than identifying or correcting error. Toni noted that when students finish her course, she thinks they are "questioning some of the beliefs they had about what it means to teach writing and what good writing is, at least in a first-year writing context." Michelle's response pointed to her hopes for GTAs' confidence in finding their own connections to the field and their own ways of teaching writing. However, she also remarked, "some potentially could walk out of it just being like, [the field is] a mess of a bunch of different things and [*laughs*] somebody, please tell me what to do within it."

Emergent Values for Teacher Development, Read Across Programs

It's one thing for GTAs to walk out of a first-semester practicum course feeling like writing studies is "a mess of a bunch of different things" and another for instructors and administrators, themselves, to be grasping for touchstones, searching for the right strategies and texts and projects to bring the field into vision for students—to design values-driven instruction. Ideally, the practicum will be a (possibly first) clear window for GTAs from the program to the discipline, one of the various sites of teacher development (and other professional development) that prepares them for the central work of the field. Finding language that identifies shared values for teacher development across programs can support this clarity of vision into this one aspect of our discipline.

As emphasized by several scholars, including Dobrin (2005) and Cicchino (2020), while we surely can keep gathering narratives about teaching or taking the composition practicum, there is a dearth of empirical evidence about the course. After identifying which of these emergent values were also evident in my conversations with WPAs about the practicum syllabus, I looked at their syllabus documents alone and alongside other programs' syllabi to see whether there was an emerging consistency across programs. Identifying this consistency would strengthen the narratives presented by interview participants and confidence in the articulation of values as well.

Syllabi are familiar genres, designed so that students can access key information about a class, and so that administrators can identify course policies and calendars. Syllabi include the times and locations of courses; information about learning management systems; contact information and office hours for instructors; course learning outcomes; required textbooks; descriptions of projects; course calendars; and required institutional language about plagiarism, student resources, and safety. The syllabi Kristi and I reviewed for this project typically included several sections outlining the core aspects of the class: learning goals, expectations for participation, readings, and projects. Policies about late work and descriptions of the way the class fits into GTAs' overall coursework typically seemed to reflect the circumstances of the local program as much as the instructor's experiences with teaching the course. For example, one syllabus in the set specifically lists behaviors that demonstrate a lack of engagement and will lead to loss of participation points; another distinguishes the difference between students' grades in the class and their (wholly separate) programmatic teaching evaluations in their own sections of FYW. These are important clarifications that convey expectations for teacher-learners in each setting. Because of these public-facing functions, it is especially important to look at what a practicum syllabus can tell us about a writing program's values; if these values are not clear, we want to know why. Are there conflicts between what an instructor centers and what a program centers? If there are, does that stymy the change work programs are necessarily doing? And, in what kinds of program environments are we conducting teacher development?

These are big questions, but to begin to scratch the surface of them, Kristi and I read and analyzed the practicum syllabi we had collected, looking to see whether we could locate the emergent values for teacher development I had identified in our home program. To begin, we each independently coded the ten syllabi I collected for the emergent values for teacher development I had identified (box 2.2); to represent our home program, we included the common syllabus produced by our program's curriculum committee in winter 2020 (see chapter 3). At times, we each labeled passages with different but related values, or one of us labeled a passage but the other did not. We discussed these moments of disagreement to achieve reconciliation or a decision. In some cases, these discussions helped us revise the ways that we phrased the values statements, revisions I then went back and reapplied across the studies of the book, ultimately reducing a list of seven potential emergent values for teacher development to five that functioned across the analyses I was conducting. These discussions also helped us refine what would count as an expression of a value in the syllabus document. For example, in one participants' syllabus, one of the course goals is "Become a reflective teacher." Because this does not reference *reflective writing*, specifically, we did not code it as EV5. We found that *reflective practice* more generally is a theme that is evident through the set of syllabi, a value that holds true across educational settings. Because of the field's interest in written reflection, however, we chose to test that specific emergent value (regarding explicit written reflection) in our coding.

BOX 2.2. EMERGENT VALUES FOR TEACHER DEVELOPMENT IN RHETORIC, COMPOSITION, AND WRITING STUDIES

EV1: The practicum should emphasize local commitments to and strategies for teaching composition courses.

EV2: (New) composition teachers need opportunities to hear and learn from experienced and expert teachers.

EV3: Teaching composition is, materially and ideologically, a shared enterprise (composition teachers regularly share materials and strategies and co-construct knowledge).

EV4: Composition teachers need to be familiar with disciplinary frameworks.

EV5: Composition teachers should learn from written reflection on teaching.

TABLE 2.2. Presence of emergent values in ten practicum syllabi

Program	EV1	EV2	EV3	EV4	EV5
A	–	x	x	x	–
B	–	x	x	x	x
C	x	x	x	–	x
D	x	–	x	–	x
E	x	x	x	–	x
Home	x	x	x	–	x
Amanda	x	x	x	x	x
Michelle	x	x	x	x	x
Stephanie	x	–	x	x	x
Toni	x	x	x	x	x

We counted codes and determined how to present the results of this coding. Table 2.2 is intended to show a range of how the codes manifested, rather than as a quantification of the number of times a code appears in an individual syllabus or across the set. Quantification of codes, we determined, might show instructors' individual investments but might also simply be evidence of redundancy in a document. What mattered more was whether a value appeared *at all* in a program's practicum syllabus.

Of the five emergent values for teacher development, only EV3, *Teachers regularly share materials and strategies and co-construct knowledge*, a value bound up in social construction, is evident across all ten syllabi Kristi and I analyzed. EV5, *Composition teachers should learn from written reflection on teaching*, one I am especially invested in as a scholar in reflective writing, is evident in nine of ten syllabi. Reflection activities are similarly noted by 71 percent of Cicchino's (2020) survey participants as "very important" (95). The other values have a strong enough presence to be in the running as shared values for teacher development across the field. EV 2, *(New) Composition teachers need opportunities to hear and learn from experienced and expert teachers*, is present in eight of the ten syllabi; Cicchino's survey finds that WPAs report many collaborative and mentoring-focused practices as valuable, including peer-to-peer presentations and discussions about readings, observing mentors and other teachers in the classroom, and designing materials for instruction (93). Sixty-six percent of respondents to Cicchino's survey report peer mentorship, which can be present in action in either EV2 or 3 (94). In this set of syllabi, EV4, *Composition teachers need to be familiar with disciplinary frameworks*, seems to be shared by my interview participants and two other practicum instructors who shared syllabi with me but not across the board. Importantly, and as I explore in the next chapter, this value was not forwarded by my program's curriculum committee in their development of a common syllabus in 2020, which included a position statement from outside of writing studies but did not recommend any from writing studies as readings for the practicum.

Values, the Practicum, and Momentum

Talking about program values and the practicum with WPAs and practicum instructors and reviewing their syllabi (both with them in conversation and in a more focused analysis) led me to three conclusions about the articulation of values in writing programs. First, while the nature of teacher development strategies in writing programs is necessarily locally driven, responsive to the ways that graduate students work in specific programs, there are evidently primarily shared values for how we want to engage this teacher development and how we want GTAs to understand teacher development in writing studies. Second, talking about program values and their evidence in the practicum highlights a distinction between individual practicum instructor values and the values of the program at large. Whether or not these individual and program values overlap, they determine the nature of professionalization in the local context. Finally, conversation about program values, values for teacher development, and the practicum shows there is an energy in teacher development in the practicum that impacts the momentum of program change.

ASSURANCE THAT SHARED VALUES DRIVE THE WORK OF TEACHER DEVELOPMENT

Regarding the emergent values for teacher development that I identified in the historical documents in my home program and look for in these interview transcripts and syllabi from other programs, I feel I am in good company. It seems that, at least with this relatively small group of WPAs and practicum instructors, I and other practicum instructors in my home program are mostly in step with these personnel in other programs. There are core values we have explicitly and implicitly integrated into the practicum that we can continue to strengthen. There are rich resources in composition pedagogy and literacy scholarship that we can draw on to bolster this teacher development.

In some expressions of the program values by participants in my interview study, articulated values are channeled through FYW (see also Ritter 2018, cited earlier in the book), the course for which they prepare teachers in the practicum. In others, we see values that consider the larger work of the writing program. The reality is, as noted earlier in a discussion of professionalization, the practicum is only one, relatively small location in the writing program workplace. Therefore, it is only one site in which we may see the manifestation of program values, with values for teacher development ideally very apparent, and disciplinary values maybe or maybe not apparent. The complexity of the work of writing programs means that the values articulated by program personnel when we talk about the practicum, like in the interviews I related, might speak to other workplace concerns, like labor, administration, assessment, or research.

There are several moments in the interviews where participants identify the presence of their individual values in the practicum syllabus, distinguishing them from program values. These moments are echoes of what was evident in the examination of the historical syllabi in chapter 1—there is often an idiosyncratic weight to the content of the practicum that demonstrates an individual instructor's investment over and above any shared articulation of program values. At times, interview participants describe the ways their investments and values are making way into program culture through things like custom textbooks, guest speakers, or shared readings. These moments provide insight into the ways that values emerge and circulate among and through writing program personnel. Program values cannot be sanitized, personless, objective values enacted by instructors through their teaching. Program values emerge from the investments of people, and from the work of these people in the sites of the program. Take antiracism, for example, one of the values that shows up in several interviews, and a practice that, were it tested, most, if not all, writing programs today, would identify as an area of focus if not an explicit value. Antiracism cannot be a program value without individuals invested in and enacting antiracist teaching practices in their writing classrooms. Values are not disembodied things—then they are only mission or vision statements. If we don't *do* values, they are not there.

UNDERSTANDING HOW PROFESSIONALIZING MANIFESTS IN THE LOCAL CONTEXT

The emphasis on professionalization in these interviews and syllabi is expected. The function of the practicum as a professionalizing site has been emphasized by Susan K. Miller, Rochelle Rodrigo, Veronica Pantoja, and Duane Roen (2005), who assert professionalization as a "central goal" of the course, one that supports GTAs in all concentrations in seeing "all of their work in the academy [including teaching composition] as scholarly" (82). That professionalization requires thoughtful attention and planning is emphasized by Yancey (2002) in the development of a heuristic for assessing TA development programs and needs. GTAs' experience in the practicum is just one part of what programs do to prepare them for the job market and their future faculty lives (Sandy 2002). As Donna Strickland notes, professionalization is a core part of the discipline; it "is what has made composition studies—as a set of pedagogical practices and a body of knowledge about those practices—possible" (53). But as Strickland (2011) and others (e.g., Hansen 2018; Wardle and Downs 2018) have also noted, what it means to be a teacher of composition and what it means to be "colleagues who teach composition" are quite different (51). Miller et al. qualify the centrality of professionalization in the practicum: "At the very least, every teaching assistant should complete the practicum with a lifelong commitment to 'effective teaching'—teaching that results in student learning" (83). The interviews help us see what is privileged in professionalizing *anyone* who is teaching a composition course for each institution and professionalizing those who aim to more formally "profess" teaching composition (Stenberg 2005; Hansen 2018). Sparking a "lifelong commitment" to teaching writing starts with time spent in classrooms, observing other teachers, and working from there to understand why we teach writing at all, and why we do this teaching the ways that we do. For those GTAs whose investment in writing studies is "minimal," as Amanda noted, it's integral that we make the work of the field "accessible."

The learning outcomes of each syllabus express professionalizing, if not in direct terms, then in other descriptors: becoming reflective teachers, developing course materials, explaining and addressing issues in teaching college writing, creating teaching portfolios. And references to professionalizing are present in other sections of the syllabi as well, in descriptions of workload, in what it takes to be part of a teaching community, in the function of peer observation and mentoring. In my discussion with Amanda, for example, she pointed out that the ways GTAs experience learning in the practicum is different from many of the other classes they take; while the workshop element of the course might be familiar, the work*load* is significantly different, providing something closer to parity of the weekly workload experience of *teaching* a writing class. What professionalizing might *mean* in each program, as described by participants, or how it might manifest in sites of teacher development, like the practicum, can perhaps tell us something about program values, and even may serve as a test of the disciplinary values cited by Wardle and Downs.

For example, a question that emerged in my examination of documents in my home program (see chapter 1) echoes in this study: What is the role of disciplinary frameworks and position statements in the formal teacher development of writing programs? This lingering question suggests something about the ways that localism, as a disciplinary value (Wardle and Downs 2018, 127–128), is emphasized in teacher development in potentially limiting ways. It is apparent that our field's professional organizations see a place for these frameworks in teacher development. This audience of reflective teachers is explicitly written into the documents. The authors of "This Ain't Another Statement! This Is a DEMAND for Black Linguistic Justice!" assert, "We cannot say that Black Lives Matter if Black Language is not at the forefront of our work as language educators and researchers!" (Conference on College Composition and Communication 2020). The writers of the "CCCC Statement on White Language Supremacy" explain, "Our goal as critical anti-WLS educators is to dismantle WLS in our field and in ourselves" (Conference on College Composition and Communication 2021b). The authors of other disciplinary position statements similarly cite teachers as at the core of the work these statements aim to do and support. But, in this small study, these frameworks and position statements only appear in the reading lists of four of the ten practicum syllabi I analyzed.

ASSESSING MOMENTUM FOR PROGRAM CHANGE

Through exercising individual program values and (shared) values for teacher development, we aim to professionalize writing teachers who, in turn, are attuned to values-driven work and can cultivate this work in their own classrooms and future programs. While institutional change work happens in committees and programs and offices all across universities and colleges, the composition teaching practicum is a core site for integrating WPA values for the writing program and beginning to enact those values. In these interviews with WPAs teaching the practicum, we discussed the ways that attention to working conditions, the labor of teaching writing, and instructor autonomy are integrated into their coursework: These topics manifest in both the readings that are assigned, the kinds of projects GTAs are asked to work through, and what they are tasked with reflecting on. But even though there are awesome possibilities, there are also limitations to what can be done in this space. Sometimes these limitations come from the influence of other faculty. Michelle described this limitation, admitting, "One of my disappointments in the class historically has been when we do all this stuff and then at the end of the day, what they turn in is basically very similar to their mentor's teaching." Sometimes, these limitations come from the force of other program priorities (and others' program priorities) pushing aside WPA's initiatives; Stephanie described this when she noted that the attention she wants to give to writing a plan for racial justice work is often getting taken by other ongoing initiatives. Despite these constant pressures, looking at program values with these practicum instructors highlights that the work of professionalizing teachers in our field is specifically bound up in an orientation toward change.

Interviewing these four participants allowed me to begin to more fully imagine myself inhabiting the role of WPA in the future. The study was a research experience that would complement the rest of the self-training I could put myself through as I looked ahead to more practicum teaching and a possible future as a WPA. The need for a "rhetoric" for new WPAs, as compiled by Malenczyk (2016) in *A Rhetoric for Writing Program Administrators*, highlights the new ground entered by those who take on the position, even when they may have a long history of life in writing programs, as undergraduates, graduate students, and faculty. Malenczyk explains that the chapters in the book are intended to "provide the reader with a basis for reflection and action" (4), a phrase that, for me, hearkens back to the "slow agency" described by Micciche (2011) as central to WPA work. I imagine encountering a workplace problem, reaching for the book, contemplating decisions in the old IKEA Poäng chair in my department office, talking through options and opportunities with my colleagues, and reviewing assessment files and previous reports before making decisions. Of course, like Monroe's (2021) counterpoint about "urgent agency" demonstrates, reflection and action are often happening quite quickly for WPAs. I see the practicum as a site where this WPA decision-making is a bit slow and urgent at the same time: The annual revision of a syllabus allows for researched, methodical changes; the responsivity required to support GTAs teaching in real time necessitates quick and resourceful thinking. It also requires a realistic assessment of what is manageable and the degree to which any single potential pressure should get one's time and emotional attention (Wooten 2020).

Enacting these decisions comes with different stakes, depending on one's institutional site and individual status. In contrast to the positions of the WPAs I interviewed for this study, and to my own standpoint as a researcher and not-yet/future WPA, Glenn (2018) acknowledges the "comfortable" administrative commitment she made when she became the WPA at Penn State in 2012:

I was established when I agreed to take on a big administrative commitment. I was not saddled with any expectations of serving as caretaker for a predecessor's agenda (as is the situation in so many places); rather, I could build upon, extend, or otherwise rethink the rich contributions of my mostly male predecessors. At least that is how I perceived my location then—and how I perceive it now. Thus, my account of writing program administration bears the ideological weight of my own body, standpoint, location, mesosystem. I cannot reduce that weight, but I can acknowledge it. (113)

Transparent about the privilege of her position as an already-established scholar and member of her program, Glenn acknowledges that in entering the administrative position, she has a particular power to develop and forward her own agenda. But moments in my conversations with participants seemed more like they might have felt like the midlevel managers I sometimes felt like in teaching the practicum. A midlevel manager role might be one deeply embedded in WPA work, particularly for those who are directly and even solely responsible for directing FYW. As Strickland (2011) writes, "The director of freshman English was the *intermediary* between the English department faculty and the largely non-tenure-track composition faculty, setting the conditions for the controlled productivity that would benefit the student-consumer" (61; emphasis mine). This "intermediary" role, while it is structured for a bureaucratic control over what happens (or to be as pointed as Strickland, over how and what teachers teach) in FYW, often comes with a feeling of powerlessness or of tabled potential, as moments in these interviews show. Micciche (2007) describes this as a contradiction between the "little power" these WPAs have compared to the expectations for management and guidance placed on them (74). What WPAs can manage—syllabi, practicum assignments, portfolio requirements—is a small counterpoint to what they can't manage—how their teachers *feel* about teaching composition or while teaching composition, how university mandates might impact what teachers experience, and whether and how they can integrate discipline-driven visions or cultural reforms. In this intermediate reality, what work could be accomplished when bolstered by the articulation of program values?

Conclusion

Analyzing interview transcripts and syllabi for this chapter has helped me identify the ways that talking about program values brings to light the degree to which these are (or are not) shared and explicit in a program. The WPAs and practicum instructors I interviewed for this chapter can easily articulate program values and their own values for teaching writing and training writing teachers, though these are not always the same. They can also easily identify places in their courses where these values are enacted, though the values are not always explicit in the syllabus for the course. Talking through these values and practicum materials with participants was a generative exercise that allowed both participants and me to reflect on our aims in teacher development, the goals we have for our writing programs, and whether and how the work of the practicum is supporting our work toward these goals.

As the interviews show, the language used to identify program values is variable. Once participants articulated these values, we had to have deeper conversation about definitions and priorities, exactly what expression of values should engage! Different university contexts, the breadth of the field, and instructors' own scholarly commitments lead to a diversity of commitments for writing programs. These commitments materialize in specific ways in teacher development, sometimes explicitly in the language of program documents, sometimes implicitly in activities and assignments. These values are evident in the local work we are preparing (new) composition teachers to do and also in how we support their professionalization such that they will do particular work in the field; when we can articulate them, but they are not explicitly evident in the materials GTAs come into contact with, we may see opportunities for making these values—and their coordinating change-making efforts—more clear.

3
Getting to Slow Agency via Slowing Conversation in Curricular Committee Work

Collaboratively minded writing programs capitalize on the social construction they value in teaching writing to acknowledge and take up these same practices in administration, research, and curriculum development. They represent communities of practice as Etienne Wenger (1998) describes them: "groups of people who share a concern or a passion for something they do and learn how to do it better as they interact regularly." About a decade ago, I captured a video on my iPad of a team of FYW instructors in my program designing a website for course instructors (Jankens 2013). In the video, the team sits around a conference table, jots down ideas, and alternatively gets excited and pensive. There is crosstalk, there are questions, and there are concrete plans. This time spent presents a significant opportunity for writing program values and knowledge to circulate through these discussions about goals and problem solving. Prepandemic, I remember weeks where I spent four or five hours in committee or team meetings for the department and university, and as many preparing materials for these meetings; many readers can recall weeks with far more.

My interviews with WPAs and practicum instructors (chapter 2) reinforced for me the value of understanding life cycles of program change, the processes for engaging action in the program, and the tensions and pressures facing the practicum and practicum instructors. Efficacious program actors

https://doi.org/10.7330/9781646427895.c003

require a more-than-tacit-or-anecdotal understanding of these forces and they need defined (if personal) approaches for how they will engage in reflective decision-making. But with our busy teaching and home lives, and, in the last few years, with the pandemic cutting a jagged line between synchronous and asynchronous work, we often spend much of our work time away from the physical realm of the program (the office, the classroom, the writing center, the hallways), with smaller groups, on more focused tasks: for example, reading transcripts with a research team, problem-solving teaching observations with a colleague, discussing the challenges of grading with a mentee. In our home program this change sometimes constrained access to information about or reflection on these myriad institutional forces. Our program work was diffused into what Etienne Wenger, Richard McDermott, and William M. Snyder (2002) refer to as "project teams," emergent from the body of the larger writing program to accomplish a task and bound together by "the project's goals and milestones" (42).

There is a practical difference between the time a researcher can take to comb through and reflect on program archives, as I did in chapter 1, and the conditions under which committees work. Experientially, we know that committees often work responsively but within limited time frames to consider the parameters of a curricular or administrative problem and to craft a solution; this work is sometimes made more complex by personal agendas and interpersonal rancor, and this complexity, without the benefit of time to allow for a committee to consider a range of knowledges pertinent to the task at hand, may forestall values-based action.

In fall 2019, I learned that my program's curriculum subcommittee would be tasked with designing and proposing a common syllabus for the two-course pedagogical practicum sequence. A change in credit hours, shifting practicum courses from three graduate credits to two, and multiple historical factors, some of which I wrote about in chapter 1, made this problem worth committee attention: Since there had often been disagreement, at least from GTAs' perspectives, about the effectiveness of the practicum courses, having a curricular stamp of approval from the program was important. As someone invested in the practicum courses but not a member of the subcommittee, I saw an opportunity to observe the team's discussions and decision-making process; I proposed a study of the committee's work to my institution's IRB,[1] aiming to understand how a committee tasked with developing a common syllabus for a practicum works through conversation and making recommendations for composing that text. This subcommittee work was a chance to produce a syllabus that reflected program values for teacher development rather than individual instructor values.

It is important for me to foreground what I found in my initial reading of the committee's recommendations, because this initial reading grounds my approach in this chapter. Early in my work reviewing artifacts for this study, I recorded these notes when I found myself frustrated by the committee's ultimate recommendations:

> 8.25.20: I'm having an emotional reaction as I really read these committee docs (email and syllabus) for the first time: there's little to no composition scholarship in the recommended syllabus. The recommended syllabus is possibly, unless I'm reading it wrong, a suggestion for a course primarily in educational theory with some practical activities related to FYW scheduled (not scaffolded) in. My concern is, how can this course, at 2 credits, be both a course in educational theory and a course in practical matters of teaching our FYW course? What in the committee's conversations led to this emphasis?

The committee's recommendations seemed to lack or discount knowledge present in program archives, including examples of disciplinary scholarship taught in previous practicum courses, and to echo the same challenges of idiosyncrasy posed by the very charge they were responding to. Every time I have reviewed these notes in the process of putting together this chapter, I remember the day I stood up from the chair at my desk, shutting my laptop, mumbling in frustration. I had an emotional, vexed reaction to both the committee's conversations and the resultant recommendations. Because I have worked closely with several members of the committee over the last decade, I also faced an interpersonal predicament: How do I present people whom I call friends in what is, really, a small picture of their work? My solution was to step back and look at their committee discourse in light of the kinds of knowledge circulating in these committee conversations, to understand better how the kind of slow agency that is so valuable in writing program administration (Micciche 2011) could be better enacted in a committee setting.

In this chapter, I present the curriculum subcommittee's work in light of three kinds of knowledge—intuition, experiential knowledge, and institutional knowledge—showing the strength of the first and the need for growth in the latter two, growth supported by local knowledge and articulated program values. The juxtaposition between recent local program history (presented in chapter 1) and the contemporary program decision-making described in this chapter highlights both important tensions in the local site and the need for a refined and strengthened triad of knowledges to influence the practices of project teams or committees, one that includes developing a shared understanding of program values through meaningfully slowing down conversation to access these knowledges. This study, read in light of the themes presented in chapter 1, reveals the contrast between a "slow agency" approach to program work (Micciche 2011) and work that is done under pressure, particularly in terms of the ways particular knowledges are employed. I argue that in addition to employing their intuition in discussion, members of project teams or committees (and WPAs themselves) can better attune to a more whole program experience through gathering, acknowledging, and considering (others') experiential and institutional knowledge as well as program values. As I explore the artifacts from this committee's work also in light of disciplinary scholarship on the ways these kinds of knowledges manifest, I also suggest that while in writing studies we may be quite attuned to making knowledge and knowledge transfer explicit in the composition classroom, we may work at being better at doing this in our other daily work. The committee conversations I highlight in this chapter demonstrate moments for this explicit inquiry and acknowledgment.

Developing a Practice of Slow Agency Through Attention to a Triad of Knowledges

In her description of the practice of slow agency in writing program administration, Micciche explores how "agency as action deferred" adds to a WPA's repertoire of problem-solving and initiative-building tools. Micciche writes about "pacing, agency, and administration, a triangulation of issues that simultaneously vex and energize WPA work at alternative turns" (75). Micciche draws from an argument for "hypermiling" with driving, "slowing down in order to increase energy consumption," to shape her look at slow agency (75); when a WPA slows down to make decisions, the resultant pacing allows for a quality of deliberation not always possible in a writing program and university environment that values quick results (79), and documenting the process in its phases allows for administrative control over how others perceive the process (84). Allowing us a glimpse of the curricular development she undertook with a "composition advisory committee," Micciche writes,

> Developing a curriculum philosophy and description for intermediate composition took nearly eighteen months. Some of our discussions were difficult

and tense, punctuated by serious concerns about how both to define and structure a course and to create opportunities for teacher-invention. Without our bi-weekly discussion and debate, we would not have achieved a flexible curricular model, one that established a coherent assignment sequence with some built-in flexibility for experienced teachers. Slowing down helped us to create a collaborative space where program matters became the subject of engaged, often spirited dialogue resulting in curricular revision that represented our collective and diverse expertise and value systems. (82)

For "engaged" dialogue to have space in and shape committee meetings, we must give way to time, become open to "difficult and tense" conversations, and make room for addressing "serious concerns." Micciche notes that the result of this slowing down is a revision representative of the "collective and diverse" nature of collaborative practice, wherein contribution from multiple players may be both complicated and generative. She does not get into these specific discussions, into the nuance of the "spirited dialogue" she reports, but somewhere in that dialogue there are clues to how slowing down becomes effective for a committee when kinds of knowledge are attended to and built upon in meetings. Micciche's description raises questions for me: How can we learn to do slow agency at all if not better than we are already doing? How can we practice this slowness in our discussions in teams? Does that help us better bring shared values—or any values—to light in our collaborative program projects?

The committee I describe in this chapter is, as all committees and projects teams are, limited by the boundaries of time and shared space, though perhaps more dramatically so, as their spatially communal work begins in February 2020 and is arrested by the COVID-19-induced campus closure in March. Despite these boundaries, the conscious construction of group norms—for any working group—impacts the overall output of the group. As Wenger et al. (2002) note, a community of practice constructed "actively and systematically" realizes sustainable benefits (12). Offshoots of the writing program community of practice, like the project teams or committees composed of writing program personnel who carry out problem-solving work, likewise also benefit from active cultivation. With the time it takes to develop a (mutually invested) set of practices, there is also the opportunity to co-construct functioning circuits of information and practical ways of engaging these circuits of information in committee meetings. While personnel may take on familiar roles in their committee-based work (the one who volunteers to take notes, the one who is willing to ask hard questions, the one who always has a story of an experience to explicitly problematize a solution, etc.), a cooperative "cultivation" of practices may make it more likely that the whole program can "achieve [its] full potential" (Wenger et al. 2002, 12–13).

Studying the process of assignment or curricular development at the level of committee work is, as LaFrance (2019) acknowledges in the introduction to her chapter on a "linked gateway" assignment, a way to "reveal a good deal about the granularities of work within a writing program, classroom, or teaching initiative" (50), including the impact (or lack of impact) of "moments of resistance or divergence" and the power particular faculty hold over curricular development (68). Importantly, as LaFrance points out, what GTAs, in particular, do or do not say about their experiences teaching is influential in what the program comes to understand about the curriculum (72). Thus, what program personnel are invited to contribute, and when their offerings are or are not taken up in discussion, ultimately shapes the work produced. Understanding the right moments for slowing down committee conversation, then, might strengthen productive contribution from program personnel, including GTAs.

DEFINING KNOWLEDGES FOR READING A COMMITTEE'S WORK

Wenger et al. reiterate that "A community of practice is a unique combination of communities of three fundamental elements: a *domain* of knowledge, which defines a set of issues; a *community* of people who care about this domain; and the shared *practice* that they are developing to be effective in their domain" (27; emphasis in original). A committee or project team has a distinct function, set apart from the larger community of practice of the writing program; its domain is more specific, the community of people comprised of necessarily fewer members, and their shared practice either heavily or minimally influenced by the community at large. In the situation I study in this chapter, the community is defined narrowly by the membership of the curriculum subcommittee during the particular semester I examined, and more broadly by the writing program this committee aims to represent. The specific domain of this particular committee is teacher development via the curriculum of the pedagogical practicum; as I have explored in the introduction of this book, teacher development, generally, is one of the core domains of the discipline to which this writing program belongs, a set of knowledge that "creates common ground and a sense of common identity" to the field of writing studies (Wenger et al., 2002, 27). What I hoped entering this study was that the knowledge practices of the curriculum subcommittee would be attentive to explicit program values rather than to idiosyncratic values or aims. In this case, "knowledge practices" can mean both specific tasks enacted in the course of the team's work and the knowledges that drive these tasks or actions; they are the "frameworks, ideas, tools, information, styles, language, stories, and documents" the subcommittee members share and drawn on as they work through their task (Wenger et al., 2002, 29). As I will describe, based on my initial readings of the team's meeting transcripts and then further established in the analysis I present in this chapter, I see it is possible that, for better or worse, three more abstract aspects of knowledge that support the practices of a committee serve as drivers of change in writing programs: intuition, experiential knowledge, and institutional knowledge. Ideally, these three aspects work in concert with each other; however, as I show in this chapter, for that to happen, members of a committee must explicitly draw on each, and build each knowledge practice up, in particular ways. To understand how this uptake might better happen in the work of a committee or project team, I needed to be able to see these discrete discursive practices in action, and to do that, I needed to define and operationalize them, which I do in the sections that follow.

A Way to See Intuition

To consider how to define intuition for this project, I looked at Patricia Conners's (1990) "The History of Intuition and Its Role in the Composing Process," valuable because of Conners's position that intuition can be analyzed (77). If intuition can be analyzed, then we can consider how it functions as part of this triad of knowledges, and I might be able to see evidence of it when I look at the committee's collaboration. Interested in investigating what is often presented as an "elusive" but integral aspect of composing, Conners wades through scholarly takes on intuition's role in the writing process. Conners reviews, among others, Maxine Hairston's description of the writing process as involving both "non-rational" and "rational" elements in its activity; James E. Miller's reflection on the "audacity and clarity" of intuitions' manifestation in writing; Richard E. Young, Alton L. Becker, and Kenneth L. Pike's description of intuition "as the bridge between incubation and illumination"; and Janice M. Lauer's replacement of "insight" for "intuition," which thus further presses on its function on bringing an idea to light (72). Conners asks what all of these descriptions and definitions might have in common with "new rhetoricians' references to aspects of the inquiry process" (72) and notes the problem of intuition being seen as both necessary and "unteachable or incomprehensible" (73). How can intuition be both a *known* and unseen part of knowledge making? Turning to contemporary explorations allows Conners to see intuition, instead, as tied to *inference* and thus to "a habit of consulting a wide information base relatively quickly to find potential solutions to problems" (77). Conners writes, "Because *intuition* is sometimes quick, unconventional, and unobserved does not mean the activity cannot be consciously analyzed and studied" (77; emphasis in original).

And here's where intuition plays a critical role in the knowledge practices of committees or project teams, when and if this role is played correctly: It cannot be only "quick" and "unobserved," and it *must be* "consciously analyzed and studied" to be useful. One way for that conscious analysis to happen is to triangulate intuition with experiential knowledge and institutional knowledge.

From Experience to Experiential Knowledge

The sharing of experiences in conversation often has the quality of anecdotal evidence: Interlocutors reference personal experiences as they relate to a topic under discussion. Experiential knowledge, however, goes beyond description of one's experiences (though it may manifest in descriptions like, "When I was in that class, we..."). Gwen Gorzelsky (2013) provides a rich description of the role of experiential knowledge in literacy practices and how literacy practices can *change* experiential knowledge. While Gorzelsky pursues an approach to studying literacy practices in larger scope than what I intend in this study—she is interested in observing and studying "individual and community changes" across space or time as literacy proficiency develops (415)—what I pursue in this chapter is a much more microscopic look at a particular literacy practice: participants' engagement in the collaboration and discussion that occurs across a short-term committee charge, an engagement that is, nonetheless, designed for systemic impact through the development of a common syllabus.

If literacy scholars draw from and analyze procedural, conceptual, and experiential knowledge, Gorzelsky says, they will better see the ways that experiential knowledge "most directly shapes people's actions and thus our participation in larger systems" (399). Arguing for this "experiential approach to studying literacy" (399), Gorzelsky analyzes and illuminates these three knowledges at work in the guided meditations of Thich Nhat Hanh and demonstrates the ways that attention to experiential knowledge ("conscious recognition") highlights how personal change and systemic change are linked (402). Further, she argues, we can understand how people work with conceptual and procedural knowledge and how this work reshapes their experiential knowledge—their subjectivity—to effect systemic change (405). The first two categories of meditation practices Gorzelsky identifies include visualization exercises and mindful attention to negative states; these two practices draw the practitioner's attention inward at the same time that they help them find balance in their environment. An especially significant contribution of Gorzelsky's analysis to the study in this chapter is her identification of the third category of meditation exercises: "The third encourages a felt understanding of the ideas of emptiness and interdependence. *Emptiness* is the Zen term for the belief that no one has an inherent nature separate from the multiple causes and conditions (from the genetic to the familial, political, economic, cultural, and ecological) that produced one's 'self.; *Interdependence* is the Zen term for the relations among such multiple causes and conditions" (407). Emphasis on emptiness and interdependence, in these terms, may draw one's attention to the ways that their own experiences are neither wholly separate from others' nor, necessarily, impactful in the ways that the individual might perceive; that is, I think, a recognition of these concepts may help the individual seek to better understand the experiential knowledge of others, and not to assume their own experiences as singular and ultimate.

Attention to experiential knowledge can be a significant part of what determines committee decisions. But without explicit attention to factors like the impact of institutional systems and information on an individual's experiences, say, in a practicum course or on an administrative team, experiential knowledge may not be as effectively utilized or taken up in discussion; this knowledge may rest and remain only in the anecdotal.

Institutional Knowledge as Complementary and Necessary

In the case of committees and project teams, seeing the link between individual change and systematic change might then depend on also seeing the ways that institutional knowledge manifests in the group's literate practices. In my reading, institutional knowledge covers a lot of ground; the "institutional circuits" in which committee members participate and intervene and which drive their work are textual, historical, and discursive (LaFrance 2019, 43–44). In the case of the study described in this chapter, to the degree that the discipline of writing studies is an institution, institutional knowledge would range from disciplinary scholarship on teacher development (i.e., what the discipline has deemed as core to teacher development in our field) to local curricular information (i.e., previous syllabi, course learning outcomes, etc.). Institutional knowledge may also work as what Peter Smagorinsky and Michael W. Smith (1992) define as "community-specific knowledge" or what Anne Beaufort (2007) calls "discourse community knowledge," as "writers in different communities produce texts of similar structure in quite different ways because of the demands and customs of the particular communities in which they participate" (Smagorinsky and Smith 1992, 288); in the case of committee work, this may mean not only how the team drafts syllabi and memos but also how they work through deliberation of ideas.

Because not every committee can build a coordinated and collaborative practice over time (ad hoc committees serve important short-term functions), the presence of local program histories can supplement work in curricular development, assessment recommendations, teacher development, policy, and the like. While published narratives of program work are often, themselves, "too hastily" ended (Davies 2013, 82), programmatic archives, though difficult to maintain, are made accessible by the presence and interpretation of program actors (Davies 2013, 85). Institutional knowledge is, at times, the most historically tangible of the three nodes I explore in this chapter, and it is the knowledge I explored deeply in chapter 1. It can exist in paper and digital archives; it may be found in meeting minutes and collections of syllabi. It can also, however, be largely archived in the memory of individuals and groups, making it "fragile" (Norgaard 2017, 145). Writing about labor conditions at UC Boulder, Norgaard (2017) explains, "If one insists on the purity of the memory, it can easily become dated and ossified, and voices for its support can readily seem shrill and out of touch. On the other hand, if memory becomes all too malleable and all too willing to accommodate new views, it ceases to serve as memory at all" (146). Institutional knowledge, then, is complementary to other knowledges; its value is conditional and contextual but undeniable.

For this project, I define institutional knowledge as recognition of common practices or historical experiences in the local context; while program personnel may have experienced these *commons*, institutional knowledge is exercised when they acknowledge these experiences and practices exist outside of themselves. In the historical program documents I explored in chapter 1, references to a "Wayne way" of teaching writing reveal a shared notion of a common practice of teaching writing and training GTAs in teaching the FYW course. This limited definition of institutional knowledge serves the purposes and context of this study; I acknowledge that institutional knowledge, in a broad sense, also encapsulates knowledge about systems-at-large or systems in abstract.

For a Triad of Knowledges

While employment of a particular knowledge may be determined "as a matter of choice, preference, and personal forms of identification," because the practices of work are also influenced by other structures—"by the common ways of doing, knowing, and being that are active social and professional norms in local settings"—they are determined by specific tasks or rules of order, which is what makes them worthy of study (LaFrance 2019, 25). When these three knowledges work together, we both begin to understand intuition and can explicitly employ intuition as *part of* an analytical process for problem solving (Conners 1990, 77). When these three nodes work together, not only do we begin to identify experiential knowledge; we also may see it as a cooperative, reflexively developed knowledge domain (Gorzelsky 2013). And when these three elements work together, institutional knowledge becomes accessible to all members of a committee or team; in addition, we may see the systems it represents as available for intervention, in need of upkeep, or functional for reasons we did not notice before.

There are multiple knowledge frameworks at work in the committee discussions in this study that I am not using to analyze the team's discourse and recommendations. In some cases, like in Beaufort's (2007) description and definition of knowledge domains for the activity of writing, these knowledges are employed across time; one's rhetorical knowledge, for example, is not only drawn upon at the outset of a writing project, in response to a prompt, but also across the life of that writing project, even after composing is done and the author considers circulation. These knowledges are thus drawn on in deliberative ways. In the activity of a committee meeting, however, the quality of the discussion with its many goals and many participants, is such that knowledges are typically drawn upon in immediate and responsive ways. In my initial readings of the transcripts, what stood out to me was the heavy presence of intuition and individual experiential knowledge and, sometimes, the admission of a lack of institutional knowledge, when that information was necessary to the development of an informed and collaborative proposal. These initial readings urged on the analysis I undertake in the next section, rereading the transcripts in light of intuition, experiential knowledge, and institutional knowledge to better understand the presence of these, their natural weight in committee conversations about teacher development, and how we might approach committee discussions differently, especially in light of a shared understanding of program values. All that is to say, there is substantial knowledge presented in the speech acts of participants in these two committee meetings that I do *not* analyze in this reading because I am primarily interested in presenting the weight of these three sometimes tacit or even unexplored knowledges.

To summarize, for the purposes of this study, *intuition* can be defined as the activity of quickly drawing from one's broad wells of knowledge; *experiential knowledge* is the bringing of one's own history and subjectivity to the discussion at hand, as well as finding meaning in the experiential offerings of others; and *institutional knowledge*, in this study, refers to explicit references to resources, common practices, and historical experiences in the local context. I suggest, through the analysis that follows, that the committee's practice can be better actualized through strategies for taking up and interrogating experiential knowledge and seeking institutional knowledge. In addition to uncovering ways that we talk about teacher development and specific programmatic changes in our daily work, this analysis further moves this book project toward its central argument: that articulation of values bolsters the work of writing programs, activated through the design of teacher development and those who design it, especially as they work to instigate programmatic change.

Studying Committee Work in My Home Program

While much scholarship stakes a claim on the content of the practicum, rarely do we see the decision-making process behind practicum syllabus design. One example is present in Guerra and Bawarshi's (2005) "Managing Transitions: Reorienting Perceptions in a Practicum Course" in Sidney Dobrin's *Don't Call It That* collection. In their chapter, Guerra and Bawarshi describe the process of revising an orientation and practicum course for graduate students teaching FYW; they emphasize that the transition period after a new WPA is placed as an especially important time for examining how the practicum course introduces the content of the discipline of composition to graduate students (54). Further, they describe how the practicum "contributes to the creation of coherence" between disciplinary scholarship, teacher development, and the content of the FYW course (44).

Guerra and Bawarshi's text thus provides a useful example for conceptualizing a study of the development of a common syllabus for the two-course practicum sequence at Wayne State, and reviewing their context especially illuminates key additions to their work provided by the study presented in this chapter. Guerra and Bawarshi capture the work of a tenure-track faculty and graduate student administrative team revising their orientation and practicum syllabus for new GTAs teaching FYW. This problem-solving team is perhaps more typical in writing programs where the WPA is also the practicum instructor (like the WPAs I interviewed in chapter 2). But our local context is different, and, in reality, WPAs cannot be on every acting subcommittee. The study I lay out in this chapter captures the input of non-WPA faculty and graduate students whose committee work centers on curriculum development. Specifically, it is important to consider what is gained by looking at curricular conversations that happen between these non-WPA stakeholders, these program participants who are in "liminal spaces," somewhere between being students and teachers (GTAs) and faculty-but-not-graduate-faculty (full-time NTT faculty) (see Macauley et al. 2021). As LaFrance (2019) emphasizes, "How people are positioned within a site will often dramatically impact not only what people do but how they do it" (30).

For many years in my home program, a large cohort of NTT lecturers has worked closely with the director of composition to exercise problem-solving and planning related to assessment, curriculum, and mentoring and professional development.[2] Chairs of individual subcommittees or ad hoc, semester-long "task forces" have undertaken specialized projects, some at the behest of the director of composition and some of their own volition, and have reported this work to a committee of all members of the composition program.[3] The result has been a relatively energized and generative and collaborative group of faculty who have the rare experience (I'd say) of working together over a long time and who are joined in their work by GTAs in the program who are keen to become better teachers and gain professional experience. Though the cohort has experienced some turnover in the last several years, at the publication of this book at least seven other members of this cohort will have worked in our program as faculty for over a decade. This history suggests the possibility of access to rich institutional memory and diverse approaches to problem solving. It suggests there may be something to see in studying how these collaborative insights come together.

My original plan for data collection was to sit in on the committee's meetings, using an audio recorder and note taking to gather data. While the audio recorder would capture the conversation, I could, as an observer, record other physical and affective aspects of committee meetings: eye contact, long pauses, moves from reading a text to talking about a text, gestures, sketching on the whiteboard, sighs, and other verbal and nonverbal expressions and interactions not evident via the recorder. However, I was also the most recent practicum instructor, and there was concern about the degree to which my presence might influence or hamper the committee's conversation. I acknowledged this as a potential workplace challenge, despite my self-assurance that I could appear an objective listener. Sharan B. Merriam (2009) notes that a researcher's presence in the observed setting may "elicit more polite, formal, or guarded behavior" at first, though I believed such behavior was not likely to be sustained in an already-established social setting, where we had practice with productive dissension (127). Nevertheless, we decided it would be best if I reviewed committee artifacts rather than be present. I used audio recording to ensure that committee members engaged in their assigned work as normally as possible, without the addition of another "member" (me, the researcher) to the room.

I visited a subcommittee meeting on February 7, 2020, to describe my study and provide team members with consent forms, which were collected by the chair of the committee and given to my recruiter to retain until the close of the study period. The participants included two graduate students in rhetoric and composition and five NTT lecturers; they represent seven of the nine members on the subcommittee.

Throughout data collection, which spanned the length of the committee's in-person and online meetings that semester, I was provided with access to committee materials, including readings, agendas, and collaborative drafts. Prior to the beginning of each meeting in which the committee discussed the common syllabus during winter 2020, I set up and tested two audio recorders, one on either end of the conference table in the meeting room, to ensure all conversation would be audible as recorded. Committee members introduced themselves at the beginning of each meeting to aid future transcription of audio recordings. Following the adjournment of the in-person meetings, I entered the room and stopped the recorders. I also took pictures of any meeting notes written on the board that were relevant to the discussion of the common syllabus.

However, suddenly abridged by the campus closure due to the COVID-19 pandemic, the committee's synchronous work happened across only two meetings, then shifted to asynchronous work on their recommendations. While the campus closure truncated committee meetings and thus also the production of some amount of committee materials (e.g., typed agendas, drafts of recommendations, conversation notes recorded on the white board), I could nevertheless work from the following documents to conduct an analysis of the committee's work:

1. transcripts from the 2.21.20 and 3.6.20 meetings;
2. a 4.13.20 email from the committee chair to the committee outlining tasks;

3. an April/May 2020 draft of the syllabus and schedule including marginal comments from committee members;
4. a 5.29.20 memo from the committee chair to the director of composition, including copies of the committee's recommended syllabus and schedule, sans comments.

I obtained written permission from the director of composition and the chair of the English department to use those documents in my reporting and analysis.

Audio recordings were held and not reviewed until the conclusion of the study and were professionally transcribed. I redacted contributions of committee members who did not consent to participate before I analyzed the transcripts. Then, I replaced the names of participating members with pseudonyms. As I do in other chapters, I used a "hybrid-institutional approach to naming" (Lamos 2012, 163) in which actual names of institutional places, sites, committees, or programs are used alongside pseudonyms of participants. For the purposes of this chapter, leaving several participants more anonymous by identifying their titles (e.g., Lecturer 3, abbreviated as L3; Graduate Student 1 as GS1) and using nongendered pronouns (they, them, their) separates my colleagues—with whom I may have long-standing working relationships and, therefore, of whom I have significant interpersonal knowledge—from these transcripts, in which I want to analyze the presence of knowledge domains. It is a personal and analytical decision.

While my positionality as a member of the program I am studying provides me with useful local knowledge and insight for my overall analysis, this positionality also carries with it some challenging intimate knowledge, or knowledge about the research interests and working approaches of my colleagues on the committee. As a result, I elected to use content analysis to develop a discussion of the knowledge practices present in the committee's conversation, as well as to identify the presence of articulations of the values I identified in my analysis of historical program documents in chapter 1. However, other studies of committee work might also employ discourse analysis to analyze turn taking, digression, and expression of disciplinary knowledge or discourse community knowledge, or analysis of power and authority, which would have even greater implications for understanding the nature of knowledge making in committee work in writing programs.

Using the framework just outlined, I read the committee artifacts I gathered for evidence of intuition, experiential knowledge, and institutional knowledge, to understand whether and how strengths or cracks in these core knowledge

TABLE 3.1. Coding for knowledge domains

Knowledge Domain	Definition
Intuition	the activity of quickly drawing from one's broad wells of knowledge
Experiential knowledge	the bringing of one's own history and subjectivity to the discussion at hand, as well as finding meaning in the experiential offerings of others
Institutional knowledge	explicit references to resources, common practices, and historical experiences in the local context

domains of the committee manifest (table 3.1). I worked through three analytical moves while I read and hand-coded meeting transcripts. For each meeting, I first read the whole transcript and composed a summary of the major moments of the meeting, defining "moments" as periods of discourse spent on discrete subtopics. Then, I coded the transcript using the list of five emergent values for teacher development that I identified in the historical documents. Next, as described earlier, to better understand what may have contributed to the emergence (or absence) of these values in the committee's discussion and recommendations, I read the transcripts for evidence of the influence of institutional knowledge, experiential knowledge, and intuition.

I must note that while I could identify moments where these knowledges are at work, it is more challenging to identify them as discrete, to carve the transcript up into wholly coded and distinct sections, especially because of the nature of discourse in the meetings, where anyone may talk at any point, though someone else may have the floor. Further, as noted earlier, there is a lot of other knowledge at work, including task knowledge and procedural knowledge, for example, that I am not accounting for in this chapter. Therefore, I do not quantify the presence of these knowledges but work to showcase representative moments that provide evidence of patterns in how the committee members draw from these knowledges. In the text that follows, I present narratives of two committee meetings organized via this triad of knowledges; organized by knowledges, instead of chronology, these narratives demonstrate the weight of specific knowledges in each meeting, and I discuss the impact of this distribution. Then, I examine the presence of the emergent values for teacher development identified in chapter 1 and reinforced in chapter 2, to further understand the tie between the committee's discourse and its recommendations and program values.

THE FIRST MEETING ABOUT THE PRACTICUM SYLLABUS PROJECT

While the subcommittee had met before, the first meeting I recorded, on February 21, 2020, was also the first where the team was discussing the practicum syllabus project. To prepare, the group had split up a reading list to provide them with a foundation in scholarly issues and teaching approaches in and for the practicum and came to the meeting ready to discuss what they had read. Their agenda for the day was to "share maybe one or two helpful insights" from each reading ("not to do grad seminar discussions"), divide into teams for working on the practicum syllabi, and "set some expectations" for the upcoming meeting. Most of the meeting time was dedicated to committee members sharing their responses to the readings and reviewing the exigence for their work, before they planned steps for the project and assigned tasks for the next meeting.

Highlighting a recent contextual change, L1 posed their stance on revising the syllabi. The recent funding of MA students in addition to PhD students requires pedagogical shifts, L1 believed, and they asserted, "I think we can be a little bit more intentional rather than sort of like—rather than responding to that as we have in the last couple years. We have the chance to now get ahead of that by thinking about how do we design a [practicum] that supports students who are probably new to the idea of teaching just period?" L1 noted that at other programs, students may be coming out of MA programs and into their doctoral study, so they have teaching experience, but that perhaps at our institution, "it's a different kind of preparation that needs to happen" when students are sometimes funded through assistantships at the MA level.

Additionally, L1 acknowledged the focus group data I reviewed in chapter 1, especially GTAs' comments on valuing "practical," "day to day" concepts for teaching FYW over rhetoric and composition theory. They note that this feedback will have a tangential impact on revisions to the practicum courses:

> And I think as the course moves to even smaller accredited hours something has to give, and I think we're determining that rhet/comp theory is going to be a thing that gives . . . we want to keep ourselves focused more on what are the things the students need to know to just be good teachers. That's our goal. We're going to need to be good teachers of writing, second. What do they need to know about rhet/comp scholarship in order to support those two goals? That's how we think about including rhet/comp scholarship.

As the committee addressed these perceived constraints in the discussions that follow, they worked to prioritize helping GTAs "to just be good teachers," subverting disciplinary scholarship in the process.

Intuition: Acknowledging Perceived Programmatic Tensions

Committee members had been tasked with drawing on their intuition to present insights from the reading they did in preparation for the first meeting. In their brief presentations, they each began with a quick paraphrase of topic and argument of each reading and began to knit threads across the discussion. In several moments, committee members acknowledged perceived programmatic tensions. These acknowledgments were moments where committee members intuited a connection between these tensions and the decisions they would make as a committee. For example, in reporting on their reading of Jessica Restaino's (2012) *Graduate Students Teaching Writing: The Challenge of Middle Ground*, L2 described their takeaways: "So it was often about... how do we get these students who actually feel like they have no interest in teaching... that's not what they want to do. They don't want to teach writing or whatever. How do we bring them in, in this practica, so it doesn't seem like it's just extra work that they're going to resent more? Which is stuff I've heard from graduate students too." In response, L1 acknowledged they had heard similar feedback.

While the topic of GTA resistance paused there for the moment, it was taken up again throughout the conversation. A few minutes later, GS1 reported their reading of Sally Barr Ebest's (2002) "When Graduate Students Resist," and they noted that it might be better used as background or "back up" reading for the practicum instructor, because "it provides some good case studies of very difficult graduate students." Later, GS2 picked up on these early conversations when the group continued talking about other readings, noting the varied interests of incoming GTAs: "Not everybody's coming in with... concentration towards composition." Reflecting on E. Shelley Reid's (2017) "On Learning to Teach: Letter to a New TA" on "composition training... coming from all faculty in terms of being cross-disciplinary," GS2 found cross-departmental contributions from faculty to the practicum as potentially useful for addressing the diverse group of GTAs in the course. L1 also acknowledged students' diverse backgrounds, agendas, and experiences when they referenced the department's funding of MA students and the need to support GTAs who have not previously taught in any setting.

In the moments recounted here, committee members reflected on readings on teacher development in light of programmatic, departmental, and institutional tensions, and this reflection sparks a handful of conversational threads that could influence their recommendations: which readings may be useful for instructors of the practicum courses, how cross-departmental contributions from faculty may support GTAs in their teacher development, and how instructors need to understand undergraduate students' diverse backgrounds. Echoing LaFrance's (2019) sentiment, "These were not issues that could be ironed out in a single meeting" (65). However, as team members drew from their knowledge about the program, the department, and the needs of GTAs, and put this knowledge into conversation about scholarship on teacher development, their intuition was beginning to lead them toward discussions about what information and ideas GTAs require exposure to, and how.

Experiential Knowledge: Unheeded Rhetorical Bids

In this first meeting, there were only a couple of times that committee members drew on their personal, previous experiences as GTAs to use that experience as evidence for an assertion. For example, GS1 assessed Dylan B. Dryer's (2012) "At a Mirror Darkly": "And I thought that might be something cool to read at the beginning of the class because there's these case studies and . . . research that actually goes into how the GTAs felt when they came in versus how they felt when they left. And I think just my experience coming in and feeling inadequate or like an imposter or whatever." GS1's reflection demonstrates how their experience influenced their recommendation of Dryer's text for the reading list for the practicum: They felt "inadequate or like an imposter" and, perhaps, like the GTAs in Dryer's article, did not wholly feel that way anymore as they sat in this committee meeting. In a second example, L1, describing their previous graduate work in another discipline prior to working as a GTA in rhetoric and composition, asserted that some instructors will need to know "rhet/comp a little bit" through their experience in the practicum: "So, I know how to teach, I just don't know how to teach rhet/comp versus the person who needs to know how to teach [and] also needs to know how to teach rhet/comp."

These experiential assertions about the outsider experience faced by many GTAs are not taken up in conversation within the committee—that is, no one acknowledges them verbally or asks follow-up questions about them—and this may suggest divergent implications: (1) on one hand, experiential assertions may be perceived as mere digressions or as rhetorical moves meant to emphasize a point (e.g., *I am an example of a person who would have benefitted from this reading*; *I am an example of someone who came into the program with teaching experience*); but, (2) because experiential evidence may provide a window into the shared experiences of people not represented in a committee, committees need to consider how their work will honor and take up this knowledge. This committee happened to be composed of all white members, with many of their diversities less visible; at times, these diversities only come out in references to their positionality within the writing program as this positionality regards labor contracts or, like in the example GS1 describes here, novice teaching status. But the offered experiences and suggestions of minoritized or marginalized members of project teams are indispensable, and inquiring into these experiences, with the right (read, nonharmful) power dynamics at play in a committee conversation, can ensure the circulation of knowledge is inclusive.

Further, slowing down to acknowledge and ask about these rhetorical offerings affirms group members' knowledge and experiences and ideally reduces patriarchal, racist, and sexist dynamics. Asao B. Inoue (2021) offers this committee experience from his time in one WPA position (I abridge the anecdote here, but please read the chapter it comes from in *Above the Well*, where Inoue presents the complex interpersonal nuance of these interactions):

> I was in a meeting about student success. I was the only person of color in the room, which was typical . . . I suggested that we might gather data on the racial identities of student respondents in a survey we were discussing. We might add a few questions about the racial climate in classrooms. We might even ask about Whiteness, about students' perceptions of it on campus . . . As my voice was slowing down, pausing, one of the meeting's attendees, an older, male, graduate student from Ireland spoke up—rather, he interrupted me . . . he reiterated what I just said and suggested the survey questions. He even re-explained what I was saying just moments before, as if I'd not said anything. He looked right at me, as if he was teaching me things about being Brown in an all-White school. I remember his passion and my own anger at his racialized mansplaining. No one seemed to notice that he had just taken my idea and my rationale with no reference to the words I had just spoken. (175–176)

The interruption of experiential evidence—paired with the uptake of someone else's ideas—is (too) common in the "collaborative" conversations of committees who must work under time constraints to develop solutions, and who work within social and institutional structures that have privileged the "passion" and last word of white male group members over the expertise of team members of color, women team members, or other marginalized team members (176). If the too common academic discourse that has won out in classrooms and department meetings and conference talks is that the loudest, longest talker carries the day, the discursive action we mindfully take in committee meetings is actually no small matter. Team members' authentic, invested responsiveness to minoritized and marginalized members' offerings of experiential evidence and experienced recommendations can be a game-changing spark for local program action.

Institutional Knowledge: Ask When You Don't Know

While the committee discussed their assigned readings in the first meeting, they drew heavily on their intuition and individual experiences to provide feedback. However, there were moments in the discussion in which members raised questions or acknowledged gaps in programmatic or departmental information that would supplement and sometimes usefully complicate the presence of intuition and experience. The absence of some information suggests evidence of a need for more local knowledge for the tasks at hand. For example, in describing the upcoming work of the committee, L1 explained, "I haven't looked, I don't think there are set course outcomes for this . . . I'm not sure—I haven't looked at the past syllabi yet to figure out if there are consistent outcomes across those syllabi or if they're varying a little bit. Or if they just don't include outcomes, 'cause I don't know if it's a requirement to have outcomes on graduate syllabi or not." Two significant task-oriented deficiencies appear in this statement: a lack of knowledge about past syllabi for the course and a lack of knowledge about the nature of learning outcomes and graduate courses. This deficiency was addressed later in the conversation when the committee divided into two working teams, and GS2 outlined what their team would like to accomplish:

> GS2: Well, first, I think what you mentioned before in terms of, you know, looking back to prior syllabi and seeing if there are objectives or learning outcomes. I think that would be a good starting point.
>
> L1: I agree.
>
> GS2: Yeah. I thought there were, I'd find it shocking if they didn't have them.
>
> L3: Yeah, I mean knowing these people, I'm sure they had outcomes.
>
> GS2: So then from there determining . . .
>
> L3: . . . Do they need revision?

The team members' commentary here is fairly innocuous: They are not sure about outcomes, but they understand they should review them to figure out what to do with them. While there is a bit of a misunderstanding about how learning outcomes work in the department (they are not determined by individual instructors), and the group rightfully assesses that starting with these required outcomes is important, it is worth noting that they seem to have begun this work *without asking anyone who might know*. It's a difficult moment for me to read (as someone who might know, someone they might have asked) with moments in mind like one Staci Perryman-Clark (2019) describes in a chapter on workplace bullying:

> At this meeting, my department's undergraduate committee presented a proposal to revise its curriculum for English majors and proposed eliminating an introductory literature course and shifting its graduate teaching assistants (GTAs) over to sections of first-year writing (ENGL 1050), without discussing these changes with me, the WPA. The proposal also stated that ENGL 1050 simply taught "the basics of rhetoric and writing," while the proposal areas that pertained to the creative writing and literature courses included carefully crafted and thoroughly detailed course descriptions. Both of these instances infuriated me because no one from the committee took the time to discuss with me how these changes would impact the writing program or to find out exactly what happens in our first-year writing courses. (127)

In Perryman-Clark's experience, the weight of attention given to the creative writing and literature courses, as compared with the slight description of ENGL 1050 and the committee's inattention to Perryman-Clark's institutional knowledge, as WPA, illustrates how this inattention can function as a power play to disregard a colleague. While the practicum project team is nowhere near bullying in their musing about learning outcomes, passive disregard for the institutional knowledge held by others or available in the documented work of others may be a slippery slope to active disregard, to limiting perspectives, and to strange and small groupthink. Infuriating, indeed. While institutional knowledge is readily available in the myriad documents we produce each semester and in the minds of our program personnel, we best seek it.

THE SECOND MEETING

In early March 2020, the committee held their second meeting focused on discussion of possible revisions to the syllabi for the two-course practicum sequence. The meeting began with several minutes of collegial conversation about external committee work, reading each other's syllabi, grading workload, travel plans, FYW class discussions, and where to buy good clementines. Then each group tasked with reviewing previous syllabi reported their progress on their work. They discussed practicum assignments they "love[d]" from the set of previous syllabi and they talked through the challenges and needs of the pre-semester orientation for teachers.

The employment and uptake of knowledges in this committee meeting reiterate patterns in the previous meeting, though now the group had begun to think through specific examples, experiences, and ideas.

Intuition: Weighing What's "Too Much" and What's Not Enough

Throughout this second recorded meeting, the committee identified several programmatic tensions that might shape their work: arranging the pre-semester orientation after the beginning of lecturer and GTA contracts but soon enough before the first day of classes; annually responding to the changing nature of GTA anxieties upon entering the program; feedback from former GTA cohorts that there was "too much reflection" in some iterations of the practicum; shifting the work of the practicum into a two-credit course from a three-credit course.

GS1's intuition about the place of reflection in the practicum came out as the team discussed sample syllabi and assignments:

> I think something that is kinda missing that I think should be required, is I think that GTAs should have to write a reflection about their teaching every time that they teach. Like, we should have, and I would say even do this instead of reading responses, like you should have to write 250 words after every single class that you teach and then turn that in, too . . . And then turn that into like an end, we had an end reflective essay for Adrienne's class, and I think that could really build toward like a longer reflective project at the end.

In this example, GS1 drew from both the sample syllabi the committee was consulting and their own experiences in my class as part of their broad wells of knowledge as a graduate instructor; they added to these experiences a pedagogical suggestion. This suggestion was then affirmed and expanded on by GS2: "I do think that's smart, and I think the reason why it's so smart as well is because it begins to form a philosophy of teaching on its own."

When the team turns to discussing the pre-semester orientation, we see another example of experience shifting into brainstorming and problem-solving, of the expression of intuition developing from the confluence of considering scholarship on the practicum, institutional reality, and committee members' own experiences with our pre-semester orientation. L4 noted that many of the readings the team discussed describe programs that have several days, if not a week or more, of orientation for new instructors before they begin teaching. Our program, however, has new GTAs teaching after a short orientation (see Wallis and Jankens 2017 for more description of this process), and the committee wrestled through the labor considerations the program must attend to and their ideas for what happens in orientation, some of which emerged in this moment:

> GS1: Yeah, and I think as far as my experience having just gone through it, the one day that I had as, like, my GTA orientation for the department was five million times more helpful than the university-mandated one... So, I like the idea of that being two days, like, I think it would have been really helpful to have a day of that kind of onboarding conversation, things like that, but then another day of like, well, what do I do the first week?
>
> L1: Right.
>
> GS2: Well, yeah, it's a huge concern.
>
> GS1: Or just reading the syllabus, the common syllabus, together would be sweet. Even something that simple, like a reading group the next day would be great.
>
> L4: So maybe, you know, those two days don't have to be super content heavy where people would have to prepare.
>
> GS2: It could be like a workshop.
>
> L4: Yeah.
>
> GS2: ... That could be a space as well that opens up to, okay, we, if we're understanding this assignment properly, what, what might you do with it? What are your thoughts? How are you going to come at this? How are you, you know what I mean? I just think it's really a space for people to bounce ideas off of one another.

GS1 followed their initial experiential offering (comparing the helpfulness of the program orientation to the university-mandated orientation) with an intuitive suggestion that aims to solve the challenge of our program's quick start into teaching for GTAs. L4 and GS2 provided affirmation but also extended this moment with their own intuition. L4 asked GS2 to comment on how they felt their cohort would respond to a more in-depth orientation:

> L4: ... Trust your gut.
>
> GS2: I think people would be okay. I'm going to be straight honest. They're going to bitch at first, but I think they're going to be like, oh that was so much better than it used—you know, like, I feel more confident. I feel like I got something from it. I think that if it was solid and it was meaningful, and it was helpful, we're fine with that.
>
> L4: So, it's really the value. If you think it's of value to your time and preparation. If you feel that the university has a little of that. "Oh, the university's trying... to cover their ass on A, B, and C."

GS2: Right, right.

L4: So, but if you felt no, no it's valuable. I feel better prepared, I feel less anxious.

GS2: I think it puts people in a position where they're really gonna have to confront what's going to happen in the next couple of weeks. It's just reality.

In this exchange, L4 invited GS2's honesty, asking them to speak and hypothesize from their wells of knowledge and experience as an incoming GTA and not only as a committee member. When committee members encourage each other to engage their intuition in this conversation about orientation plans, there is an increased opportunity for often unheard perspectives to enter the discussion.

In these examples, participants draw from reflection on experience, institutional knowledge, and consideration of scholarship to make an intuitive recommendation; this move demonstrates a step beyond the ways experiential knowledge is often presented in the context of these meetings. When participants apply intuition, demonstratively drawing from multiple sources of information, their perspective seems to be taken up by the team. Especially valuable is that GTAs' intuition has space and is honored in the discussion.

Experiential Knowledge: Offerings Affirmed and Left Alone

While the preceding example demonstrates GTAs reflecting on their general experiences with pre-semester orientation as part of moments of intuition, in this second meeting about planning for a common syllabus for the practicum, experiential knowledge more often emerged in small blips across the transcript; when it was offered in conversation, it was not taken up or developed. Table 3.2 represents these three minor moments.

Like in the first meeting, these offerings emerged in terms of experience-as-evidence: evidence of what is necessary and valuable in new teacher orientation, of how participants will respond to specific topics, and what works in selecting assigned readings in a class. And like in the first meeting, while there were sometimes responses to these offerings in the discussion, they were simple affirmations ("Yeah"; "That's cool"), and the experiences were not interrogated further. If they were, GTAs' anxieties about grading, or the typical observed responses of longtime part-time faculty may be better understood, and approaches operationalized.

TABLE 3.2. Experiential evidence offered in the second curricular subcommittee meeting

Conversational Topic	Statement of Experiential Knowledge [responses in brackets]
Foundational concerns to discuss in orientation	Because I find the grading always ends up being last when I think that it's a huge stressor for a lot of GTAs coming in. What do I do? How do I grade? How do I allocate time for it? How do I, you know? So I'm just, that's just an example. *[Yeah]*
Organizing program-run orientation for new and returning instructors	The established PTF [part-time faculty] are going to do what the established PTF are going to do.
Selecting assigned readings for the practicum	I like giving my students, here's excerpts of the thing. But also, something that I appreciated as a grad student was the instructor who like, you had your syllabus, you had your readings. But then they would also hand you, here's a bibliography of, like, everything that I have read on this subject that might be relevant to the assignments... *[That's cool. That's cool. Smart.]*

Institutional Knowledge: The Need for Local Knowledge (Reiterated)

In this second meeting, as subcommittee members reflected on the labor realities and conditions in which our program's NTT faculty, PTF, and GTAs work, they drew often on their own experiences with orientation, their knowledge about contract calendars, and memories of the events of previous program orientations. Because they had read and reflected on a set of previous syllabi for Practicum I and Practicum II, they also had the opportunity to add those syllabi into their developing institutional knowledge, and they touched on course learning outcomes in their discussion. The two teams in the committee sometimes asked each other questions about assignments in these syllabi.

There were times in the meeting, too, when the team acknowledged their need for more of this institutional knowledge: checking the official course descriptions and outcomes in the department's graduate bulletin, identifying labor boundaries around the pre-semester orientation, and asking questions about previous practicum assignments (like a question GS2 asked one of the lecturer team members about a peer observation assignment in their class).

The need for sharing knowledge about the local site was asserted by L1 in a moment focused on university demographics:

> L1: ... I would like us to continue to be aware of how our instructor demographics do not mirror our student demographics.

L2: Yeah, yeah.

L1: ... and how we, how we continue to, how we build our instructors into having awareness of what that means as well. I think that is ... Wayne State is a unique place to teach. Every campus is a unique place to teach, but I think there are unique aspects to Wayne State that people who come from like Ohio State would not be aware of for instance. Or that people who come from the Pacific Northwest would not be aware of.

L4: No, I think you're 100%. You are super right, you are super right, yeah.

GS2: So right.

GS1: Yeah, how do we build that in?

L1: I don't know, but I think it's something we should think about.

While the committee was "super right" that the demographics of our university are "unique" and integral for teaching faculty to be aware of and responsive to, attention to these demographics was, at least in part, already a part of the orientation sessions in the historical period presented in chapter 1 via documents the committee also had access to. Additionally, the committee did not seem to have accessed all available syllabi for Practicum II, L1 noting that the course has "only been offered twice," though it was offered three times during the program's recent history and several times before the 2014–2015 academic year, with which I begin my program history. All of that is to say, had the committee been gifted with more face time to work through the complexities of bringing these knowledges to bear on making recommendations for a practicum syllabus—or if, like Micciche's (2011) committee, they had "pulled back" in the face of the myriad pressures (83)—they might have deepened this institutional knowledge such that they found more resources from which to draw and continue their problem solving.

RECOMMENDATIONS FOR THE COMMON SYLLABUS FOR PRACTICUM I

The team closed their second meeting excited about upcoming travel and spring break and then, a week later, our campus closed because of the COVID-19 pandemic. An April 13, 2020, email from the chair to the committee included steps forward after a break of several weeks. As they had been asked by the director of composition to "write up a sample syllabus with a weekly calendar outline," the chair suggested that, in addition to writing learning outcomes and assignments, the group draft a calendar with suggested readings. The chair invited committee members to identify missing topics or add reading suggestions in the document. Committee members collaborated asynchronously to a degree, in shared documents, as evident in the presence of marginal comments, questions, and suggestions. The group ultimately produced a sample syllabus and schedule for Practicum I, including proposed learning outcomes (not the official department graduate-level learning outcomes), a menu of assignments with suggested weights, a menu of educational theory readings, and a suggested timing breakdown for a single class session. As their memo to the director of composition concluded, the second part of their team's task, recommendations for Practicum II, was "put on hold until Fall 2020 due to time constraints created by the coronavirus pandemic during March-May 2020."

Some residual impact of the committee's discussions about assigned practicum readings in both meetings is evident in committee documents created during the campus closure and the committee's asynchronous work, though much of the individual work of committee members is invisible to me. While I cannot identify which committee members made suggestions for specific readings in the suggested schedule submitted to the director of composition, I can see in three cases connections to previous syllabi, and, only to a small degree, references to the committee's earlier conversations, which I had recorded and studied.

Two texts listed in the sample schedule had been used in previous sections of the practicum: Laura Bolin Carroll's (2011) "Backpacks vs. Briefcases: Steps Toward Rhetorical Analysis" (used in the FYW class and in three iterations of the Practicum I syllabus) and a chapter from Beth L. Hewett's (2015b) *Reading to Learn and Writing to Teach: Literacy Strategies for Online Writing Instruction* (full text used in three iterations of the Practicum I syllabus and in two iterations of the Practicum II syllabus). One text listed in the schedule, Mitra Dunbar and W. Douglas Baker's (2014) "Teaching as Emotional Labor: Preparing to Interact with All Students," I recognized as an assigned reading in a pedagogy seminar taken by GS1 and GS2. Two texts, Douglass Brent's (2013) "The Research Paper and Why We Should Still Care" and the Association of College and Research Libraries' (2016) "Framework for Information Literacy for Higher Education," were listed as readings for the fifth week of the course, when GTAs would be preparing to begin a research unit with students.

The remaining suggested texts were listed in two sections, "Educational Theory / Theorist Reading Idea List" and "Pedagogical Concepts." In the first list, the committee included a mix of education, critical pedagogy, and rhetoric and composition scholars, along with sets of theories: "Lev Vygotsky, B. F.

Skinner & Behaviorism Learning Theory, Cognitive Constructivism, Social Constructivism, Maslow's Hierarchy of Needs, Bloom's Taxonomy, Chickering & Gamson, Gagne, John Dewey, Paolo Freire, bell hooks, Networked Learning/Connected Learning/21st century learning, Ira Shor, James Berlin, Henry Giroux, Bartholomae 'Inventing the University.'" Critical pedagogy scholars Paolo Freire, bell hooks, and Ira Shor were also represented on the Fall 2018 Practicum I syllabus (see chapter 1 for an examination of historically assigned readings). However, none of the other texts listed as suggestions in the recommendations were represented in the historical syllabi for the course. Under "Pedagogical Concepts," the committee linked three websites, "Transparency in Learning and Teaching (TILT)" (University Center for Excellence in Teaching n.d.); "Design for Learning (UDL): What You Need to Know,"[4] and "The Future of Learning and How It Could Change Your Classroom" (McMurtrie 2018). In all, these listed texts seemed to suggest the teaching practicum in composition is a site where GTAs will develop background knowledge in educational theory, critical pedagogy, and universal design/accessibility in teaching and learning, a tall order for a two-credit course.

The moment in the first meeting where L1 presented their stance on the committee's task may clarify the appearance of a heavy set of education texts in the recommended readings for the course: hearing the complaints of GTAs in previous focus group sessions (chapter 1), L1 suggested pivoting away from an emphasis on rhetoric and composition scholarship and toward "thinking about how do we design a [practicum] that supports students who are probably new to the idea of teaching just period." The syllabus recommendations and the committee conversation seem to suggest that the committee members contributing to the recommendations interpreted "practical training" in teaching FYW as including a developing background in educational theory, critical pedagogy, and universal design/accessibility over and above more direct training in teaching FYW based in scholarship in composition pedagogy. This interpretation of what is required in the practical training of GTAs teaching FYW is at odds with the tradition of practicum instruction outlined in the historical documents. That is, its rationale seems to be heavy on intuition but light on institutional knowledge. This bolstered my investment in understanding whether and how the emergent values for teacher development I identified through my historical program research (chapter 1) were at play in the committee's decisions.

Reading the Committee's Work for Values for Teacher Development

The scholarly tension present in the committee's recommendations—the subversion of scholarship in composition pedagogy—was both curious to me and traceable to their original discussion. I wondered, though, whether tacit values influenced their discussion. Though I ended the first phase of my research for this book project (and chapter 1) by identifying five emergent values for teacher development in our historical program documents, and tested these values in an analysis of syllabi from several other writing programs (chapter 2), reading the committee's transcripts for these values required some reading between the lines, looking for key terms that tie to these emergent values or suggestions that show ways these values may be employed (box 3.1). Early in this first meeting L1, reporting on their reading of some texts from the reading list, said, "This is sort of a potentially useful reflection moment for us and a good opportunity for us to articulate what are the values that we have as we move into designing the practica? What are the values the program has around the practica?" A reference to "values" is also present in the proposed learning objectives of the course: "Teacher-learners will produce instructional materials that demonstrate command of the Composition Program's pedagogical values and curricular goals." However, the committee did not explicitly work to identify values throughout their conversations, even though members' repetition of ideas might have conveyed their values. For example, L3 made it clear that they value currency in scholarship when they repeatedly stated the years texts on the reading list were published, and explicitly explained, "This book is from 2002 and there are things that I skipped out of here because it's from 2002." The currency of scholarship may or may not be centrally valued in a program's teacher development, but this relatively innocuous example shows the ways that assertions in committee work may manifest as either personal preferences or as program values.

Nevertheless, while the committee's task was not to outline values for teacher development in the practicum, their discussion, shared tasks, and recommendations demonstrate ways that the values I could identify as historically evident were either definitely part of the work and talk of program members or were not. Here, I further illuminate moments from these two meetings, and in some cases, the committee's documents, organized by evidence of these specific values in the committee's discussion, or places where these values might have been better highlighted and activated through attention to institutional knowledge, experiential knowledge, and intuition. Some assertions by committee members may evidence more than one value.

> **BOX 3.1. EMERGENT VALUES FOR TEACHER DEVELOPMENT IN RHETORIC, COMPOSITION, AND WRITING STUDIES**
>
> EV1: The practicum should emphasize local commitments to and strategies for teaching composition courses.
>
> EV2: (New) composition teachers need opportunities to hear and learn from experienced and expert teachers.
>
> EV3: Teaching composition is, materially and ideologically, a shared enterprise (composition teachers regularly share materials and strategies and co-construct knowledge).
>
> EV4: Composition teachers need to be familiar with disciplinary frameworks and position statements.
>
> EV5: Composition teachers should learn from written reflection on teaching.

EMERGENT VALUE 1: THE PRACTICUM SHOULD EMPHASIZE LOCAL COMMITMENTS TO AND STRATEGIES FOR TEACHING COMPOSITION.

In the first meeting, L1 referenced the need to support GTAs in teaching WSU-specific courses over and above general approaches to teaching FYW, and the group decided to review previous practicum syllabi before their next meeting. Otherwise, Emergent Value 1 (EV1) is not materially addressed in the first discussion. In the second meeting, local commitments to responsive teaching begin to emerge. As reported earlier, L1 asserted the value of attending to the differences between instructor and student demographics, "I think the teaching at Wayne State is a unique place to teach. Every campus is a unique place to teach, but I think there are unique aspects to Wayne State that people who come from like Ohio State would not be aware of for instance. Or that people who come from the Pacific Northwest would not be aware of." L4 agreed, "No, I think you're 100%. You are super right, you are super right, yeah." The group briefly discussed the value of these demographics being shared at orientation.

Assignments from previous syllabi and included in the sample syllabus further speak to this value, particularly an assignment to create a unit for FYW that can be submitted to the director of composition for approval for the GTA to use in an upcoming semester. This assignment, originally one I designed at the request of the director of composition, was a safeguard in place to both limit rogue unit plans and to better provide GTAs with constructive feedback that ensured their inventive approaches meet the learning goals of FYW in our program.

However, in the two meetings I was able to record before campus shut down and the committee's conversations ended, there was no explicit discussion of "local commitments" to teaching writing. Accessing these commitments goes beyond identifying the learning outcomes of general education composition courses. These are epistemic commitments, as Germano and Nicholls (2020) point out in their discussion of the work accomplished by a course syllabus, commitments not only about outcomes but also about practice. "In fact," the authors write, "that is its [the syllabus's] most important function and the underlying motivation for its content. *This is the evidence we will consider. This is how we will consider it. These are the ground rules for how we will work collectively through it*" (19; emphasis theirs). What comprises a "Wayne way" of teaching writing must speak to both learning outcomes and the strategies teachers use to support the actual students who attend our courses. That this "Wayne way" or set of local commitments is not explicit in the program documents explored in chapter 1 or in the committee talk explored in this chapter, suggests again a need for a process of making these commitments explicit. Are they wholly bound up in the course learning outcomes? Or do other commitments and values inform instructional decisions in general education composition courses, and thus in the way we prepare teachers to teach these courses? Clarity on these questions, achieved through the coordination of institutional knowledge, seems central to the beginning of a process of articulating program values for teacher development.

EMERGENT VALUE 2: (NEW) TEACHERS NEED OPPORTUNITIES TO HEAR AND LEARN FROM EXPERIENCED AND EXPERT TEACHERS.

The committee's brief conversation on new instructors needing or seeking mentoring from experienced instructors began when L2 reported their reading of Jennifer Grouling's (2018) "Training Writing Teachers":

> She was trying to get the ... TAs to sort of interview and ... read the materials of their mentor teachers in their program. To sort of be able to start a map of values that exist among the faculty and also kind of trying to map the departmental values ... if you want to get a sense of how well your teachers are reflecting, sort of the values in your curriculum, it's kind of a valuable thing.

After some digression on the assignment Grouling recommends in the piece, GS1 raised a question:

GS1: If I may? In that assignment, are they all comp students or comp GTAs talking to other comp instructors?

L2: Yeah.

GS1: Because I wonder just how our department is made up because we're going to have GTAs that are lit students and film and media studies students that might not, I don't know, like who are they going to talk to? Are they going to talk to other comp instructors or are they going—I just, like thinking of these questions, how we might work that into all of it?

L2: Yeah, yeah, yeah. Fortunately, I won't have to make that decision.

L2 acknowledged GS1's questions as relevant to thinking about the assignment and asserted the limitations of their role (which they are correct about), after which the discussion moved on. I would suggest, though, that at least deliberating these particularities, while not fit for the limited time the committee had in that meeting, was within the scope of the knowledge the subcommittee had to work through to determine whether this assignment was worth putting on the list of possible projects for the practicum. Without pinning the question for future discussion or adding it as a note in the possible assignments, GS1's question fell into a kind of black hole in the middle of intuition, experiential knowledge, and institutional knowledge. GS1 knew, from experience and observation, that GTAs outside of rhet/comp will have particular challenges working through some practicum assignments, and GS1 also knew that some work on the part of the instructor (or instructional team) can produce scaffolding that supports student success. So, there are payoffs to working through questions like those GS1 presented but to a limit. If the committee spent too much time on this discussion, it could veer into anecdotal evidence or conjecture; if they spent no time on it, they would miss the chance to explore and actualize a program value. Nevertheless, intuition, experiential evidence, and institutional knowledge had to be pressed to more fully consider whether and how this assignment would be adaptable to our practicum context: For example, how does the instructor cohort Grouling describes compare to ours? How is mentoring for teaching structured for literature and film students in our department outside of the composition program's efforts? How might a practicum instructor navigate the relationship building that would have to be done to support GTA success with this assignment, as GTAs engage with faculty inside and outside of the composition program?

EV2 was present in the second meeting in slightly more practically minded or forward-thinking moments. The committee discussed the value of hearing from experienced GTAs and PTF at the pre-semester orientation. L2 asserted the value of integrating personnel from across the department in the practicum sessions. GS1 commented on the value of the teaching observation assignment, wherein GTAs watch another GTA teach and write a reflection: "I thought that was really cool." Similarly, GS2 highlighted an assignment in another practicum where mentors visited the GTA's classroom and offered an informal observation and conversation. Suggestions to integrate experienced GTAs into pre-semester orientation conversations also reflected this value. Ultimately, however, this value was only minimally integrated into the recommended sample syllabus, in an "extra credit" assignment to "visit another (more experienced) instructor's class."

EMERGENT VALUE 3: TEACHING COMPOSITION IS, MATERIALLY AND IDEOLOGICALLY, A SHARED ENTERPRISE (COMPOSITION TEACHERS REGULARLY SHARE MATERIALS AND STRATEGIES AND CO-CONSTRUCT KNOWLEDGE).

As noted earlier, in the first meeting the group decided to begin their work on recommendations by looking at the learning outcomes in previous syllabi. In the second meeting, when the group had spent some time discussing these previous practicum syllabi, GS2 commented on learning from others' experiences: "I like this whole idea of having a pool or some sort of you know, collection of strategies and methodologies in different assignments that people had tried in the classroom and if they have those reflections, what worked, what didn't, how it can be changed. But just seeing other people's ideas I think are huge." GS2 also asserted that conversations about assignments with experienced GTAs would be a helpful part of the pre-semester orientation. L2's appreciation of the integration of other teachers into the practicum also highlighted this value. Again, this value was minimally integrated in the sample syllabus, in a suggested assignment in which GTAs present a lesson plan to their peers, but as the committee discussed the value of having multiple teachers share teaching ideas and strategies in the practicum, we can see that committee members see a place for experiential evidence *in* the practicum.

EMERGENT VALUE 5: COMPOSITION TEACHERS SHOULD LEARN FROM WRITTEN REFLECTION ON TEACHING.

Explaining their thoughts on the book *New Ways in Teacher Education* (Freeman and Cornwell 1993), L1 described one of the classroom activities described in the text, and commented, "So this is essentially a way to think through, how do you guide new instructors into being reflective practitioners ... that is one of the cores I think of our teacher preparation here within the comp program, is that we prepare our instructors to be reflective practitioners." Here, when L1 used the phrase "one of the cores ... of our teacher preparation," they identified a value.

Though other committee members do not discuss reflection in their comments during the meeting, L1 returned to the idea toward the closing of the meeting, noting their reading of a chapter wherein the author describes students keeping teaching notebooks, and L1 recommended further discussion of the use of teaching notebooks for all GTAs in the practica. Through repetition of assertion, L1 reinforced the place of reflection, and written reflection, specifically, in the practicum, both for the instructor of the course and for students.

In the second meeting, this value was taken up when GS1 asserted the importance of regular reflection, presented at length, on the subsection on intuition: "I think that GTAs should have to write a reflection about their teaching every time that they teach." GS2 followed up this comment about scaffolding reflection: "I do think that's smart, and I think the reason why it's so smart as well is because it begins to form a philosophy of teaching on its own."

The committee included in their sample syllabus several examples of reflective writing assignments from previous practicum syllabi and their reading list: weekly reflections, a teaching notebook, a teaching vlog, and a learning encounters assignment I had previously adapted from Stenberg's (2005) description of such encounters in *Professing and Pedagogy: Learning the Teaching of English*. Reflective writing was also included in the proposed learning objectives for the course: "Teacher-learners will demonstrate the ability to use reflective writing to critically engage in their learning and development." The presence of this emergent value for teacher development is, perhaps, the strongest value explicitly integrated in the local context, despite the resistance to reflection voiced by GTAs in previous focus groups (see chapter 1). Further, the inclusion of reflective writing in the practicum syllabus is the strongest representation of institutional knowledge coming to bear on the committee's work, as an investment in reflective writing is present in historical practicum syllabi as well as in the instructional approaches of the larger writing program.

SO, WAIT, WHERE IS THE VOICE OF THE "DISCIPLINE" IN THESE RECOMMENDATIONS?

While, as just described, four of my initially identified emergent values are taken up by the committee in their conversation, one clearly did not appear in these recommendations: EV4, "Teachers need to be familiar with disciplinary frameworks and position statements." If I am looking for whether and how the values of the discipline are evident in teacher development alongside local values in our program, it would seem this is not only a crack but a gaping hole in the committee's recommendations. As Adler-Kassner and Wardle (2015) explain in the introduction to *Naming What We Know*, disciplinary frameworks and position statements provide researched and agreed-upon talking points that local writing program actors can use to describe disciplinary commitments and knowledge to interested or invested parties outside of the discipline (6). LaFrance (2019) outlines the weight of these resources in describing how ruling relations function in sites of writing:

> Professional statements not only provide educators with a generalized sense of the ideals of practice and prevailing sensibilities within writing studies, but they are also useful to programs and departments in making crucial arguments about the value of the work faculty do in their classrooms and within campus communities, the working conditions necessary for success, and appropriate types of teaching practice to administrators and colleagues who may have different ideas about how writing courses should be organized, staffed, or situated within a curriculum (34).

These disciplinary resources are rhetorically imperative for the work of writing programs, broadly, and teacher development, more specifically. The practicum instructors and WPAs I interviewed for chapter 2 seem to agree. Not only do those engaged in sites of teacher development in writing programs benefit from the support and guidance provided by these disciplinary statements, but these statements also provide a vocabulary for working in the field, and within the values of the field, for those who are new or newer to the community. The exclusion of these statements in the recommendations of the committee blocks a channel for values-based program action.

While one disciplinary framework is recommended in the syllabus ("Framework for Information Literacy for Higher Education"), it is nevertheless from an adjacent-though-relevant-to-FYW discipline, authored by specialists in library science, the Association of College and Research Libraries. It appears as an idiosyncratic commitment, similar to the idiosyncratic appearance of scholarship and frameworks in the historical practicum syllabi presented chapter 1. These limited references to disciplinary frameworks and scholarship might suggest a hyperlocal vision of teaching writing, one that implicitly insists that it knows how to function in spite of the long asserted best practices of composition pedagogy, that reifies the challenge of idiosyncrasy highlighted in chapter 1 and does so without further outlining what a "Wayne way" of teaching writing means. Further, the exclusion from the recommended readings of disciplinary frameworks for teaching composition (e.g., *Framework for Success in Postsecondary Writing* [Council of Writing Program Administrators 2011]) suggests, as noted earlier, that, ultimately, the committee views the teaching practicum for composition as a site for helping GTAs develop theoretical background in education, rather than specific, research-based practices for teaching FYW as represented in composition scholarship. Though previous practicum courses took up these frameworks to a degree, that knowledge has not come to bear on the recommended syllabus. What, indeed, *is* a "Wayne way" of teaching writing?

Thus, the committee's represented values for the content of the course, as seen in their recommendations, seem somewhat at odds with the multiple instances of their discussion of a need for "practical" work in Practicum I. If teacher development at the program level is the material work of a few, but the site of decision making for all, then explicit articulation of shared values for teacher development is necessary. How do we get there?

There are ruling relations functioning in the committee's work, but they do not include—yet—an articulated set of values for teacher development. The historical idiosyncrasies of the course may function as a ruling relation that while urging the committee toward a common syllabus only reify idiosyncrasy. The recommendations represent, on top of the historical idiosyncrasies of the course, idiosyncrasies that are purposeful but also problematic, and they potentially emerge from this lack of articulation. To contend with these forces, the committee would need more time and a different quality of dialogue.

Rhetorical and Relational Implications of this Analysis

In reality, the limited face time and short-term deadlines of curricular committees make this kind of depth of real-time analysis and enacting of knowledges, well, unwieldy and impractical. At the same time, however, without an explicit expectation of the presence and triangulation of intuition, experiential knowledge, and institutional knowledge in collaborative committee work, teams may risk missing the mark of values-driven program goals. And, if nothing else, this lack of explicit attention to the depth of presence of these knowledges might have a rhetorical impact, as it did on me, as a colleague, when I first read through the committee's recommendations, as I described in the beginning of this chapter.

I certainly brought my own triad of intuition, experiential knowledge, and institutional knowledge to bear on my reading of the committee's recommendations and the rest of their discussions. I know from having taught the course and having read about the challenges of deciding what to do in a practicum, when there are so many options and so little time, that "covering" the practicum's work in two hours a week is a stark challenge. I know that our graduate students value the practical "stuff" they need to do in FYW but bring their own theories to bear on their teaching whether we introduce them to specific theories or not. And I know that when what we have been trained in is composition theory and pedagogy, and not wider educational theory, then maybe that's what we should be teaching. The practicum is, after all, designed to support GTAs in teaching a very specific course: FYW.

The work of writing programs is situated in and coordinated in local ways and we cannot ignore the way that systems and people bring this work to life (or halt it) (LaFrance 2019, 5–6). The conversations of committee meetings are not isolated from these contextual influences; as it is in this study, the committee's acknowledgment of contextual influences occupy significant discourse during the just less than two hours of transcripts I was able to examine: contract timelines, GTAs' areas of study, undergraduate student demographics, the upcoming spring break. Nevertheless, there is the potential for a real, material impact on the discourse of future curricular committee conversations through an examination of the discourse (if not the whole subjectivity) of committee participants.

However complicated my perspective in this site was or is, my position as a former practicum instructor, mentoring committee chair, and administrator of teaching observations, while it provides me with significant insight toward the program's overall work in teacher development, has also provided a useful subjective lens for analysis. My reading helps me consider potential core questions toward a simple heuristic to guide committee work in writing programs, one I will certainly present to the committees with which I work:

- What institutional knowledge (history, bylaws, materials, interpersonal/personnel knowledge) is required for the committee to productively approach its task?
- Who in the committee needs this knowledge to begin work and how and to what degree will it be shared with all members?

- How and when will committee members use question-asking and response to develop intuition and experiential knowledge into shared knowledge?

This study also helps me think about the ways that, as a WPA in the future, I might better take up a practice of slow agency that mindfully seeks institutional knowledge, experiential evidence, and intuition outside of my own. Micciche (2011) notes, "As most WPAs already know, acting overwhelmingly in response to ever pressing urgencies frequently prevents us from coming to terms with a larger circumstance. It also creates barriers to occupying spaces of deliberate uncertainty in hopes of achieving a renewed standpoint on a situation" (79). While the sometimes-urgent requirements of quick responses on decisions are a reality of WPA life, a practice of regularly seeking this triad of knowledges in coordination with other program personnel may produce returns in those hurried moments. As I will explore in chapter 5, structuring this coordinated knowledge sharing into the practicum (or other program sites) as one node in a programmatic feedback loop can support a more habitual (programmatic) slow agency.

Aside from these potential rhetorical, relational implications, there are also implications of this study for how graduate students on curricular committees may experience professionalization, broadly, and teacher development, more specifically, via the quality of their participation. As Ashton Foley-Schramm, Bridget Fullerton, Eileen M. James, and Jenna Morton-Aiken (2018) describe, their development of a Graduate Student Praxis Heuristic arose out of their experiences "in more marginal or unauthorized WPA roles," not as official graduate assistant WPAs (96). Like the two graduate students on the curriculum committee I examined, GS1 and GS2, the authors negotiated their understanding of institutional (program) dynamics. They consider how these dynamics shifted between when they participated in an assessment project and afterward as they were the project experts who remained when their cooperating faculty member moved to another university and they, as graduate students, lost their foothold on the project (92–93). Their developing expertise on the project matter was honored at first, then it wasn't. The authors' experience demonstrates the tenuous expertise of graduate student members on project teams like the one presented in this chapter—their experience is essential during the process of the team's work, so it is worth making sure their contributions "count," hence the development of a heuristic for strengthening and assessing professionalization. One question in Foley-Schramm et al.'s heuristic stands out to me as highly relevant to the situation described in this chapter: "What kinds of institutional structures, power dynamics, and embedded cultures are graduate students experiencing at play in this project?" (95). This question points not only to the confluence and interruption of experiential knowledge and institutional knowledge at play in the work of the curriculum subcommittee but also to the double layer of experiential knowledge these graduate students must negotiate: their experiences as teachers of general education composition courses, and their (limited) experiences with the discourse of program committee work, work that may directly impact their teaching.

Thus, this committee work influences teacher development in two ways (and therefore impacts all GTAs in the program, and GS1 and GS2, specifically): both through recommendations about the content of the teaching practicum and through discussions about curriculum that may have a tacit or explicit influence on the work of these two graduate instructors. And this analysis of committee work highlights the ways that a nuanced attention to committee discourse has the potential to affect the pacing of this discourse such that more equitable deliberation leads to more inclusive results.

Conclusion

In this chapter, I have outlined the exigence for a curriculum subcommittee's attention to making recommendations for a common syllabus for the teaching practicum; read their meetings for the presence of intuition, experiential knowledge, institutional knowledge, and program values; and located possibilities for better developing these often tacit and unexplored layers of collaborative discourse. To trace one of the threads I introduced in the opening of this book, this study is useful for me in determining which teacher development values I identified in historical program documents actually "stick" when put into conversation with the committee's discussions of recommendations for the Practicum I syllabus. It also, however, demonstrates something significant about the role of experiential knowledge, institutional knowledge, and intuition in curriculum committees and has implications for the ways such committees might pursue their work.

When teams purposefully slow their conversation to develop these knowledges, they may better account for the experiences of program personnel, the institutional circuits in which they work and, therefore, they may also more fully support the professionalization of GTAs on the team. Further, they may better ensure the desired rhetorical impact and sustainability of their recommendations via engagement of program values. While compositionists have become very familiar with the role of explicit prompting in supporting students' knowledge transfer, it's possible that we are less experienced with the need to activate specific knowledges in our work outside of the classroom, that we are less aware that to support the development of a committee that works as a satellite of the larger community of the writing program, we need to explicitly bring these various knowledges to bear on conversations and collaborative tasks.

Among the cracks left by gaps of institutional knowledge and the bulging weight of unattended individual experience, however, the beginning of something grows. The subcommittee's concern with assigned readings in the practicum is shared by the instructors I interviewed in chapter 2, especially Stephanie, who shared with me her rationale for sequencing a complex and valuable set of readings for her practicum course. Determining the reading list not only takes significant time for practicum instructors (or WPAs or programs designing the practicum) but conveys messages about what the program values in working with undergraduate and graduate students and teaching writing. This committee, halted in many ways by the onslaught of the COVID-19 pandemic, expressed a lot of thoughts about what specific readings might offer to practicum students or instructors; however, ultimately, most of the readings they discussed did not make it on the recommended syllabus.

In addition to practical implications for the discourse of project teams who aim to better attend to program values and the rhetorical offerings of their members, to effect a more impactful agency, this study also provided me with clear next steps for my teaching and research. My analysis of the committee study artifacts coincided with my preparation to teach Practicum II in winter 2021 and therefore shaped my planning work with a small committee, which I describe at the beginning of chapter 4. I was able to use the committee's conversation and recommendations, along with my own conversation with the director of composition, to outline an approach to the practicum in line with the teacher development values shared across program sites and conversations. Pushing ahead on my own agenda as a practicum instructor, to structure implicit program values more explicitly into the practicum course, how would my attempts play out? This is the question I explore in the next chapter of my research story.

4
"But Here We Are!" Still Learning How to Teach About Language

The Practicum, a Revised Curriculum, and the Pandemic

> What would happen if all TA training and practicums were just readings in antiracism, ungrading, and Jacques Ranciere's "The Ignorant Schoolmaster"???
> —*Will Duffy, tweet, 9.17.21*

For the first three years I taught our program's Practicum II course, I modified the course in response to GTAs' feedback and requests from the director of composition, who, from a labor standpoint, needed these GTAs to be ready to step into various teaching roles, perhaps teaching our IC course, technical writing, or basic writing, based on each year's demands. While it was challenging to wrangle training for the *possibility* of teaching new courses in the composition sequence and the *possibility* of teaching online into one syllabus and schedule, I relished the chance to share my experiences with online teaching, my expertise as a licensed high school English teacher, my institutional knowledge, and the scholarly and institutional knowledge of the colleagues I brought in as guest speakers. I balanced Practicum II assignments with a mix of reading responses, practical applications (lesson plans, instructional videos), and professional documents like teaching philosophies. I wanted to contribute something to GTAs' ongoing teacher development and professional development to help them realize professional possibilities in teaching outside of our department. Sometimes GTAs thrived in the course, excited about their sense of developing agency in our program. Sometimes they attended the class and its required teaching circles begrudgingly. My excitement at teaching my first graduate-level courses was sometimes blotted out by students who skipped class but were on campus, who faked watching their classmates' presentations while they surfed the internet, and who used class discussions as a chance to exercise the same problematic social dynamics they exercised in the GTA offices (though I did not know that back then).

My long-standing goal was to use the practicum to spend time with other teachers talking about exciting scholarship that I hoped would impact our local teaching. One year, we labored over Asao B. Inoue's (2015) *Antiracist Writing Assessment Ecologies*. As focus group notes from that W18 semester indicate, we did not have enough time to work through all the discussion needed to deeply reflect on assigned pedagogy readings in theoretical and practical ways: "We read a lot of texts about teaching that we didn't get a chance to talk about." In the weeks we read Inoue's text, we worked through written reflections and potential applications alongside our classroom conversation, imagining possibilities for antiracist assessment in FYW. But in our limited discussions, a repeated script emerged, a refrain: *If racism is inherent in the institution, what happens in one classroom isn't going to make a difference—what I do in my FYW class won't ultimately matter.* I could take you to the spot in our practicum classroom where a GTA sat and weekly expressed this frustration and resignation; I can still see him there—I could tell you which chair he sat in. It was an experience that, while it might have broken my teacherly spirit, only made me want to push harder to see what work I could do.

However, my assignment to teach Practicum II in the winter 2021 semester, after a three-year break from teaching the course, was one I approached with some trepidation. Following my first readings of the curriculum subcommittee's notes and conversations (chapter 3), I experienced frustration not only about my ongoing research on program values for teacher development but about the ways that both the pandemic and (sometimes resultant) modes of committee knowledge-making had potentially impacted the curriculum for the practicum courses I would be teaching in subsequent semesters. I had an opportunity for curricular intervention, though, in fall 2020, when I made my way onto a subcommittee with two graduate students and an NTT colleague. Our goal was to make curricular recommendations for Practicum II. This was an opportunity for me to collaborate, in a heavy-handed way, on addressing the problem with course readings I had identified as I reviewed the recommendations for the first course (chapter 3). Through a series of biweekly meetings, the four of us identified possible readings, strategized their organization, discussed assignments for the course, and crafted a course calendar.

This chapter is the story of the winter 2021 Practicum II course we put together, one that, like others I have read about, carried the weight of doing too many things in too little time (Trubek 2005). Because I knew I would want to reflect deeply on the confluence of curricular changes, teaching experiences, and pandemic education that I would see and hear in our weekly Zoom meetings, I filed for IRB approval to conduct a teacher research study so that I could craft an account of teaching the course and of what I could learn through examining how we worked with the readings we incorporated.[1] In this chapter, I begin from the big picture, the role of the practicum course in supporting GTAs in working with the diverse language and literacy practices of students. Then, I zoom in on the ways four students and I experienced learning a revised IC curriculum, learning how to continue teaching in a pandemic, and addressing our investments in supporting these diverse language and literacy practices. I use this story to show the generative tensions that emerged when GTAs and I took a tacit program value and an explicit pedagogical value we shared (activating antiracist writing instruction) and worked through learning how to enact it in IC. The Practicum II course was a chance for me and these now experienced GTAs to work on pushing our understanding of teaching differently; as this chapter's epigraph suggests and as I show in this narrative, we understood pedagogical change as imperative at our urban research university in this pandemic semester.

Through the evidence of this chapter, I argue that the practicum can be an empowering site for instigating program change and activating tacit and emergent program values when instructors attune to the tensions experienced by GTAs in engaging these changes and values. Additionally, I demonstrate how these tensions may be revealed through the juxtaposition of disciplinary scholarship and local requirements. In structuring practicum discussions in which GTAs and I worked to apply writing studies scholarship on social justice, antiracist teaching, and linguistic justice—emergent values of our program at the time—curricular and instructional challenges in the local context rose to the surface in new ways. Specifically, these discussions highlighted GTAs' feelings about pandemic isolation, the need for boundaries, and the limits of their authority; they also highlight the ways that, because of my experiences working with these GTAs over several semesters, I was able to better support them in navigating these tensions.

The work of this chapter contributes an important perspective to scholarship on the composition teaching practicum. As both Jessica Restaino (2012) and Meghan Brewer (2020b) have emphasized, GTAs learning how to teach composition in their first semester are in a "tenuous position of being a graduate instructor" expected to manage their classrooms and promote the values of the discipline, particularly regarding "confronting discourses of oppression" (Brewer 2020b, 38). Brewer argues, and I dig into this in chapter 5, that it is the role of WPAs and mentors to help GTAs develop strategies for this work. I wholeheartedly agree and focus narrowly in this present chapter on the integration of readings and discussions attending to this work. I also present this work from a different vantage point: looking at GTAs in their fourth semester of coursework, and with experience teaching in our program, as they learn to teach IC for the first time. Through this study, then, we can begin to see difference between the ways that first-semester GTAs experience working through these tensions (e.g., as represented in the studies presented by Restaino, Brewer, and others) and the ways more experienced GTAs encounter them; we can also, thus, see what tensions remain regarding teaching values and teaching practice after several semesters of teaching within one writing program. This study contributes to important conversations about linguistic justice and antiracist teaching in postsecondary institutions, teacher development in writing studies, and the integral value of developing teacher research that may be placed in conversation with wider, ethnographic and quantitative data on the work of institutions of higher learning.

The Big Picture: Supporting the Diverse Language and Literacy Practices of Students

"Antiracism" and "linguistic diversity" may more and more be common vocabulary in the hallways, meeting, and documents of writing program work—certainly of the social media feeds and conference talks of members of the discipline—but as Frankie Condon and Vershawn Ashanti Young (2017) reflect in their introduction to *Performing Antiracist Pedagogy in Rhetoric, Writing, and Communication*, academics doing antiracist work in the contemporary university must still explain the necessity of this work to colleagues and administrators (3). In the same collection, Mya Poe (2017) describes the multiple institutional frameworks in place to address issues of race and diversity, arguing for a reframing of the ways local programs and institutions work with race, by paying special attention to the actual students with whom they are working, framing assignments and assessments specifically for those students, and learning more about the connection between multilingualism and race.

This localized classroom work is important; teachers need to be aware of the ways that even the texts of their classrooms and curricula may include microaggressions and contribute to systems of oppression (Diab et al., 2019). General education writing classrooms, as sites in which almost all university students will spend time at crucial threshold moments in the university experience, are locations where this attention and reframing can happen in more systematic ways, where instructors can engage in "rhetorical and pedagogical interventions" (456). For example, exploring the implications of the integration of antiracist writing assessment practices in FYW, Inoue argues for the reframing of writing assessment such that it acknowledges students' labor and does not disadvantage students not steeped in white, hegemonic literacy practices. Inoue's (2019c) argument for reframing writing assessment helps writing teachers and writing program administrators consider the ways that institutional change related to language practices can begin in the classroom, where the habits of white discourse can be interrogated (399). We can also be mindful of the reflective curricular inquiry Ritter (2018) encourages us to engage in regarding the ways that international, multilingual, and minority students experience the curriculum: "What are these students' particular needs, and how must our programs evolve to meet them? How does the 'standard' curriculum address their needs—if at all? What must we do to make these students feel like a genuine and valued part of our writing programs, and not unwelcome interlopers in them?" (62). These questions speak to the curriculum subcommittee's reflection, recounted in chapter 3, that new GTAs need to learn about the demographic makeup of our diverse student population if we are to support their learning.

Supporting GTAs in developing these antiracist practices in their classrooms requires acknowledging their working conditions too. As Jennifer Slinkard and Jeroen Gevers (2020) note, GTAs and other writing instructors are not always positioned to change assessment policies and practices, beholden as they are to the demands of their departments and institutions. Additionally, Staci M. Perryman-Clark (2016) demonstrates the challenge of instructor resistance to writing program initiatives regarding social justice and linguistic justice: Through WPA leadership in such initiatives, "white, monolingual instructors and graduate students are challenged to work differently from the practices to which they have been accustomed, and by working differently, white, monolingual instructors and graduate students often see themselves as unsure of what exactly they should do" (210). As Cecelia Shelton (2019) asserts, writing as a Black GTA working in a business writing classroom, writing programs need to design intersectional training and assessment of GTAs; such training can better support their thinking about and integration of antiracist instruction and discussion of race, linguistic justice, and social justice issues in their writing classrooms. Teacher development practices like the dialogical and dialectical models Judith Goleman (2002) advocates for may support GTAs' work with integrating new literacy models into their own teaching. These models require GTAs (and their students) to critically reflect on the knowledges produced by discourses and social functions of these discourses (87). That reflection engages a reflexive response in the GTA as they consider their subjectivity and their pedagogical decisions (89). Employment of models that allow students to reflect productively on their comfort, discomfort, vulnerability, and positionality within "safe" spaces can prepare them for the needed justice-oriented work of the writing classroom.

Beyond the classroom, such work has real implications for the future working lives of GTAs and those who work with them; as Perryman-Clark (2016, 2019) highlights, white allyship is a significant antidote for the bullying WPAs of color can face at the hands of graduate students and colleagues. The practicum, thus, is a site where GTAs experience and consider the possibilities of action in its many forms (Restaino 2012); it is a site where allies and "accomplices" (e.g., Martinez 2018, 231) in linguistic and social justice can begin, or contextually reconfigure, their work. Arguing that "neutrality in the classroom is only ever a performance," Brewer (2020b) positions the assignments and readings in the practicum as key for helping GTAs "recognize the embodied, performative nature of teaching" (29). This recognition is integral for GTAs to process and consider what they will *do* with the materials and concepts they encounter in the practicum, and *how* they will do it.

Because composition courses include and depend on a significant amount of reading and reading instruction, GTAs also need preparation for how to work with texts with their own students; this preparation is especially important for the study presented in this chapter, as GTAs and I consider whether and how we can use texts focused on social justice, antiracism, and linguistic justice with our students in IC. As emphasized by Yu Ren Dong (2008), new teachers may benefit from reflection on moments of sociocognitive conflict in classroom discussions, avoiding initiation-response-evaluation patterns and supporting their own students' learning through discussion. As I describe in more detail in this chapter, strategies like jigsaw discussions engage students in learning, owning, and teaching subject matter to each other (Lebaron and Miller 2005; Amador and Mederer 2013; Jay et al. 2021), shifting the role of the teacher in managing classroom talk. There are also material considerations for GTAs learning how to work with students on reading, in either online or face-to-face classes.

So, integrating this critical work into the writing classroom may not be a question of whether, for GTAs, but of *how* and how *not*. Octavio Pimentel, Charise Pimentel, and John Dean (2017) address the limitations of a "colorblind" approach to teaching writing, wherein instructors position students as nondistinct in terms of race. This colorblind classroom, based in the same meritocracy that American education has systematically and historically held itself to, "rarely works to the advantage of people of color" (109). Making the writing classroom "multicultural," argue the authors, does little to change the system or even to benefit students of any race in the class; positioning multicultural texts as "other" than White European American (WEA) texts only "reinforces the status quo" that WEA texts are part of a cultural standard (110). The authors demonstrate further that when WEA texts are not interrogated as also cultural (and white students are not supported in interrogating their whiteness), "the diversity approach . . . can do more harm than good in classrooms," (111). In enacting an antiracist approach to teaching writing, the authors explain, teachers and students need to understand the pervasiveness of racism *and* rhetoric. "Whether one is racist or not, one produces racist discourses"; that is, racism is not something that resides wholly within an individual (112). "Students and teachers do not leave their race, ethnicity, sexuality, gender, or class in a heap outside the classroom door," the authors remind us, "so nor can they dismiss themselves from their inclusion in dominant discourses" (112). Working through the narrative analyses of two instructors who "examine whiteness in their own teaching pedagogy," Pimentel et al. emphasize the necessity of identifying, interrogating, and addressing "white talk" (2017, 119) if antiracist approaches are to gain any ground in our writing classrooms. The "logic of racism and white privilege" are ever present in these spaces (121).

Explorations of assessment ecologies help us understand that antiracist writing instruction requires attention throughout these ecologies (Inoue 2015; Wood 2020); the practicum, with its already-present teacher support structures, is a place to develop this attention. While the practicum must be responsive to myriad institutional pressures, it must also function to support GTAs' practice and familiarity with theory- and research-based approaches to teaching writing (Latterell 1996; Dobrin 2005); this imperative can lead to a diversity of content in the course itself (Pytlik and Liggett 2002). Brewer (2020a) positions the practicum as an opportunity for GTAs to investigate their conceptions of literacy; As Poe (2017) and others assert, this kind of work requires an understanding of linguistic diversity and of the language and literacy practices of the students with whom GTAs are working. In the first chapter of her book *Linguistic Justice: Black Language, Literacy, Identity, and Pedagogy*, April Baker-Bell (2020) writes pointedly, "There really is not a legit reason why any teacher in the state of Michigan should walk out of a teacher education program unaware and ill-prepared to address Black Language in their classrooms, but here we are!" As a literacy educator entrusted with the training and preparation of GTAs in English for teaching general education composition courses at a university in Detroit, when I first read Baker-Bell's critique, I took it as an immediate call to action.

Of course, Baker-Bell is not the first to critique or highlight a lack of attention to teacher preparation for addressing linguistic diversity, antiracist instruction, or social justice issues. A review of even just scholarship from within the last decade shows that writing studies and English education scholars are concerned with whether and how writing and education programs prepare and support teachers to do this work (e.g., Boudreau Smith 2017; Condon and Young 2017), emphatic about the need for sustained attention to the work of "race justice and activism" in literacy instruction (Kinloch 2020, 204). But these conversations go far back: Nicole Boudreau Smith (2017) describes a history of fifty years of unheeded calls for revolution in the teaching of writing; Kate Vieira and coauthors (2019) describe the multiple, historically evidenced ways that literacy and literacy education has "the potential to liberate and oppress." Outlining the history of language education for Black students, Geneva Smitherman writes in 1977 (from my university) about the ways that this education needs to be reformed not only at the level of subject matter but also, significantly, teacher disposition: "What is needed to prevent further miseducation of black kids is a change in teacher attitude and behavior, a complete reordering of thought about the educational process and the place of black students in that process. The belief sets, the philosophy, the world view, and the pedagogical ideology of the teacher are all intertwined and interrelated" (217).

These conversations parallel graduate students' potentially narrow exposure to diverse scholarship in the wider curricula of graduate programs in rhetoric and composition; in *Counterstory*, Aja Y. Martinez (2019) asserts the narrowing impact of disciplinary histories written by white scholars being the texts typically frontloaded in graduate curricula (74). Russell (2020) demonstrates, through analysis of syllabi and interviews with practicum instructors, the problematic lack of attention to the integration of course texts and discussions on critical language awareness and social justice issues, noting that often these are integrated sparsely or nominally. This highlights an important trouble spot: the lack of practicum instructor preparation or readiness to facilitate these conversations. Indeed, as I explored in the first chapter of this book, a study of practicum syllabi from my home composition program documents, including practicum syllabi, from 2014–2019 shows not only a minimal integration of texts on these topics but a lack of explicit or coherent structuring of GTA engagement with these topics and issues as part of their training within and in addition to the practicum.

This is not a local challenge. As Cicchino (2020) points out, one of the categories of writing pedagogy education (which Cicchino abbreviates as "WPE") that WPAs most wish they could change is the timing and length of this training (91). We don't learn all we need to know about teacher development for GTAs from just this first year. Cicchino explains,

> GTA WPE seems to mostly occur when GTAs need specific directions for surviving the classroom but ceases before GTAs are ready to use their theoretical knowledge to develop their own composition curriculum. If we consider these GTAs to be emerging faculty, it becomes a question of where and how these teachers of writing learn about curriculum design if not in [sic] through WPE and how this local curriculum both can and cannot serve them as future faculty in a different local context. (100)

With most of this WPE ending "before the end of year one" (91), we have, as a field, both little time to engage in teacher development with new teachers of (college) writing and little evidence for how to do this best. Showing through survey data that most of the ways we engage WPE have not changed much in a century but that we do agree on the integration of several approaches, Cicchino expresses hope that as a field, "we can begin to move towards the development of evidence-based best practices" for GTA preparation, and beyond the often local accounts and narratives she cites in her literature review (88).

In the study I describe in this chapter, I take up these charges and notable gaps, by examining the integration of social justice, antiracist teaching, and linguistic justice texts and conversations across the semester in a composition teaching practicum course enrolling experienced GTAs. Specifically, I explore two research questions:

- How do practicum students work with and respond to specific course readings on social justice, antiracist teaching, and linguistic justice?

- Does the integration of course readings and writing assignments on social justice, antiracist teaching, and linguistic justice register in GTAs' contemporary teaching work? If so, how?

Teacher Research as Part of the Institutional Whole

In this chapter's work, I use a teacher research approach to build a pathway from my subjective teacher experience to ongoing curricular revision. I work to employ critical self-reflection on my role as practicum instructor and curriculum designer. Specifically, I attend to classroom texts (both assigned readings and student compositions) and classroom discussions and the ways these demonstrate GTAs' responses to and engagement with theories and practices related to social justice, antiracist teaching, and linguistic justice. This focus allows me to demonstrate the public reflection of teacher development I practice in this book (Stenberg 2005).

I see and experience teacher research as methodical and intentional, as a way of taking experiential knowledge and positioning it within institutional knowledge. Through engaging in teacher research, practitioners do not only capture classroom experiences but also build bridges between single classrooms and programs, departments, colleges, universities, and communities. As Ruth Ray (1992) argues, teacher research is conducted in the interest of forwarding change. Thus, as much as it is conducted in an effort to improve teacher effectiveness (Ray 1992), the work of teacher research in individual classrooms provides valuable data for programmatic initiatives, and eventual institutional change, including by bringing student voices to bear on the subject of inquiry (Ray 1996). Teacher research is a method and methodology with a productive impact on classroom instruction, student learning, researcher development, and program policy (Ray 1993; Fleischer 1995). In light of discussions of antiracist teaching, the self-work and collaborative learning inherent in teacher research can function as a means of making "actionable commitments" to racial justice (Diab et al. 2017, 20).

DATA COLLECTION

Our Practicum II class meetings during the winter 2021 semester were held on Zoom while our campus remained largely closed during the COVID-19 pandemic. I video-recorded most class sessions, both for the purposes of student access and for research. During class sessions, I captured key topics of conversation or themes on a yellow legal pad; this jotting aided in the eventual development of course themes described in the sections that follow (Emerson et al. 2011). I organized and collected course texts and student work as a part of the regular work of the class, on Canvas, the course's LMS. Following the end of the semester, and the submission of course grades, I downloaded relevant student assignments to add those to the folder of materials for analysis. I used Otter.ai to produce and check transcripts from the Zoom recordings. Then, I reread transcripts to construct a narrative timeline of the class, identifying key moments for closer reading. Finally, I worked between field notes, transcripts, and students' writing to develop themes and to present what and how participants (four students and I) contributed to class discussions, especially class discussions about the assigned readings.

In analyzing the work of that semester, I read the classroom materials as a whole to understand the degree to which we successfully attended to course readings—in classroom discussion and in writing—in a way that positioned texts by minoritized or marginalized authors as central to our learning about teaching, rather than in "tokenized" ways (Russell 2020). To craft the chapter, I read these materials to bring together experiential knowledge, teaching practice, and the scholarship we were engaging with both inside and outside of the course: Would we use these texts with students, and how? And what else do we learn about our teaching through our discussions about these texts? While I pursued research questions in my exploration of the data (transcripts, field notes, students' writing), I allowed these artifacts to speak back to me, to show me what themes emerge in GTAs' experiences while they work through these texts, teach a new course, and continue to think through several semesters' worth of pedagogical questions. To that end, what I write about in the rest of the chapter is the assigned course texts, yes, but also the tensions and possibilities that emerged in the discussions around these texts.

PARTICIPANTS

Four of the six students in the class consented to participate in the study: three students in rhetoric and writing studies and one in film studies. While these distinctions in academic emphasis are often used in descriptions of practicum courses to show differences in the dispositions of GTAs from across English studies toward the practicum or teaching composition, in the case of this study these dispositional distinctions are not evident. I reference these distinctions here because maybe it matters that we worked through this course together after having already worked together in another practicum and in other courses for a year and a half; we each were familiar both with each other and with teaching in our program. I allow the profiles of these four students—Dylan, Hunter, Kristi, and Lauren—to come through their voices in this chapter, especially in the interest of relative anonymity. They each reviewed early drafts of this chapter with me and have indicated whether they prefer to be represented by a pseudonym.

One noteworthy piece of demographic information, however, is that each of the participants in my study is white, a limitation similar to one presented by Brewer (2020a) in her study of first-semester GTAs (13). The project at the center of my inquiry—the whole package of the class, the whole teacher research study of that class—though it asks a question about better integrating texts by BIPOC scholars into the composition teaching practicum, is an artifact representative of an inherent problem of teacher development in university writing programs and in education in our country overall: We are mainly preparing white teachers (e.g., Berchini 2015).

The Context of Practicum II: Learning How to Teach IC

As noted earlier, Practicum II was in place to support GTAs in teaching a new (to them) course, our intermediate college writing course (what I call IC in this chapter). The course, focused on supporting students in learning how to write from a scholarly perspective in their academic or professional discourse communities (often, more simply, their majors) and drew from writing studies and composition scholarship on discourse communities and research writing. Its curriculum designed in 2015, the class was intended to function as a bridge between students' experiences in FYW and their writing-intensive courses in their majors. For example, psychology majors in the class might research the psychology discourse community by learning about academic journals in the field, interviewing practitioners, reading about contemporary issues, and conducting research on a question of professional interest. The class was initially designed to include significant in-class workshopping. When I taught sections of IC online, which I did for several semesters, I included demonstrations of this workshopping and of the research and writing process in my instructional videos and relied heavily on one-on-one conferences to support students through their individual research. However, in consideration of the time management challenges I had observed in students suddenly taking all online classes during remote pandemic teaching in 2020, I asked my colleague Chris Susak to work with me on revising IC for manageability for both students and instructors working in the course during the pandemic. In our revised version of IC, teachers supported students through four (instead of five) projects: a multimodal "research guide" with interview, a multimodal presentation of their research in progress, a literature review essay, and a reflective essay. We piloted these revisions with GTAs enrolled in the winter 2021 Practicum II.

The readings for this revised Practicum II thus balanced attention to (a) teaching IC; (b) teaching online; and (c) teaching with attention to social justice, antiracist teaching, and linguistic justice. This heavy reading load reflected the complex balance managed in previous Practicum II courses I had taught, which always necessarily had to do the work of several practica courses (i.e., preparation for teaching our program's various intermediate writing courses, preparation for teaching online, and continued exploration of pedagogical and scholarly issues), but, as described in chapter 3, now in the space of a two-credit course rather than three. That is all to say, if the balance of readings seems complicated or strange, it is. However, each reading was carefully selected by our committee to support one of these three goals.

The two-credit, hybrid class, which included both asynchronous and synchronous components, met on Tuesday afternoons from 2:30 to 3:15 on Zoom, with supplementary videos posted online for students to view across the week and, at students' request, some conversation time built into the Zoom room starting at about 2:15. In these class sessions, we did regular weekly troubleshooting, talked about lesson planning and grading, and provided feedback on each other's teaching. For example, in a session in early March, we discussed student drafts of the literature review assignment from previous semesters and how we would give feedback on these drafts. The group raised points and questions about paragraph organization, the purpose of an abstract, and the place of students' opinions in a literature review. I include this example of classwork outside of discussing assigned readings to show other ways we used the forty-five minutes for our own, real time, pedagogical workshopping.

Despite all of the other problem-solving we had to do, centering discussion of readings was important. I wanted to avoid the peripheral treatment of readings that sometimes happens because of this intense focus on the day-to-day work of teaching a course. In addition to having students prepare written responses to the assigned readings (and to questions I posed about the readings), I scheduled modified jigsaw discussions several times across the semester to help us bring experiential knowledge from teaching IC together with the arguments and ideas presented in the readings. After GTAs shared their responses, I worked to draw ideas from these responses together in a "plenary stage" response (Jay et al. 2021, 127). While I knew that class discussions in online classes are often tough to navigate, I understood that jigsaw discussions, in which students prepare individual contributions on assigned topics in advance of group discussion, have proven especially successful in higher education for managing the problem of class discussion, student engagement, and student confidence in online courses (Amador and Mederer 2013; Lebaron and Miller 2005; Jay et al. 2021). Alongside our other weekly conversations and problem solving, I hoped jigsaw conversations about assigned readings would help us strategize how we could also bring these topics to our IC students, and I hoped that because everyone had the opportunity for equal space to share in the discussions, our conclusions, as IC teachers and program participants, would be crafted from this more even participation and listening.

Course Themes: Connecting Our Previous Conversations, Practicum Readings, and Teaching IC Online, in a Pandemic

In this section, I work from transcripts of class sessions, field notes from these sessions, and course artifacts like the LMS and students' writing to craft themes from Practicum II focused on our discussions about how to work with course readings. I focus on our discussions (sometimes supplemented with GTAs' writing about assigned readings) to demonstrate how our work with readings influenced our experience at a few levels: learning how to teach IC (and for me, supporting GTAs' work through a new curriculum), continuing to learn how to teach online during a pandemic, and addressing our investments in supporting students' diverse language and literacy practices. Under these three core themes that characterize the nature of our discussions, I explore themes that transcend individual class sessions and point to GTAs' feelings about pandemic isolation, the need for boundaries, and the limits of their authority, as well as my reflections on the degree to which I, as their practicum instructor, could support them in working through these tensions.

TEACHING THE IC CURRICULUM: PROBLEMS OF CURRICULAR ALIGNMENT AND PROGRAMMATIC POWER

The IC course at our university requires undergraduate students to engage primarily with scholarly texts in their disciplines. Because teachers in our program typically come from English studies backgrounds, the course's emphasis on genre analysis and reflection supports both teaching and learning: We have to be able to support students in humanities, social sciences, and pre-professional programs in working through the common assignments of the course.

In our first Practicum II session in early January, we focused on sharing examples of scholarly writing to talk about textual and paratextual features. This discussion was intended to work as an initial connection point between conversations we had had in previous seminars, the texts we would read for Practicum II, and the work GTAs would do with IC students. It was, in part, to prepare us for leading similar lessons in IC in the following weeks. "What is academic writing? And what is scholarly writing?" I asked them. "Those mean a little bit different things." I asked students to drop their examples in the Zoom chat, and they each took turns describing why they selected these examples. Our goal was to begin to compile a list of example features like they might draw on or develop with their own students. Unsurprisingly, GTAs and I each drew examples from our own scholarly research interests; we looked at sections of texts on critical pedagogy, linguistic justice, rhetorical listening, multimodality, and ethnographic research. Identifying and talking through these examples drew our attention to various possible features of scholarly writing, which we named in our discussion: code-meshing; an organizational pattern moving from concrete to theoretical; explicit building on a previous scholarly conversation (evident at the sentence level in references and citations); synthesis of others' work; pop-out quotes; and author positioning.

Our first jigsaw discussion at the end of January had us beginning to reflect on various threads we were holding together in Practicum II, including students' work with multimodal composing (and our own) and larger concepts of language ideologies. I asked GTAs to read an excerpt from Elizabeth Kleinfeld's (2019) chapter on multimodal composing, universal design, accessibility, and inclusivity and Vieira and coauthors' (2019) chapter on the liberatory and oppressive features of literacy, and to choose either an article by Asao Inoue (2019c) on classroom writing assessment or Jennifer Slinkard and Jeroen Gevers's (2020) article on language ideologies. I selected these readings to help us work with students on their multimodal composing and to help us think about how we would be attending to languaging, both in IC discussions and lessons and in our assessment of students' work. I posed these questions for our discussion: "As we work with students on engaging the scholarly literature of the discourse communities they are studying this semester, how do the required practices of our classroom liberate and/or oppress? Where do we support student access? Where might there be roadblocks?" In still learning how to manage all of the responsibilities of synchronous Zoom sessions, I failed to record this first jigsaw. However, my notes on the discussion capture the questions GTAs brought to our conversation: How can assignments that worked in secondary ELA for investigating discourse—like rewriting scenes from Romeo and Juliet—work in FYW or IC (Kristi)? Will first-year students understand terms like *white racial habitus* and how can we not get in the way of students understanding what they need to do in the class (Hunter)? How can we work with students to articulate what "language standards" are, and how do we do this work in asynchronous courses (Dylan)? How can we have students practice putting authors into conversation with each other before writing the literature review assignment (Lauren)? These questions provide evidence that from the beginning of the class, GTAs were reflecting on the multiple threads that would pull at our attention across the semester.

While GTAs had formed inquiries to guide their own reading and teacherly refection across the term, the misalignment between the IC curriculum and the program's emergent goals—addressing antiracist writing instruction and social justice—was continually in front of us. In my own attempts at tying our readings to the teaching problems GTAs brought to class each week, I often found myself bouncing between ideas. A February session, centered on April Baker-Bell's (2020) *Linguistic Justice*, had us thinking about the language knowledge students bring to IC, especially in response to her pedagogical reflection: "When discussing the features of Black language, I was careful not to reinforce culturally irresponsible approaches to language instruction by treating the students at LA as if they were not experts of their native language. They use the language everyday just like me. Therefore, I wanted our study of the grammatical and rhetorical features to reflect our collective knowledge" (74). I used Baker-Bell's caution as a way for us to consider bringing students' prior knowledge into class work on the literature review essay:

> Think about the collective knowledge that our students have about the writing that they have to do in the literature review essay, and the ways that they talk about texts when they agree or disagree with them, not their approximations of how they're supposed to do it, because their approximations of how they're supposed to do it often include dropped quotes, and really strange signal phrases, and not how they would actually talk about something if they were explaining their ideas about a text in a conversation. So, that is not to say that conversation, the way we speak, automatically translates onto the page in the same way, because we know that it doesn't, but it is to say that our students already are experts at talking about their ideas and what they agree with and what they disagree with. And that maybe there are some connections there that can help them think about the kinds of ways that they write themselves into these conversations.

While the pedagogical and critical concepts Baker-Bell presents in *Linguistic Justice* are worthy of discussion in their own right, in the brief time we had together in class we had to work to respond meaningfully to both her scholarship and our questions about teaching in that week, without giving either short shrift. As I describe in part in a later section of this chapter, our discussion of *Linguistic Justice* also included discussions about language ideologies and linguistic double-consciousness (Baker-Bell 2020).

As we increasingly felt the tension of these dual goals (working through the IC curriculum and developing our discussion on assigned readings) in the second month of the class, I began our second jigsaw discussion in February with a monologue about our class as a community of practice, trying to sort our multiple goals: "As a group together, we're working on teaching IC. This is our workplace challenge ... with all of its various contextual factors. But we're also working ... on our development as teachers in the long run. And part of that is our engagement in this shared inquiry of thinking about linguistic justice, social justice, critical language awareness, all of the shades of thinking about language in the institution." I invited students to bring their problem-solving questions to class, as the agenda responsively changed each week. To prepare for our February jigsaw discussion, we read Koritha Mitchell (2015) and Cecelia Shelton (2019) on instructor positionality and curricular resistance alongside several texts related to teaching IC. For our discussion, I had invited students to speak generally about the readings for the week or to respond specifically to this question: *Where do we see places in IC to discuss power and power differentials in developing scholarly writing?* The jigsaw offerings in this class meeting demonstrated GTAs working through how to bring theoretically powerful ideas to IC alongside working with students on practical aspects of writing literature reviews. These offerings also highlighted the emotion that comes along with this reflective teaching work.

As Dylan put it, when he prepared to share this response, he was "hung up" on the ideas and experiences Shelton presents:

> And I have a lot of very confused and not very thoughtful points about [Shelton's article]. But I, I've also been reading, like, ideology and ideological state apparatuses by Althusser, and thinking about the ways of trying to negotiate teaching things that you have different ideological goals than the thing you're teaching, which is then kind of reinforcing this mode and this way of being in the world. And just anytime I read about things in HR terms and talking about students as employees and things like that, I just immediately shut down. So, trying to read things like this on its own terms

and appreciate like some of these pedagogical moves that Shelton is doing and thinking about power and seeing it on its own terms without getting all messed up about the fact that it is about preparing students to be employees, which is something that she's kind of dealing with. But something that turns me off immediately when I read. Anyway, I've just been rambling. I don't really know if I said anything just now, but Shelton was really difficult for me to read. And I don't know, I hope other people have cool things to say about it.

Dylan's response included his reading of Shelton not only alongside his teaching in IC but also alongside his reading for other aspects of his graduate coursework. His reflections on these, brought together, resulted in an emotional response, one that he hoped his classmates could help him think through.

Plagued by the challenges of participating in an online class with a troubled Wi-Fi connection, Lauren's contribution began with apologies for missing some of the conversation while she was offline. Reflecting on the example of Shelton teaching a curriculum that was not her own, Lauren explained: "Black GTAs faced power disputes with their students when these aren't even, this isn't even the lesson plans that they've devised on their own, these are, you know, stock ones from the department, but yet they are the ones getting harshly held to standards by students for pushing agendas, which I thought was really upsetting." Lauren's audio cut out, and I asked her to share ideas in the chat so we could hear from her another way.

Kristi picked up the conversation thinking about how students are positioned in the IC curriculum:

> I want them to evidence that they're understanding and they're processing and they're responding to the research and the experts and the scholars that they're trying to synthesize. But they also have to bring their own voice in and determine where those gaps are or how they can contribute. And I think that that's really possible in the multimodal presentation that they're working on currently, but that can't go completely into the lit review as we're asking them to contextualize that lit review within something else.

Kristi pointed out the problem of alignment we had been feeling. The scholarship we were reading in the practicum on centering students' voices and literacy experiences felt especially at odds with the constraints of the IC literature review assignment: While students could very explicitly demonstrate where their perspectives fit into the scholarly conversation in the process-focused multimodal presentation assignment, "we [were] asking them to contextualize that lit review in something else" (a conversation between published scholars).

Instead, Kristi posited using the topics presented in the week's readings as a way to help students develop inquiry into the practices of their own discourse communities: Where do they (or their interview participants) see or experience racism or sexism in their profession?

Finally, Hunter's jigsaw contribution shifted attention from IC students back to GTAs, almost bringing us full circle to addressing the frustrations Dylan expressed at the opening of our jigsaw:

> I think the Shelton article is the perfect example of what might happen if you try to do that [push back against the system] . . . not that you shouldn't be discouraged from doing it, but just that it's a more fraught situation than Mitchell maybe positions us to think about it as. To pivot to IC then, we have students who are either neophytes in their discipline, or who are looking to engage with this discourse community that they might be joining in the future. So, it's an opportunity for us as instructors, and especially as GTAs, to pull back the curtains a little bit on how we are situated within our own community . . . [W]e are, like, the least powerful instructors—maybe adjuncts—depends on the institution, right? So, it would be an interesting conversation, I think, to place it in context with the students thinking about their own discourse communities, and where we are positioned to the ones that maybe we want to join.

Hunter's frustration with the readings comes from the lived experience of what it means to have the positionality of a GTA. While, as he noted, GTAs may not feel they are positioned to push back against the system or help their students to do so, Hunter's suggestion was that teachers might use their own personal positions to relate to students: GTAs are working to make their own ways into a profession too. While their position as "the least powerful instructors" has them, in ways, on a "neophyte" plane with students, there is pedagogical power in being able to relate to IC students in this way. Essentially, Kristi and Hunter's responses suggested it was more possible to think about integrating these texts to support IC students' professional reflection rather than their direct work with writing the literature review.

In my few minutes of response, I tried to tie together the threads of our conversation, and to be responsive to the emotions GTAs presented. I began by bringing Lauren's contributions back into the discussion, reading her comments in the Zoom chat:

> Lauren says, "I really liked [student's] point about power differentials between students in different levels of faculty relating back to the reading by Jackson and Smitherman [2002] where [B]lack GTAs were held accountable

by their students for the content of the course, even when these are university department curriculum, as pushing their own agendas on the students, which is really frustrating and upsetting. This is something that I've discussed with a student for IC that at the beginning of the semester, I was still learning how the course is going, which she replied, must be frustrating. But it makes me reflect on what I would change in the course, which might be seen as me pushing an agenda as a woman in academia."

Lauren's reflection was important because it hinted at her perceptions of limitations in her power to address or critique aspects of the program-prescribed curriculum. I saw Hunter's response as a way to dig into what Lauren was saying:

> I think maybe just to reflect on what you were saying, Hunter, in your position as a GTA, is it the most vulnerable position? Or ... at what level can you push an agenda? It's really interesting, when we're thinking about power, about how GTAs in many cases ... do have some, at least, conversational influence on the curriculum because you're working more closely with faculty who are designing it, in ways that maybe part time faculty do not. But then also, you know, you're also taking classes and working with professors as your advisors. So, there's inherent power differentials in those situations. So, when you say the word "fraught," it's the best word ... But I also want to point out that you're talking about being transparent about your positionality as a student, and Lauren's comment in the chat reflects that as well. Being able to talk with students about what your position is, and even as a scholar, what are you doing when you are reading in your discipline and trying to position yourself and your dissertation work, as somebody who's trying to enter the field's conversations, I think that could be a powerful demonstration of how that works, too.

In these wrap-up comments, I tried to validate GTAs' difficulty in enacting changes, including justice-oriented actions, in their classroom work. Their concerns about potential power differentials are founded, but they also seem to have identified ways to address their intentions with students, through transparency about their roles and teachers, students, and writers. Their sense that the work is "fraught" does not seem to be stopping their work; they are frustrated, sometimes, but not halted.

TEACHING IC ONLINE IN A PANDEMIC: LEARNING HOW TO TEACH IN NEW WAYS

Much of our class time was spent reflecting together on teaching a new class, online, during a pandemic. Unless these GTAs had participated in an early pandemic summer session our program provided for teaching online, they had not had instruction in teaching online before taking Practicum II. Much of what they learned had been through their experiences finishing their winter 2020 classes online after the campus closure and then in continuing to teach online in fall 2020, when our university continued remote instruction. One small sure moment of preparation was the online mini lesson I had them create in Practicum I in fall 2019. However, online teaching (and teacher development in this area) during the pandemic was undoubtedly different than before this era (e.g., Saidy and Sura 2020). So, our class discussions in Practicum II helped us especially consider how reading, written feedback, and grading were working differently in our composition instruction in this season of remote teaching and learning during the pandemic. These discussions on reading, feedback, and grading in the online writing classroom helped us consider the function of instructional relationships, developed through feedback (Hewett 2015a, 2015b; Borgman and McArdle 2019) as well as through negotiation and articulation of expectations with students in the various media of the course, including assignment descriptions and grade contracts (e.g., Inman and Powell 2018; Formo and Robinson Nealy 2020).

Some of our time together was spent providing feedback on recorded teaching demonstrations that GTAs could then use in their asynchronous IC courses. Because of our limited shared time in Zoom sessions, GTAs provided feedback on each other's video-based teaching demonstrations in the LMS discussion board. In our Zoom meeting, then, GTAs who presented had a chance to ask the group questions back. For example, commenting on one peer's demonstration, Hunter and Dylan provided feedback on how to contend with large blocks of text in online videos—breaking up the text, adding italicized words to emphasize core ideas. I encouraged returning to the same quote or passage more than once in a video or class discussion, to help students dig into that passage. The group shared other strategies they had tried since watching each other's videos: writing a script for a video rather than ad-libbing, using PowerPoint presentations to organize and present ideas, and using wait time to allow students watching the videos moments to reflect.

As much as we were working through our own complex discussions of readings, we were also working on how to help IC students do their assigned reading, something that felt less possible to manage in online courses. In an early February session, Hunter, giving feedback on Dylan's teaching demonstration (an online video), raised a question about how to work with readings in online sessions:

So, Dylan, you do this thing that I find myself doing a lot, which is sharing your screen and being on the text. And I just don't know what to do with that. But it occurs to me when I do it in my own classes that there has to be a better way to do this... I think, whenever I do that, okay, what are the students actually getting out of looking at the reading, because they're not reading it, right? And even if I'm moving my cursor, it's hard to follow that when you're not the one who's directing it. So, I'm curious if there are better ways that others have thought of to kind of tackle that?

In this moment, Hunter moved beyond thinking about *what* we are having students read to *how* we engage them with reading in online classes—how we *read with* students in online classes. The group offered responses ranging from using slide decks to highlight passages, audibly annotating the features of passages while reading aloud to students, and modeling reading, note taking, and inquiry based on shared classroom texts. In the discussion that followed, GTAs wrestled with their pessimism that students were likely not reading assigned texts. Hunter resolved this tension by suggesting we use assigned class texts as the examples we talk through with students in upcoming assignments, like demonstrating annotating and creating Cornell notes.

We also worked together to understand how feedback loops were working in our online IC courses. Facilitating peer review was certainly different than in face-to-face or even online synchronous classes. Having had a little less classroom teaching experience than the others did, Lauren asked the group for feedback on how to outline "supplementary tools" for students to use to guide their own peer review. Dylan responded that he asks students to summarize their peers' texts rather than to provide mechanical feedback; Hunter echoed this, drawing from his writing center training and explaining how he works with his students on "privileging global feedback over surface level feedback." I shared a set of peer review questions I used in a previous class to help students engage as authentic readers.

Our discussion about reading Hewett's (2015a) *The Online Writing Conference: A Guide for Teachers and Tutors* had us thinking about our own written feedback on students' *language*, specifically, important in an online class focused on scholarly writing. In a mentoring meeting before one of our class sessions, Dylan had previewed for me that he was working through some critique of Hewett, and I related to the group that since then I had been reading with curiosity, anticipating his response. I offered an example from my own research that spoke to Hewett's criticism of "particular pedagogical mindsets" (i.e., expressivism) and the ways that these mindsets influence and perhaps impede students' uptake of teacher feedback on writing. I asked the group what they thought. Hunter, like Dylan, felt "put off" by the ideas of several chapters and found Hewett's tone "dismissive" of particular approaches. He explained that his previous writing center training "is so far ingrained" in his commenting practices "that it will never really go away." Dylan noted that he didn't "really have a problem" with the "eclectic" approach to feedback Hewett argues for but rather with what he characterized as "straw man" arguments:

> I think that's what kind of frustrated me about it, is you're saying all this [criticism of expressivist, Marxist, and post-process pedagogy] just to say, "be eclectic." And it's like, well, you can decide to be any of those things and still take an eclectic approach to teaching a student how to write a sentence, to tell them that they mixed up "granite" and "granted." You can be any of those things and still tell a student . . . how you explain what you know.

While our conversations about diverse language and literacy practices were in the background of this conversation, I see a connection to them in Dylan's last sentence here. In focusing on working with students on writing "how [they] explain what [they] know," Dylan started a refrain that we would hear echoed in our classroom discussions across the semester: that students have both expertise and developing knowledge they are drawing on as they work through IC projects, and our role as instructors providing feedback is to work responsively with our actual students and their knowledge to craft that feedback. In this online, asynchronous, pandemic semester, this feedback was the essential mechanism for building classroom (reader-writer) relationships (Hewett 2015a, 2015b; Borgman and McArdle 2019).

The group described their feelings about the chapter and their approaches to giving feedback, acknowledging that we had all given unhelpful feedback sometimes. Needing to wrap up the discussion at the end of the call, I asked the group to think about audience:

> [Hewett's] audience is people . . . who are teaching online for the first time, or have been in teaching for a long time, and really need to rethink, like, how they are doing it. And so we are different readers in that sense. And also readers who are steeped in pedagogical theory right now, and in thinking about a lot of different things . . . the critical ways that you're all reading this text are really valuable, and we might read it differently if we were just, like, "I need some help teaching online."

I gave the example of a student in my IC class asking me questions about an assignment description and my reflection on how I could read the description differently than she did because I was reading from a curricular structure perspective and she was reading from a task-oriented, learning perspective. This reflection helped us consider the texts of our courses in an additional way: It was important that we considered not only the subject matter of assigned readings and course texts as we worked through them with IC students but also the rhetorical nature, and, more plainly, the usability of these texts for accomplishing specific purposes in IC.

Our concerns with learning how to more successfully do online, pandemic-era writing instruction were possibly most evident in our discussions of grading. In early March, we invited Chris, my collaborator on the IC revision and an NTT faculty member, to talk about his grading contract for IC. While a few GTAs in the course were already using labor-based grading contracts, I structured time for the discussion to further promote reflection about grading and revised grading practices for our program overall. I asked the group whether they had any pressing concerns they wanted to raise or successes they wanted to share before Chris explained his process. Hunter shared this reflection:

> I don't know if this is a pressing concern. But something that I've been thinking about a lot when I've been grading this semester is just how weird the in-between place we're in with respect to the pandemic is making grading. Because, when we switched to emergency remote instruction, and then last semester, also over the summer, my explicit aim in grading was to be extra compassionate and graceful to students' needs. But I'm wondering, like—and I'm still trying to do that this semester, mostly in policies of when I'm accepting work and things like that—but I'm wondering, and this isn't like a question I expect anyone to have an answer to, but I'm wondering, when do I start to think about things as like, well, this is just school, so, . . . I need to grade like I normally would, or is this a situation where, like, maybe we reevaluate holistically how grading works, and is done. That's something I've been thinking about a lot this semester.

This was one of the moments of the semester that most stuck with me in the semesters that followed. When I reflect on the whole semester—the whole study—this is the moment I remember first, so it is worth attention here (and it reflects some discussions I had with WPAs and practicum instructors in the study I present in chapter 2 as well). Hunter's question was both for the moment and about whether his teaching (and our collective teaching practices) would be changed from that moment forward. Chris responded, "There really is no good time to be, like, all right, the pandemic has resolved itself . . . here's your A and here's your C+ . . . I think we've hit this paradigm shift, which everyone is fond of talking about, but we have a hard time recognizing that this is a very recognizable paradigm shift." Chris's response acknowledged both the difficulty of a large-scale change in grading practices and the undeniable reality that grading—and a lot about teaching—had, in a "very recognizable" way, changed during the pandemic.

In discussion, Chris acknowledged that for those who are not comfortable with shifting toward wholesale grading contracts from traditional grading, there are ways to infuse the transparency of the contract into more traditional practices. He and Dylan talked back and forth for a few moments working to reconcile how this transparency might function for and with students. Dylan described how he created with students more individualized expectations that were more responsive to their circumstances. Chris responded that he has found that using the grade contract has benefitted his busiest students by taking out the "guesswork" of what they must do to succeed in class: "It's no longer, 'is this good enough for you?' It's, 'I've ticked my box, I can move on.'" He described revisiting the contract with his students midsemester to collaboratively revise some components. Dylan acknowledged that not everything can be made fair for everyone and related his frustration with the problem of quantifying labor—the individualized approach seems to work better for his students. Chris encouraged him to develop a flexible practice rather than focus on individual cases, meeting somewhere in the middle.

We discussed matching instructional goals with feedback labor to manage the time spent providing written comments on students' work, and in my own interjections into the discussion, I acknowledged the struggle we spoke about in the previous week's jigsaw:

> Across teaching, there's that challenge of, you want to make sure that you're doing both what's best for your students, but also making sure you check the boxes in terms of your responsibilities. And so hopefully, this has changed a little bit about how we see what the norm is. Maybe our responsibility is supporting and providing appropriate feedback to our students more than it is the letter grade. What's going to happen to the grading part? I know it's not going to go away, but it might change a little bit of the expectation.

I was thinking about the centering of feedback loops in classroom activity, about shifting weight toward feedback and away from grades. My comments picked up conversations I had had with these students the previous year in our discussions in a pedagogy seminar about the classroom impacts of labor-based grading—conversations that would continue to evolve over several more semesters.

Our reflections on online teaching culminated when we met for a "bittersweet" final class session at the end of April, a chance to reflect on teaching after two years of course work together. I asked GTAs whether they felt they got better at running a Zoom during our remote learning year, because, as was evident in the closing of the final jigsaw, I did not. Hunter reported that he thought a lot about the way the Zoom functioned when he recorded one of his synchronous sessions to send to the faculty member doing his teaching observation. He described himself as "maybe not better, but at least aware." Dylan described realizing how easily he got distracted as a student in synchronous Zoom sessions—checking email or the news. He prefers asynchronous online learning. Though the brevity of our class sessions (under an hour) felt manageable, "the long Zooms are hard." While teaching via Zoom had constrained our instruction in some ways, doing this alongside teaching a new curriculum had shifted the quality of our attention to classroom relationships and how we could support those through feedback and other messages and structures in the LMS.

TEACHING IC WITH ATTENTION TO LINGUISTIC JUSTICE: WE WON'T TACKLE LINGUISTIC VIOLENCE IN THE NEXT EIGHT MINUTES, BUT WE CAN KEEP THINKING ABOUT IT TOGETHER

Our limited time together each week meant that we could not often do the deep collaborative work we wanted or needed to do to strategize our IC instruction, especially regarding our shared desire to support linguistic justice in the course. However, one refrain was certainly evident across each of the threads of the course I have described: Dylan's reflections highlighted the ways we can treat students "as experts of their own language," as Baker-Bell (2020) asserts (74). Reviewing our conversations, it seemed we felt unified on this aim but struggled with bringing explicit discussions about diverse languaging practices into IC because of the requirements of the curriculum.[2]

Partway through the semester, when we had read the first half of Baker-Bell's *Linguistic Justice*, I asked the group to prepare to think about the assigned chapters and our own experiences teaching IC so far. We talked through a passage on page 82 that helped us consider the idea that our conception of a "standard English" is not universally definable, "not based on linguistic facts." After walking through the passage with students, I invited their responses "on that sort of idea of standard English being actually an ideology and not a language with discrete features."

Hunter responded that it may be that he is "in the bubble of the Academy" but that he did not think his composition students, including "cis white students," would challenge the ideas in Baker-Bell's text. I responded, in part, that it's important for us to keep in mind that "as we talk about language issues and ideas in our classrooms, [our students] may be experiencing those conversations differently than they've experienced language messages in other educational settings." Dylan remarked on the racial diversity of students in our university and the general metropolitan area and on the amount of change that has occurred between 2013, when Baker-Bell conducted her study, and 2021, when we met for this course. Lauren responded to my question about ideology by positing a way a standard language ideology might be understood: "Like, we're implying your tool of language is defective, and you need to use this tool that actually functions, or some other analogy like that . . . how do we change that? How do we change the tools of the institution?"

Dylan picked up on this problem in his response to Lauren, and they had a brief interchange:

> DYLAN: . . . there's this part in the book where [Baker-Bell] starts to talk about how even speaking white, or whatever, won't save you, like you're still gonna get killed, even if you're speaking "correctly," or whatever . . . a few of us . . . were in [another seminar], and these accounts that we read again, and again, of it doesn't matter, like you can fulfill all of the things that the institution wants you to do . . . they can just choose to ignore you . . . because of that identifier . . . class, race, ethnic, whatever that identifier is that doesn't fit, you can be dismissed . . . it's like the ability to kind of pick up and put down these tools, but also recognizing the way that power just can, like, cast you aside. That's really depressing.
> LAUREN: Like, sometimes you can't even use—like you're just prohibited.
> DYLAN: Yeah.
> LAUREN: Not that you're physically incapable or intellectually incapable, but you're not allowed to use that tool.
> DYLAN: Yes. Yeah, absolutely.

Dylan mentioned a "double deficit" for IC instructors of helping students reflect on both their own language practices and the practices of their discourse community; he shared that he had "really pulled back from" feedback on and evaluation of grammar and mechanics and was responding more to "ideas and intention." He noted that he was in "brainstorm mode" about how to assess ideas and intention more in "something like a literature review." I offered the group reflective questions for their teaching journals about when and how they integrate language instruction. Once again, our vibrant forty-five minutes of problem solving hit its end.

At the opening of our final jigsaw in mid-April, I expressed dissatisfaction with the ways I had presented the week's question, which was, "How does the way we explicitly address language in our lessons, syllabi, feedback, etc. reflect our understanding that the impact of language is not felt only inside our classrooms or outside our classrooms?" I added that I "want[ed] us thinking about the level to which we make our stances on languaging explicit to our students." We had several possible readings to draw from for the week: Jabari Courtney (2018), John McWhorter (2019), and Koritha Mitchell (2018) on the use of the n-word (all identified by the curriculum subcommittee as possible texts), the "CCCC Statement on Recent Violent Crimes Against Asians, Asian Americans, and Pacific Islanders" (2021a) (which had been recently published), and Asao Inoue's 2019 CCCC's chair's address (2019a). I had just attended several of the online sessions for the 2021 CCCC Conference, so, like the GTAs, I was working to tie together significant listening and thinking not only about the readings but about the conversations we had had across several semesters and about teaching IC.

Because we had had practice with our version of jigsaw discussions, and because we were weaving so many conversational threads across the semester, I include larger excerpts from this jigsaw transcript shortly to show how the readings and GTAs' teaching had come together by mid-April. Like the previous jigsaw, this conversation includes some emotion (Dylan names this as "excited") as GTAs consider what the readings mean for teaching IC and in our school generally.

Dylan offered to begin the discussion: "I have five pages of double-spaced notes. I'm not going to read all those, I just, I had a lot of thoughts about this. And I really appreciated the prompt. So, I just want you to know, my brain is also buzzing. And if I am not coherent, I apologize in advance." Dylan's excitement demonstrated to me that he understood these excited five pages (and their author) had a place and voice in our classroom discussions. Focusing his response on Inoue's 2019 CCCC address, Dylan returned to a problem he had explored across the semester regarding the tensions between our required IC curriculum and antiracist pedagogy:

> So, Inoue gets at a debate I think we pretty consistently have in our discipline: in the classroom with my students, in discussions with many of my peers and mentors, and reading lots of current composition scholarship.

I think most of us end up agreeing that a single standard for assessment is racist and/or teaching Standard English at all is racist, but that we need to do it because we want our students to succeed in the real world. This is something that Inoue disagrees with, quote, *"We must stop justifying white standards of writing as a necessary evil, evil in any form is necessary is never necessary, we must stop saying that we have to teach this dominant English because it's what students need to succeed tomorrow, they only need it because we keep teaching it."* ... According to Inoue, the pragmatic approach of teaching Standard English, but discussing the power dynamics present in teaching Standard English, isn't enough. What I think Inoue fails to discuss is that it's not just teachers who reinforced this standard. It is also writing program administrators, deans, college presidents, United States and state government officials, corporations, students themselves, and on and on. There's this entire culture of austerity capitalism and the university that tells us to do this. It's not just teachers individually deciding to ... In regards to our immediate context ... we need to think about what we teach in IC. I think a lot of what our class does is teach students how to write in white collar jobs. We're teaching them how to interview, we're teaching them how to write academic literature, reviews, research and write about professional organizations ... [T]his puts us into an immediate contradiction when it comes to respecting students' different languages ... I'm sure that you would say I should just ignore this, because creating the antiracist classroom is more important, it's the right thing to do ... So, if we're thinking about [IC] I think he makes a great point. But it's only a fraction of what we need for doing antiracist pedagogy ... So, I hope I wasn't yelling, I got, I was very excited. Anyway, that's my thought. Sorry.

In enacting an antiracist pedagogy, Dylan reminded us, we need to also attend to curriculum. Our IC curriculum was evidence of our fraught position, working to enact emergent program values (and personal values) related to antiracist teaching while employing a curriculum responsive to the general education demands of the university.

Hunter shared his response next, focusing on Courtney and McWhorter's texts on "the n word, and can we refer to the n word, and who can, and what context." Hunter's jigsaw offering focused on making decisions about classroom language along with students:

As an instructor, especially as a het, cis, white, male, I feel like I'm doing violence to students, sometimes, when I make that decision [about language use] for the classroom. And I'm trying to think through a way, if it's possible, to have a conversation with students early in the semester about the kind of language practices that are acceptable in that particular class. And obviously, that's something that will maybe change throughout the semester, or, you know, there's a lot of variables there . . . I think the most important position for me as an instructor is to try to be compassionate to students with respect to those things, and if I'm making a value judgment, like, with good intentions, sometimes that's going to do a really bad thing for the class. I don't know.

Hunter closed by asking his classmates if they had feedback on how to work through those language decisions with students. Kristi spoke next, beginning with a response to Hunter:

> Just to go off of what Hunter just brought up in terms of ideas, or how to kind of determine how to tackle those conversations or make it most comfortable for your students, because they change semester to semester or course section to section. I wrote some notes earlier in this conversation, too, about how I found myself addressing languaging much more in FYC than I did ever in IC. And I think that was completely separate from being online or in person. It was just the nature of what was discussed in the class.

Kristi acknowledged the lack of opportunity in the IC curriculum to talk about language in contexts outside of scholarly writing, a challenge we worked through from the beginning of our time together in Practicum II. Nevertheless, she made a tie to understanding students' perspectives on languaging in the classroom:

> [Inoue] brought up Ratcliffe and empathy. And I thought that was interesting in terms of really rhetorically listening and what we are hearing from our students in terms of these community spaces and what makes them comfortable, what they're okay with, and how they want to talk about language. And I think that that's really good in terms of, again, practicing rhetorical listening, but also giving our students a sense of control or agency in that space.

When Lauren entered the conversation, she highlighted the idea of "mystifying that which we take as natural," which she had gleaned from Inoue's speech. She proposed that discussions about different cultural experiences with words and language, via Peter Elbow's (1973) believing game, may be an inroad to classroom conversation about linguistic justice:

> By playing the believing game we can interrogate why [dissent] could be useful for everyone . . . Being in the university gives us this very specific positionality to discuss these things and be critical of them. And we need to share that with our students. Because power dynamics obviously play into whether they feel comfortable sharing their dissent, or advocating for

themselves, or considering authority in that way that we are not just teaching them, but that they need to be active . . . it needs to be a constant discussion that we need to repeat in order to reassess, because those opinions might not always show up.

Lauren's point that this discussion about language and power should be a "constant discussion that we need to repeat in order to reassess" was a reminder that learning how to navigate classroom, scholarly, and institutional discourse is not a one-time classroom lesson but something that students—and instructors—would have to learn over time, and with support.

In my "plenary" response to the group (Jay et al. 2021, 127), I worked from my notes to bring together the threads of our conversation. I began with a response to one of the GTAs:

> You said it's important that we know like that we're clear in our classrooms what will be tolerated. And certainly . . . we can talk put those guidelines for language use in syllabi, but I jotted down right after that, I think we also need to be clear about what is expected in our classrooms in terms of what will we *do* with language, so not only will we *not* use terms that are offensive to other people, but also we *will* . . . like Lauren, when you use the phrase "mystifying that which we take as natural," right, like taking something that maybe we haven't thought about critically, and starting to think about it critically instead . . . So, what *will* we do with languaging? Maybe we could say that we *will* think about where our languaging comes from, we *will* talk about why literature reviews are constructed this way. It's not the personal, community kind of languaging discussion that can happen in FYC. It's different in IC. I think, Kristi, your point that we don't do the same talking about languaging in the class—we *could*. We didn't construct the [IC] semester to really dig deep into it. But we could theoretically look at, well, why is scholarly writing the way it is? I don't know, part of it is institutional. But like we know from reading Aja Martinez last semester, we know that it could look different. We know from looking at April Baker-Bell this semester, that scholarly writing can look different. So why does it look the way that it does? And what happens when we start to write it in a different way? Maybe that's some of the ways that you know, we can think about what we are going to do in our individual classrooms with languaging,

I continued my response turning back to Dylan's offering at the beginning of this jigsaw—important because he spoke about something he'd been working through all semester: "And you know, Dylan, I'll acknowledge your point that you want us to be critical about conflating different kinds of violence as having the same impact. But maybe we can agree that racism manifests in different ways and that it can manifest linguistically. And it can manifest in physical violence, and it can manifest in other structural inequalities. But maybe the violence is different."

Dylan gestured in the Zoom window that he wanted to reply. "Go ahead," I said. He explained,

> Yeah, just to clarify that point. I do think that linguistic racism is a huge problem. I think that I'm just thinking about, like the rhetorical choice that Inoue makes to compare, like doing a single standard of grading, comparing that to being killed. I don't know about that rhetorical choice. I think that like when we start equating those things, like physical death becomes devalued, when you make those comparisons. That was kind of my point.

This talking through allowed Dylan to clarify what had challenged his mind about Inoue's language; it also allowed me a chance to listen again and to admit that I needed to think more:

> Yes. Thank you for restating it. I think when I hear you express that, I don't have a clear response. I feel like you're putting it out there and saying we need to interrogate this more, like this is worth us thinking about more, what's the choice of using this term "violence" to talk about what happens with linguistic racism, which of course we won't tackle in the next eight minutes, but we can keep thinking about it together.

In this response to Dylan, I acknowledged the work of time and reflection in thinking through and addressing linguistic racism in scholarly and pedagogical ways. Our persistent reflection across the semester had been proactive but not conclusive. There were logistical and curricular hurdles we were working through as we tried to understand what linguistic justice looked like in this specific context of teaching IC, online, in pandemic conditions.

Our readings and encounters with scholarship had provided us with some inroads to rethinking the IC curriculum, however. I shared with students my reflection on Young's 2021 CCCC chair's address, which I had watched over the weekend, and his emphasis that our curricula should be designed so that students in our classes read scholarship from authors that share their backgrounds. I reflected to the group that while I had not interrogated the backgrounds of the scholars on our reading list for IC, I certainly could do that for the next semester. Beyond assessing the reading list for IC, however, our conversation had led me to think about how we need to assess the more theoretical objectives of the course and the ways those manifest in the practical work we were asking students to do: "Dylan, but I'm really interested in talking more about the idea of the employment curriculum and what that means for—I think that's the term that you used—what that means for our classes. Is that what our intention is in IC? . . . Do we have a different goal, but if it's manifesting as a sort of, like prep for employment, what does that mean, then?"

Also in my mind was the work I needed to do as a practicum instructor, and I needed the group's input on how to do that in the best way when it comes to addressing language and the curriculum:

> I also want to address the challenge of teacher readiness for doing this kind of work. And I think I want to talk about—I think Kristi's point that she talks a lot more about languaging in FYC than in IC is the first thing that made me think about it, as I'm preparing to move back into teaching first semester graduate students next fall, and working with them in Practicum I, and thinking about the things we've been doing this semester, and how we know that they apply to FYC . . . I've got a lot of reflecting to do on how to support first semester teachers and doing that work. And, so, I think, either today or in the ensuing weeks, any thoughts that you have on that, I think I would really welcome, because you're able to look at this from a perspective of, after four semesters at Wayne State. I look at it from a perspective of twenty semesters at Wayne State. So, I've got you know, a little bit, in a different position. So, your insight is really useful to me.

It was important for me to acknowledge the *reflective* privilege I have as a long-term faculty member in my program. This privilege comes from knowing the long story of our general education composition courses because I am one of many coauthors of that story. I can apply my critiques and amendments to my own classroom curricula whenever I like, because, as a full-time faculty member, I am not beholden to a common syllabus. And I feel safe improvising in response to tough questions in the classroom space after over two decades of teaching.

Lauren provided a perspective on power in response to my inquiry:

> What I also was trying to point to Inoue for this week is just that any position of comfort comes from being at the top of the hierarchy. And there's no minority position that will exist without discomfort, because it is the minority. So African American students in our class, or Arab American students in our class, or any other racial or ethnic minority in our classes, are going to naturally be in a state of discomfort. And not only that . . . as we are all white instructors, we will have some level of comfort in the classroom, and that we have to learn to exist to make our comfort discomfort . . . it might be

uncomfortable to have to justify why you do or don't use specific terms in your class. But that's our role. We set the precedent.

Kristi offered a pedagogical inroad to support Lauren's idea, returning to the importance of conversations about languaging in the first several days of class: "I think in forcing yourself to create spaces where students are asked to talk and encouraged to share their experiences is huge. And you're kind of doing two things at one time where you're kind of tackling this really important thing, but you're also establishing a relationship with students."

This final jigsaw had to end as our class time ended; in my final words to GTAs, I acknowledged we were not done thinking and working on the problems we set out to tackle:

> My brain is still firing, because here we are at the end of—close to the end of—basically two years of working together on what it means to be teachers at Wayne State, but also to think critically about what it means to be . . . in a position of power, relative power, to make changes, at least in our own classrooms. And then to start to think about systematically what that can mean. But even that work can't come uncritically . . . I need to be more transparent about—be transparent at all—about reflecting on positionality, thinking about the choices that I make in presenting a concept with a particular term, like violence. What does that mean for what my students are going to understand about languaging? . . . I'm happy that we've been able to talk—to start to talk through a lot of things together.

I let GTAs know they could stay in the Zoom call to continue talking while I left to pick my children up from school; there was so much more talking and thinking and working to do.

GTAs' reflections on their instructional decisions come through in this final jigsaw. Dylan described the ways that an instructor needs to consider students' desires and needs for learning when making choices about how to teach language. Hunter brought to light that the instructor, even when trying to be compassionate, may not always make the best judgments for students. Responding to Hunter, Kristi asserted the value of instructors practicing rhetorical listening and allowing their students the "control and agency" in classroom learning about language. And Lauren emphasized that these should not be one-off discussions but conversations that need to happen frequently and across the semester. Together, the group reflected on the ways that they need to prepare and to be prepared, as teachers, for these discussions, to be responsive to the actual students in their classrooms, and to learn how to develop this work with language with students, over time. They reflected on how they need to think about this work rhetorically and relationally. Reading the discussion over and over again as I prepared this chapter draft, I reflected on how practicum instructors (and me, specifically, as an instructor) need to support GTAs, both in the class and in the program, for the kinds of reflective decision-making they will have to make when they feel deeply that things need to change.

I didn't know that we were collaboratively writing the argument of this chapter when we had that final class meeting, but rereading this discussion many times as I piece together the semester's narrative, I see so clearly how this jigsaw discussion in the penultimate Practicum II meeting in winter 2021 brought together impressions from across this book into a sort of verbal collage. As a class, we reflected on how we could move from what we *might* do, or what we *should* do, to what we *would* do, and on what it would take to make this action more than just individual and isolated, and, instead, programmatic.

Final Reflections from Practicum II: Generative Dichotomies for Teaching in New Paradigms

In our final class session in April, I asked GTAs to record what they were wondering about as we began our Zoom meeting, and we wrote for a few minutes in our journals. We spent the session sharing the overarching themes from our teaching journals and notes, themes that focused on both teaching IC and our remote teaching online: reflections on time management, flexibility, responsiveness, and the challenge of building relationships with students in this pandemic environment. We talked about the final IC project and dealing with late work, enduring logistical problems. As I closed the session to pick up my kids from school, I asked the group to add one word to our shared slide that captured their experience teaching IC that semester. Individually, we added *responsive, empathy, compassion,* and *isolation.*

Each of these terms provides a way to read some of the experiences described in the preceding narrative in terms of overlapping themes, which I will explore in the following subsections. However, instead of exploring them only via the impressions of students during this last class session, I pair each of these terms with a second term to suggest how these impressions work as part of a problem-solution encounter with teaching IC. These pairings show ways that the GTAs and I learn to hold these different terms both reflectively and practically; in light of our curriculum-experience-scholarship triangle, these dichotomies emerge as tangible and generative experiential truths. As my friend and colleague Nicole Guinot Varty put it when I explained them to her, these dichotomies are helpful because they allow us to say, when we listen to teachers, "We know about this, we have seen this before." In other words, we can match individual experience with evidence.

In addition to providing insight about how GTAs work with course texts on social justice, antiracist teaching, and linguistic justice, the artifacts from this "pandemic semester" Practicum II course highlight other important aspects of teaching writing during this time. In the following text, adapting some of the terms we listed on that last day of class, I work through four themes, each bound up in generative dichotomies: isolation and relationship-building, responsiveness and boundaries, student (the role in which these GTAs best *empathize* with their undergraduate students) and authority, direction, and listening (actions through which GTAs might exercise *compassion*). As described, these themes present experiential evidence in light of terms that may transcend the individual classroom or semester. For program talk, these themes allow me and colleagues in mentoring or administrative positions to provide context-specific evidence to instructors facing instructional challenges. For disciplinary talk, these themes carry evidence of the values explored in other chapters of this book.

ISOLATION AND RELATIONSHIP-BUILDING

In our last class session, Dylan reflected on what he learned about how his attentive teaching was both restricted and shaped by the challenges of remote instruction:

> I'm really a relationship-oriented teacher. And I really have felt like I've been teaching with one arm behind my back for the last, like, year and a half. So, it's been both kind of good because I've focused more on the kind of content minutiae that I don't really enjoy as much. But it's good to do. Because I feel like what's ended up happening is the people who come in for conferences, want to conference, want to email me, those students are really just succeeding and blossoming. And it's beautiful. And the students who don't kind of know that cheat code aren't getting the same experience of the class. So, I'm just thinking through that, as well.

I suggested to Dylan that he centers that value of conferencing in his teaching philosophy and in his syllabus. He replied, "Yeah, just put in big, bold letters: here's the cheat code, make sure you do conferences." As Dylan noted, conferencing allowed him to work with students on "content minutiae" that he had not been addressing in in-person classes. This deeper work with writing instruction, then, shifted the quality of content in his course.

Joking with Dylan that the "cheat code" for his class could be presented in the syllabus by the note "COME TO CONFERENCES" was a final conclusion to a semester-long reflection about helping students connect with each other and with class content. Dylan began the course concerned about siloing of students as they research their discourse communities. A GTA whose pedagogy was enriched by student collaboration, Dylan asked his first question in the practicum class about finding opportunities for students to connect with each other in the asynchronous, online environment: He asked, on January 12, "Is that siloing gonna continue to happen? Are there assignments coming up that I should be prepared for where I could do more with discussion or more with discourse among students?" Dylan described adapting the first weekly task in the course from an individual submission to a group discussion board in the LMS to structure students' contact with each other.

It was not just Dylan's students that seemed to be experiencing this siloing; he was too. In an early February session, as we reflected together on students' seeming lack of experience with secondary research, Dylan commented on noticing "fatigue" in his online students and feeling a similar fatigue: "I struggle with that, because it's also disheartening to do hours of work on lecture videos and then go on Loom and see that, like, two people have watched it [laughs]. But you know, you keep doing it." I responded, both empathizing and suggesting LMS strategies for linking students directly to videos and discerning where our energy most needs to be spent.

Other students in the class echoed Dylan's feelings of isolation and fatigue alongside the need to feel more connected with students and for students to connect more deeply with each other and with course content. Lauren, despite her persistent attention to student engagement, expressed, "I felt like maybe I wasn't doing enough." She described how she had borrowed another instructor's strategy of having an open weekly discussion board for students to share their experiences via digital images and gifs. Conferencing was built into their weekly time. And all GTAs tried peer review to varying degrees of success. As she reflected on her teaching journal entries across the semester, Lauren wrote, for example, "Despite guidance towards genuine and productive feedback, peer review assignments were often met with lackluster effort. I imagine this is partially attributed to the fact that students rarely interacted in class and therefore failed to build community." As Lauren explained, while she had crafted community-focused spaces in the course LMS, only a few students in her asynchronous course participated in these spaces. While the instructors seemed to feel personally responsible for not structuring opportunities for interaction, for not "doing enough," like Lauren said, we spent less time talking about students' dispositions toward school. These dispositions became evident in our discussion of grade contracts, when our guest, Chris, noted students sometimes working in a headspace of "I've ticked my box; I can move on."

Despite these feelings of isolation and evidence of students working differently in online, pandemic-era courses than they would have in the traditional classroom, GTAs remained convinced that relationship building is core to the work of teaching writing, including and especially the work of integrating discussion of social justice, antiracist teaching, and linguistic-justice-oriented issues and topics. We were reminded of this in Lauren's point that discussions about critical language awareness need to happen iteratively and across time in the course, with that reflection engaging students with course content and with thinking about their own languaging. And Kristi emphasized her work building relationships with students through practices of listening in conferences, working with students on how to develop their agency and voice in projects, such that they can bring themselves more fully to the work they share with the class.

RESPONSIVENESS AND BOUNDARIES

GTAs' concern for individual IC students led them to reflect on managing their responsiveness to these students and the boundaries necessary for their own work-life balance. For Hunter, this tension was especially pressing. In our final class session he reflected,

> Because of the individual nature of the work the students are each doing, I need to figure out a way, when teaching this class again, to set more explicit boundaries with students about the labor that I'm willing to do for them. Because I had a couple students who wanted me to look at so many drafts of their projects that I swear if I had to look at one more draft of a certain student's assignment I'd freak out. But this semester especially I tried to be really accommodating, so I always did it. But there needs to be some explicit, like, I will look at your draft this many times, or, this is the amount of time I'm willing to work with you on this. To me, it's not fair. But also, I'm only one person.

Reflecting on this same experience in his final reflection of the semester, Hunter explained that he would like to be clear with students that he could "theoretically, give feedback forever and find different things to discuss."

This tension is present in our discussions of grading as well. In our session on grading contracts, Hunter reflected on feeling like we are in a "weird in-between place" with grading, where compassion is extra important, but we are waiting for things to go back to the way they always have been. In his final reflection for the term, though, after reflecting on the necessity of "honesty and mutual vulnerability" in classroom and conference discussions, Hunter expressed, "When my students are experiencing homelessness or losing their parents or any of the other abundant tragedies that I've heard about this semester, traditional grading seems utterly pointless." He explained that he was going to shift into contract grading for the next semester.

A way that this dichotomy has emerged in my teaching conversations since this semester is as "compassion and expectations," though the nuance is a little different, I think. What Hunter described with his changed grading practices, and I think what we all experienced, was an influx of flexibility that is hard to imagine going away. That flexibility is responsive and compassionate. It requires learning how to set boundaries, as noted here, so that instructors can, themselves, manage the tasks and rest required in their lives. It also, however, requires the expression of clear expectations. These expectations were, at times, murky for GTAs in Practicum II. Their expectations about required tasks for IC seemed to be identifiable, if frustrating to manage, at times. However, the quality of these expectations in terms of students' writing was something we only began to work through in our jigsaws; we addressed it when we talked about students working with the genre features of literature reviews and when we talked about how we gave written feedback on student writing, but we mostly struggled through bridging what we were reading about in the assigned articles and chapters for the class with the required work of IC.

While Dylan and Lauren talked through the ways this tension exists for students, who are often told how they can and cannot use their languages in academic settings, these IC instructors experienced the tension of what Dylan referred to as a "double deficit" of needing to help students reflect on their individual and community language practices as well as the language practices of their intended discourse communities, practices these students are to emulate as they write their projects. It seemed easy for GTAs to amend their policies when it came to accepting late work, instead incorporating flexible due dates; they seemed to feel confident about making that level of administrative change in their courses. However, the language-focused work that came along with responding to and supporting students in crafting their scholarly writing with linguistic justice in mind remained a challenge not fully addressed in that semester.

STUDENT AND AUTHORITY

The tension GTAs experience in their roles as both students and instructors is familiar territory in scholarship on GTA training and the practicum. Aside from GTAs' positions as students, other positional characteristics may exacerbate tensions regarding their inclusion in decision making or authority (Brewer 2020b, 29), and, even after participation in their programs' teacher development process, GTAs may not feel "agentive, self-efficacious, or adequately prepared" for teaching writing (Macauley 2021, 3). While these elements of this tension are present in this narrative of Practicum II (like when Lauren notes the challenge of learning the IC curriculum while teaching it), the other ways this student/authority tension is present in this study are especially interesting in two ways: (1) GTAs' reflections on using their position as students to encourage IC students to investigate language in particular ways, and (2) GTAs' reflections on their need for agency in instructional decisions related to supporting students' linguistic diversity, antiracism, and compassionate teaching.

Each GTA addressed issues and experiences with authority a little differently. Kristi, for example, explained in a February discussion about giving feedback to students, "I often find myself leveling with them as a student, myself, and what I find myself doing, what processes I work through, like my little tips and tricks, and sometimes that really, you know, appeals to them as a student, because it's not coming off at them like I'm such an expert or such an authority." This strategy is also apparent in the teaching philosophy she submitted at the end of the semester, when she described herself "as a person learning" and dialoguing with students about the learning and writing process. As noted above, Hunter addressed GTAs' limited authority as both a challenge and a tool; because they can relate to students in terms of their "neophyte" positions, GTAs can model ways that they work from these positions to learn and work within their discourse communities. At several points in our discussions, Lauren identified the challenges of authority faced by marginalized and minoritized GTAs, and Dylan, reflecting on instructors' responsibilities, spoke to these challenges with authority when he acknowledged the tension of being bound to a particular curriculum.

GTAs' responsibility to the common syllabus may have contributed, along with their positions, to their difficulty sometimes feeling strong about the smaller instructional decisions and revisions they had to make. Reading through transcripts of class sessions, I was struck by the nature of Hunter's frequent questions to the group. It seems like Hunter's m.o. was that he sensed a need for something to change, and then asked for permission to make that amendment. In other words, Hunter's intuition was strong but needed reinforcement. For example, in the second class session, when we were talking through preparing IC students to conduct interviews, Hunter echoed my comment that there was a lot of work for students to do in the second weekly writing assignment: Students had to identify three relevant scholarly sources in the library database, identify the textual and paratextual features of these, and write a reflection on scholarly writing in their discourse communities. The assignment description in the course LMS included ten bullet-pointed parts of the assignment. Hunter asked whether it made sense to "make some of this [assignment] not even part of the assignment, just part of a separate page or thing in the module? . . . link the assignment, so it's clear that they're very related, but maybe it isn't a whole thing for the students? I don't know." I responded, "Yeah, that's a great idea," and, in screen share, I broke up the assignment description into tasks (1, 2, 3, and 4) and talked through how I would adapt presenting that assignment to students. Hunter's suggestions were practical, helpful, and forward thinking, as one of our tasks, as a group, was to pilot the revised IC curriculum and to make suggestions for improving it. While it may be that these questions are emblematic of Hunter's discursive style (presenting suggestions and experiences as questions for discussion), they also point to a need for this kind of micro-level decision making (document and calendar revisions) to be within GTAs' power, a challenge in programs where curriculum is prescribed or even rigidly enforced.

DIRECTION AND LISTENING

As GTAs reflected on their teaching, as the Practicum II instructor I worked through tensions of my own, and the two I write about here were both surprising to me for different reasons. As I prepared transcripts for this chapter's analysis, I was immediately aware of the percentages of speaking time presented at the top of each transcript. These percentages provided me with some quick quantitative data that I found problematic. In the class sessions I recorded, I regularly spoke more than 60 percent of the time; even in our recorded jigsaw discussions, this was slightly less but still significant.

The nature and emphasis of teacher talk in class discussions are well attended in writing studies and English education scholarship, studied because of the influence they can have on students' experiences with their writing classes and the writing process. Dong (2008), whom I cited earlier in this chapter, argues for instructors to reflect on their handling of sociocognitive conflicts in classroom discussions so that classroom participants can better dwell on and learn in these moments of "productive tensions." One of Dong's participants, Sue, reflects on how her classroom strategies, in which she deferred to her supervising teacher's preferences, conflicted with her actual desires for "student centered classroom discussion." Similarly, while I structured our jigsaw discussions to secure space for GTAs to talk through their responses to and questions about the readings, my talk time in these transcripts marks ways that I bookended the discussions with business, prefaces, and culminating remarks. While I was attentive to this challenge, even in the moment, and while I have worked to amend it in this chapter by centering students' voices, I am still thinking about the amount of time the teacher in the practicum should be talking, and when that teacher should be talking, when it is GTAs who need the space to practice their own teacher talk.[3]

Earlier in this chapter I positioned this study within local and scholarly evidence that practicum instructors need to be prepared to manage difficult discussions about topics that practicum students may not yet feel confident talking about or working through in their own classrooms. While much of the story of this winter 2021 practicum has been focused on GTAs' readiness for teaching IC and working with issues of social justice, antiracist teaching, and linguistic justice in the IC course, and while I have shared ways that I approached these discussions, I admit my analysis has largely sidestepped questions of my own preparation and readiness. What the moments from the class show, I think, are my knowledgeable improvisations—not especially knowledgeable about the questions we were raising (I think the five of us were on par with each other in terms of reflecting on bringing these questions to our local context) but rather knowledgeable about who these GTAs were, what goals and experiences and questions they brought with them into their teaching that semester. It is an impossible thing to expect of a first-semester practicum instructor to have this knowledge of their students but a luxury I hope I fully took advantage of in the short time I had with these fourth-semester GTAs in Zoom sessions and in the digital spaces of our course LMS.

It is also important for me to reiterate that I came into the practicum with an agenda that exceeded preparing these students to teach IC *while* they were teaching IC, a tough enough challenge of its own. Learning how to balance these agendas is inherently part of the role of the practicum instructor, and it is a role that includes mindfulness about GTAs' knowledge and positionality. For example, writing about a graduate student, Karen's, surprising performance of neutrality in response to a student's presentation of "racist and historically inaccurate views of slavery" in a paper, Brewer (2020b) admits, "While part of me want to push graduate instructors like Karen to confront their students in less-couched terms, to do so is to force someone in a less-marginalized position to enact a role she is not yet comfortable with and does not yet have the experience to occupy" (36–37). Further, as Brewer (2020a) explores in her book, pushing students into critical work may be more difficult in their first semester; this first-semester challenge is reinforced by Restaino (2012) as she explores the myriad positions and priorities of these new instructors.

Because I worked with GTAs in their fourth semester, I was confident in their knowledge about teaching in our program at the same time that I was differently aware of their positionality than I was when they were in my Practicum I class. And, as I have described in this chapter, GTAs were explicit about their positionality and reflections on it in our jigsaw offerings. Therefore, it was important for me to listen to their own assessments of their positionality in our program—where they felt empowered to make teaching decisions and where they did not yet, where they felt secure in their knowledge about teaching writing and where they needed me to supply some direction. What I can discern from rereading transcripts and students' writing from the course is that they felt empowered to bring their curricular concerns and revisions to the virtual table in our practicum sessions and to enact them in their IC courses in that semester or craft plans for potential use. However, I can also see they did not always feel sure that these decisions would be honored outside of the bounds of the specific "pandemic semester" in which we were teaching.

Would our small group's experiments, rehearsed in the safety of a practicum course with an urgent and supportive instructor, have staying power? Or, without the security of a program-articulated curriculum and policies—without clearly articulated program values focused on linguistic diversity, antiracism, and compassionate and considerate instruction—would the conclusions of the semester fade from our pedagogical memories?

Conclusion

The threads of this winter 2021 practicum story have been, I imagine, familiar to readers balancing their own practical struggles teaching writing during the pandemic and working to find ways to amend or develop their instruction in action- and justice-oriented ways. The pressures of that time, many having persisted in the semesters to follow, led instructors to weigh personal and programmatic values and demands for teaching and to make decisions in responsive and compassionate, yet practical, ways for their students and themselves. The GTAs in the course I write about in this chapter were at the culmination of several semesters of coursework that had them reading about and planning social-justice-oriented work in their classrooms, if not also their scholarship; the realities of teaching online courses to students who had been working remotely for a year challenged GTAs' outlook and instructional goals (and my goals as a writing program actor) in many ways. As we engaged with assigned readings and the revised IC curriculum, we thought differently about the ways that we would work with students on concepts like the language of a literature review or how we would help them work with course readings in real time. This was a productive recentering and rethinking of the course content, following the hurried transitions to online instruction in previous pandemic semesters (winter 2020, fall 2020) (Collopy 2020). However, while GTAs developed instructional strategies for teaching this new course, they also grappled with how to forward their valuing of antiracist writing instruction and linguistic diversity through teaching IC.

However heavy the weight of the pandemic was on GTAs and their students during this semester, though, other structural forces emerge in their discussions of positionality and possibility. As the students in my class commented several times throughout the semester, they did not always feel positioned to take up the instructional approaches and the pedagogical topics advocated for in the texts we read, even though they (mostly) embraced the arguments and strategies presented in these texts. This is partially because they did not see the teaching assignment before them as amenable to these changes—the curriculum of the course they were learning to teach felt, at times, far from the topics and issues presented in our practicum readings. But it is mostly because, as graduate students, they should be supported from all angles in this change making, and they should not have to be the primary drivers of change. If, as a program, we successfully position teachers-as-learners (Stenberg 2005; Jankens and Torok 2023), how do we position (graduate) teachers as *do-ers*, including do-ers of the kinds of critical self-reflection required of antiracist and justice-oriented teachers? We can begin to see that the practicum and the larger teacher development scheme in which it functions require the right scaffolds for change making. In my final chapter, I pose possibilities for how, by the attention to seemingly smaller moments of articulation I have emphasized in these chapters, our field's investments in socially responsible institutional change and in teacher development can come together to produce more than just idiosyncratic values but actualized realities.

5
Between Mission and Action

Restructuring Programmatic Change Through Teacher Development

The studies in this book represent inquiries responsive to teacher development-centered changes in my local program, changes based on administrative pressures, values-based investments, and practical exigencies. As I outlined in the introduction, rather than only drawing from models of the change work of other programs, which were informative but contextually difficult to apply, I knew I wanted to look with more depth into what was happening in our own writing program talk and activity to understand the values at work in teacher development. Reading inside, in this way, I hoped to see this talk and activity anew, and as outlined in several chapters, reading inside my program helped me see both tensions and sites of discursive possibility. Once I had identified these tensions and possibilities, I was ready to read outside. Reading outside meant I needed to get out of my comfort zone, and out of my own perspective and experience, and listen not just outside of my program, like I did in the study I recounted in chapter 2, but also outside of the field.

The business aisle of Barnes and Noble is replete with discussions of values-oriented workplaces and change-making strategies. When I understood the general direction I hoped to take for this book in December 2020, I found myself one afternoon remarkably child free in the bookstore, and therefore able to leave the Thomas the Tank Engine and graphic novels areas and walk wherever I liked, a joy that had been on hiatus for over a decade of children's books and academic reading. Venturing down the business aisle, I specifically sought books on mission and values statements. I assumed I'd find something, since these statements are part of most, if not all, corporate workplaces as much as they certainly are part of university websites and marketing and program reviews, if not actually evident throughout university culture. I thought, if every workplace has these statements, then surely I'll find a book on how to write them, or interpret them, or enact them. Long story short, I didn't (and in fact, online that weekend, found only one slim self-published book on mission statements).[1] I mentally accounted for related keywords and let my eyes scan instead for books on "change." Looking for books on change might tell me more about the *action* of change making, not just the intention, I thought.

Low on the right-hand side of one bookcase I found a stack of Adam Grant's (2016) *Originals: How Non-Conformists Move the World*, a white paperback with a splash of rainbow-colored graphics circling the subtitle. In addition to supplying countless Instagram and Pinterest posts on my social media feeds, Grant is a highly read and followed organizational psychologist and author. In *Originals*, he explores examples of individual actors who recognize how and when to act on innovative ideas even when power structures might count them out. Writing about what change makers *do—how* they successfully think and strategize outside of the norm—Grant spoke to me through his descriptions of successful entrepreneurs and leaders. Specifically, the chapter "Out on a Limb" provides an entry point into the arguments I want to make in this chapter.

In "Out on a Limb," Grant explores the example of Carmen Medina, a CIA analyst who, in the early 1990s, advocated for an internet system that would allow for improved information sharing between major government agencies (63). As Grant narrates, Medina's urgent advocacy lost her friends and supporters, shifted her to a less visible position, and led to a few years of quiet (63). While she worked behind the scenes, Medina built relational support for her ideas (68). Years later, Medina chose to re-up her formal advocacy, and in the 2000s, "played an indispensable role in creating a platform called Intellipedia, an internal Wikipedia for intelligence agencies to access each other's knowledge," a system Grant notes is "radically at odds with CIA norms" (64). In setting up discussion of the ways Medina worked within and against a system wherein aspects of power and status would have counted her out as a change maker, Grant writes,

> Leaders and managers appreciate it when employees take the initiative to offer help, build networks, gather new knowledge, and seek feedback. But

there is one form of initiative that gets penalized: speaking up with suggestions. In one study across manufacturing, service, retail, and nonprofit settings, the more frequently employees voiced concerns and ideas upward, the less likely they were to receive raises and promotions over a two-year period. And in an experiment when individuals voiced their objections to racism, they were criticized as self-righteous by those who had failed to speak out against it. (65)

Grant discusses the ways that status impacts potential actors' ability to suggest change and have their suggestions accepted and supported by administrators and leaders; when personnel have not cultivated relational status in an organization or do not *appear* like others who have that status, their change-making suggestions may be ignored or they may be perceived as "difficult, coercive, and self-serving" (65). To build this relational status, Grant says, Medina "accumulated what psychologist Edwin Hollander called idiosyncrasy credits—the latitude to deviate from the group's expectations" (67).

Even though Grant writes primarily for readers working in corporate and nonprofit settings, it is easy to see how his description maps on to the experiences of GTAs in writing programs. We design opportunities for GTAs to invent their own lesson plans and sometimes even whole units within the bounds of our course learning outcomes and assignment requirements; we acknowledge their good teaching by asking them to deliver workshops; and when they teach general education classes well, we ask them to teach new courses. In a way, we could say that we reward complicity (and we reward it with more work!). Kelly Belanger and Sibylle Gruber (2005) describe the problem this way in terms of determining practicum content: "In a sense, we are putting GTAs in a no-win situation: we want them to teach what we have established as important, we want them to teach the material using a certain lens, but then we also tell them that we want to make sure—to a limited extent—that the practicum or methods course moves them beyond the framework that we consider suited for the program" (118). We teach GTAs to disrupt at the level of scholarship but to toe the line in curricular matters. This makes sense in some ways: Our composition curricula are designed to support undergraduate student success and have been (ideally) thoughtfully researched, scaffolded, tested, and assessed. They should, therefore, be pretty good, and we should expect they will be employed by every teacher in the program (with the proper instructional support). But we may not have structured enough room to grow, room to ensure that all instructors' teaching experiences are part of the input that helps us build more functional, inclusive, and even ideal writing programs.

Reading Grant's book as part of my strategic contemplation on the problem of locating program values in the practicum opened up some conundrums for me. While writing programs may be wont to resist corporate-style thinking, they often function in similar ways, sometimes out of necessity and sometimes because, well, they are workplaces in a lot of ways like other workplaces. And their workers and administrators labor and circulate tasks like they do in other workplaces (Strickland 2011; LaFrance 2019). As I described in chapter 2, WPAs might often feel more like midlevel managers, seeing the changes they would like to make but not feeling positioned well enough *yet* to enact those changes or working in the face of too many other institutional pressures that take their attention away from the visionary game they would prefer to play. And as I described in other chapters, other tensions might leave instructors feeling like what they do individually really has little support or makes little difference: When program history and the experiences of individual teachers are not taken up in conversational depth in curriculum development, we might wonder what all that previous work was for; and when teachers are given latitude to attempt changes in their individual classrooms under the supervision of a practicum instructor but are not sure whether those changes will be allowed or supported in future semesters, then daily work, even when it matches up with program values, might seem futile. Restaino (2012) puts it this way: "When we fail to pause, study, question, and think about what we ask new teachers to do in the classroom, we are inevitably allowing their efforts to be swept away like labor's harvest. They learn dangerous lessons from this experience: most crucially, they learn that the pedagogical efforts of the writing teacher do not make for serious work" (105). How do teacher-scholars build up the "idiosyncrasy credits" we need to be able to do change work (Grant, citing Hollander, 67)? And how do we support GTAs (and contingent faculty, like the committee members I write about in chapter 3) in doing this work, when their experience is that idiosyncrasy is labeled as problematic, not contributive? The strategy, I think, is to structure the contribution of experiential evidence so that it has intellectual weight in a program's circulation of knowledge.

So, in this chapter, I develop an argument that when programs are structured to promote change making, teachers can more confidently do this work; that the practicum is a significant, coordinating brace of this change-making structure; and that depth of attention to teachers' experiential knowledge is the strength of the overall structure. Through my reflection on scholarship, the studies in this book, and other professional experiences, I position focusing on the talk about and decisions around those micro-level changes—especially via structured discussions and written reflections—as core to the ways that programmatic change (key for WPAs with any level of vision) can be tied to consideration of program values. I illustrate, essentially, that because the practicum is a site where WPAs and practicum instructors typically work to integrate change and to work with teachers on new initiatives, it is also the place where values-based ripple effects of change can originate. Instead of originating from the top-down, however, values-driven programmatic change can emerge through teachers who feel confidence in carrying out these changes, both because they are participants in determining them and because the changes are meaningfully sustainable. This argument is paired, then, with an argument more strongly presented in the preceding chapters: Unless articulated through program-wide conversation, values for teacher development will remain diffused instead of distinctive, cohesive parts of a writing program's mission. This surety is especially important when the desired changes match the energies of the discipline. We cannot be talking with vision in mind but maintaining the status quo—or working toward multiple incoherent visions—in practice.

Asao Inoue reflects on these tensions in his interview with Neal Learner (2018):

> We can change our hearts and our intentions, but that doesn't change our standards, or the dispositions we've cultivated over many years about what is clear, what is valuable, what is good or bad in language practices, or what we think our students will need in their futures because others are not as enlightened as us—the delaying of activism and social justice for the sake of our students! Can you hear how foolish and counterproductive that sounds? (116)

I can. The approaches I describe in this chapter focus on the design, listening, and reflection we can undertake in sites of teacher development to move past that foolishness and into action.

Reading About Change-Making in Writing Studies

As Kelly Ritter (2018) reminds us, "No writing program can champion fixity if it wants to remain healthy and vital both inside and outside its home institution" (62). We certainly cannot rest on engaging program action, whether that's developing curriculum, strategizing assessment, bringing in new students, or retaining faculty by doing things the same old ways. If we understand our program values, how they play out at the local level, and how they connect to disciplinary values and initiatives, we may, as Rita Malenczyk and her coeditors (2018), arguing for the value of claiming disciplinarity, assert, "have the opportunity to be intentional in our actions" (7). Recent writing studies scholarship has been especially forward looking about the practical conditions for values-driven change work. Putting this scholarship into conversation with the present conditions of my home program in this section, I establish the role of explicit program values in shaping action-oriented writing program work.

I use a local problematic to frame my discussion in this literature review. Like most writing programs today, we have been actively working on antiracist initiatives, most especially through curricular revision, attention to undergraduate student support, and the active recruitment of underrepresented scholars. While minoritized and marginalized graduate students have become more represented in my home program even in the years since I conducted the studies in this book, as of my completion of the first draft of this manuscript in spring 2023, our program's faculty—comprised of tenure-line and NTT faculty—was all white. The fight for full-time faculty (FTF) searches is one we annually put up and don't win. Meanwhile, our university's student body has been highlighted on university websites as the most diverse in our state. To be allies for these students, we need to make our antiracist and social-justice-oriented goals actionable (Wible 2019, 88). At the curricular level, we are working through revising our FYW syllabus to (1) include projects that deemphasize white mainstream English and allow students to draw from their diverse linguistic resources and (2) reshape classroom assessment ecologies. This action-orientation requires a few levels of work. This work begins with attending to the status of personnel in our programs, honoring their experiences as crucial to program knowledge-making, and structuring initiatives that draw from this experiential evidence while they work to achieve values-based visions. In other words, it requires that we consider labor, power, articulated values, and design.

FIRST, ATTENTION TO LABOR CONDITIONS

Discussions about labor came up in every study I conducted for this book project; in every site I entered (our program history, interviews with WPAs and practicum instructors from other schools, committee discussions, and the practicum class itself), graduate student labor—and the labor of instructors overall—is present as a significant factor in decisions about or the sustainability of change-making efforts in writing programs. It is crucial that labor is at the forefront of everyone's minds; though compositionists have called out for attention to labor for decades, at too many institutions we still annually fight against pressures on class size and course load. And the pandemic brought a reckoning down on what is considered a reasonable work-life balance, perhaps even, for some, including me, bringing more balance into the picture.

As Amanda, one of the WPAs I interviewed in chapter 2, expressed to me, the demand for ever more sections of composition, and her university administration's conviction that adjunct labor is an appropriate response, means that the writing program's collaborative attention to graduate student and instructor labor must be a central program value. Indeed, change making that attends to labor requires a particular depth of institutional research. In their description of the planning and effect of massively increased lecturer-lines in the John Jay College writing program, Mark McBeth and Tim McCormick (2017) argue that attention to kairos is integral for WPAs hoping to make change related to labor conditions: "WPAs must interrogate the context (or predicament) of their programmatic staffing; analyze their institutional contexts and budgetary constraints, and institutional mission goals; and seize upon administrative moments where change is possible, to proactively address the too-often undiscussed status quo" (53). The WPA's skill and experience as a rhetorician, then, can bring together arguments for increased staffing, economic realities, and institutional mission to attend to labor conditions so that they are as favorably in line with the university's ever-changing financial demand as possible.

I draw on a personal example to illustrate a way that this interrogation of context might include attention to the depth of experiential evidence and historical knowledge that I argue for in chapter 2. In 2011, I was hired as a full-time lecturer in my composition program in a cohort of five. Our express purpose was to improve instruction and learning in FYW, and so, in addition to teaching 3-3 loads of only FYW, our collective service focused on curriculum development and assessment of the course. This was a function that we carried out for at least three years before the constant change of writing program realities meant we had to shift into teaching other courses (like IC and technical writing) and eventually took up other roles and responsibilities in the program outside of FYW. Four of the five of us still work in our program, having amassed, since that time, a collective CV of administrative service, community engagement projects, curriculum development, award-winning instruction, composition scholarship, and campus leadership. What began as a close-knit collaboration developed into a depth of institutional impact alongside a successful story about a relatively common problem: instructor retention.

The story of NTT labor at our institution in the period I address in this book also includes other important moments of challenges and success, but I bring up the example of my cohort here because I have recently expressed it in conversations with department-level administrators as a solution to a recent pressing problem: the decrease in student retention and pass rates in FYW since the pandemic. Having made and assessed intentional efforts and small but noticeable gains in that area in the years leading up to the pandemic, our program *and our students* have experienced—along with those in so many other programs—a crushing blow to student success in recent years. Department administration is making decisions about curriculum and assessment to best address students' challenges as quickly as possible. But I see this challenge also as one of teacher development and hiring. I have described the troubling threads in other chapters of this book and elsewhere (i.e., Jankens and Guinot Varty 2025), but the experiential and historical example of an instructional cohort brought in to deliver excellent instruction in the course at the center of this issue—a cohort that, to speak in financial terms, paid dividends—is, to me, part of a winning pitch for the hiring of more full-time faculty in composition. Hire a cohort of faculty to work collaboratively on one core instructional assignment and watch what the benefits of that peer-to-peer work will do. Is it costly to hire four or five full-time faculty? Sure. Is it more costly to watch our students struggle and fail, without the attention and responsive, creative instruction they need? Absolutely. The story of this cohort is experiential and historical evidence worth telling—to department administration, to university administration. It is available for bringing into the discussion, if someone asks, or someone asserts it.

While I assert my cohort's story here, as an example of how a story about actual labor may be brought up in discussions about labor as a value and labor as a pressing issue, I acknowledge also other pulling threads of the story of writing program labor writ large. As many scholar activists have pointed out, full-time, NTT faculty face economic uncertainty and unreasonable working conditions across institutions (see, e.g., Stevenson 2021; Fedukovich et al. 2017). McBeth and McCormick write, "While we should never end our scrutiny and resistance to oppressive labor practices, we also can't sit idly year-after-year, waiting for wholesale revolution that never arrives. After all, our writing students who march along with us need the benefit of revisionary writing programs to develop their own voices of resistance" (2017, 54). Hiring more FTF is not, alone, a strategy for developing a voice of resistance, but the instructional work that can be done across the many sections they teach, the ways that curriculum and assessment can change through their collaboration, the ways that the community can be impacted by their initiatives—our local example, worth telling at a depth I have not done here—demonstrate that it is a worthy approach.

SECOND, POSITIONING GTAS AS CHANGE MAKERS

The ways that new GTAs are explicitly positioned within the practicum—what it says to them and to others in the program about their role in that program—is also a significant part of the picture of that program's labor and change making. Are GTAs bound to the neophyte status they hold in their disciplines as they begin their graduate studies? Are they considered (merely) instructors of record, completing the task of teaching a course? Are they seen as guinea pigs, testing out new projects and curricula in program pilots? Are they positioned as teacher-learners, joining a larger cohort of teacher-learner faculty and senior GTAs?

In "Resistance and Identity Formation: The Journey of the Graduate Student-Teacher," Jennifer Grouling (2015) highlights strategies for engaging GTAs with program materials and with other professionals, supporting their participation as members of a teaching community. Grouling's final recommendation is to "Tie together research and teaching through action research projects, projects designed to research and solve a particular problem in [a] particular community." When framed authentically, drawing from the actual community of teachers in which GTAs work, "they may be able to better meld teacher and student identities." This melding of identities, then, can support GTAs' sense of agency as program participants. Grouling's recommendation reflects a version of what I asked students to do, as a group, in Practicum II in winter 2021 (chapter 4): to join me in talking through whether and how a set of readings could be meaningfully used in helping them teach IC. But as I conclude in that chapter, there are limits to the long-term power GTAs may feel they can harness through formal or informal action research; the key to supporting them in becoming teachers who make change—in programs that make change—is found in their ability to confidently work through daily teaching decisions and assess the impact of these decisions (Addison 2005; Restaino 2012, 104).

In my winter 2021 Practicum II course, GTAs regularly reflected on their positions as both newer instructors in a program (in charge of classrooms of undergraduates) and newer members of their disciplines. They were expected to be able to make decisions about the daily work of their classrooms but were beholden to a common syllabus. I had presented them with the group problem of determining whether and how we could bring readings on linguistic diversity and critical language awareness into the IC course; they were teaching the course for the first time. I trusted them—I had seen them teach and reflect on their teaching for several semesters—but they needed more surety about whether the instructional choices they might make with my support would be supported in other situations, by other faculty. Lauren talked through this with me as we discussed the chapter, saying that while she understood she had a level of instructional freedom in our program that would allow her to make the choices about projects that she was making that semester, she was also developing an understanding at that time that she might not have the same freedom at other schools. Lauren's reflection echoes Mandy Olejnik's, in "Building a Twenty-First Century Feminist Ethos: Three Dialogues for WPAs," when Olejnik recounts an experience to illustrate "the complicated hierarchy that does not always allow [GTAs] to act according to [their] principles" (quoted in LaFrance and Wardle 2019, 26). Olejnik shares that in response to a faculty member who complained to Olejnik about international students' writing, "I said nothing (despite what my principles would tell me) because I was a soft-spoken, female, MA-student, assistant director with limited power and a lot to lose if my confrontation caused trouble or created an issue" (27).

A vulnerability is also embodied by minoritized and marginalized instructors. Sheila Carter-Tod (2021), looking specifically at hiring practices, notes that "epistemological exclusion" is central to not only why we see only a "few non-traditional, or racially-based publications" but also why more Black faculty are not hired or retained in writing programs (53). This vulnerability is demonstrated in the stories shared by Inoue (2021) and Stacy Perryman-Clark (2016, 2019), recounted earlier in this book—wherein these scholars recall workplace conversations where their expertise as WPAs of color was blatantly ignored and the ideas of or information provided by white coworkers promoted. This is an exclusion that may happen in both daily local program work and more culturally at the level of the field. This epistemological exclusion and overall instructor vulnerability can be countered, in part, through a reprioritization of kinds of discourse that circulate in a program.

Hassel and Cole's (2021) edited collection *Transformations: Change Work Across Writing Programs, Pedagogies, and Practices* provides examples of programmatic change work conducted by graduate students and contingent faculty, work done "through democratic rather than hierarchical methods" (5). Their collection is one focused on "interventions that can happen in and from a multiplicity of positions and places within our programs" (8). Like Cole and Hassel point out in the first sentences of their collection, change work (indeed work in general) in writing programs is often conducted by "the most vulnerable instructors," part-time and NTT faculty and graduate students with relative job insecurity (3). In the collection, Ruth Osorio, Jaclyn Fiscus-Cannaday, and Allison Hutchison explore how change work happens in the hands of graduate students. Responding to stories gathered in their nationwide survey of graduate worker labor conditions, the authors identify that "often the biggest barriers faced by graduate students are tied to their status as workers" (2021, 21). Writing programs' active support of "grad-worker-led initiatives" can positively impact diversity and inclusion efforts as well as labor conditions for graduate students (21). In gathering graduate workers' experiences in their survey work, Osorio et al. positioned these experiences as central to knowledge-making (22). They note, further,

> In allowing graduate workers' lived experience to be evidence, we learned not just the official labor policies but what was practiced. This was what made our work unique: we trusted graduate workers to tell us the status of their labor conditions, and with that data, better understood how policies were implemented and experienced in their daily lives. By privileging the voices of grad workers over administrators reporting, we were able to paint a picture of the grad worker experience and identify specific labor practices that grad workers can organize around. (27)

This gathering of graduate student voices in programmatic attention to the material conditions of writing program work is crucial for enacting "democratic rather than hierarchical" (Cole and Hassel 2021, 5) program change.

As I go on to explore, this repositioning can result in a generative, sustainable ripple effect of change instigated in the practicum as core site of teacher development. For the people in a program to feel like they can *do* change work, like Osorio et al. assert, WPAs and other program leaders need to actively attend to the experiences of these program personnel.

THIRD, ARTICULATION OF PROGRAM VALUES

Throughout this book I have examined the articulation of program values, looking at the possibilities of this articulation, particularly for developing the curriculum of the practicum. Making these values explicit in the talk and texts of a writing program is key for coordinating action. Once program personnel believe they are being listened to—that their work experiences matter for program decision-making—then talking about values can actually matter for driving this work. This is an epistemological administrative move Joe Torok and I hoped to establish through our recounting of the years of revision to our teaching observation form and our strategies for embedding values for teacher development into that form (Jankens and Torok 2023). In explaining how we structured moments for reciprocal learning and written reflection into the form, we address key program values for teacher development that emerged in my earlier studies in this book, essentially that teaching is a shared enterprise, that teachers should learn from other teachers, and that teachers should learn from written reflection. The audience for that article is just as much our coworkers as it is other administrators hoping to align values and practice.

Talking through the practices we hoped to promote in teaching observations helped Joe and me determine, over time, the genre features we would build into the teaching observation form and the directions we would compose to guide the process (Jankens and Torok 2023). My conversations with WPAs and practicum instructors in chapter 2 similarly demonstrate how talking about program values brings both successful initiatives and programmatic trouble spots to light. These discussions lead to necessary moments of reflection: reflection on positionality and reflection on strategy. Scott Wible (2019) addresses this reflection on positionality, acknowledging that white program personnel who hope to be "allies" to or "accomplices" (see Martinez 2018, 231) for marginalized students and colleagues must engage in critical examination of the ways that white privilege impacts their daily work, "what it means to put that privilege on the line" (Wible 2019, 79), and what it will take to effectively mentor Black students (86). Intention alone does not make for allies; action does (88). Wible sees the composition of "mission and vision statements that focus our collective sights" on goals like antiracist writing instruction as a means of facilitating the reflective work that accompanies the provision of instructional strategies and resources (93). Without a shared understanding of why a program enacts a particular curricular scheme, program personnel may not be able to effectively execute it.

FOURTH, ATTENTION TO DESIGN

Yes, our statements of mission and vision can focus our collective goals, *and* we need to work toward these goals (Beavers 2021). Yes, sites of teacher development need to attend to the promotion of linguistic diversity and antiracism. And, as I have demonstrated in previous chapters, these sites need to support graduate students in our field as do-ers, alongside faculty and administrators who are also doing the work for which they argue. Even with program personnel theoretically on board with a shared vision, for any "antiracist" curricular work to hold water in a writing program, it must be accompanied by other structural revisions. Tyler S. Branson and James Chase Sanchez (2021) say regarding antiracist program policies what I hope to say more generally: We cannot "merely . . . *suggest, align with,* or *vocally support*" things like antiracist teaching and curriculum development; we must change our program policies and practices to align with our stated values (74, emphasis in original). Branson and Sanchez position curriculum development as the primary location for antiracist programmatic policy change (72); they suggest moves like integrating antiracist readings and readings from nonwhite authors into FYW courses as one means of practically approaching such policy change (72). "The premise of such an exercise is not that mandating diversity changes attitudes. It often doesn't. However, it does reflect the values of the program," the authors note (72). Scholars have also provided measures of assessment for antiracist action. Natasha Jones, Laura Gonzales, and Angela M. Haas (2021), for example, arguing for the necessity of care in framing antiracist action, present a set of qualities integral to this work. These items can draw program actors' attention to and reflection on the degree to which they engage the reflective, coalitional, pro-Black, iterative, and other work necessary for antiracist action (32–33).

This structural work can happen within individual projects or at programmatic or institutional levels, and change work can be part of structural design from the first iteration. Jeffrey T. Grabill, Sarah Gretter, and Erik Skogsberg (2022), writing about the Hub at Michigan State University (a "project-based organization" [15] providing a collaborative workspace and facilitating design-based problem-solving) and about the larger scheme of design work in *Design for Change in Higher Education*, approach the structuring of programmatic and institutional change as most sustainably emerging from a central perspective of design. For these authors and change-participants, learning experiences and conversations can be designed to bring together all necessary change agents (including students) in the university. The moment in their introduction when they position their argument for redesigning higher education is where I want to look even more closely for possibilities for teacher development:

> Our argument is that the only way to achieve what Davidson, Bass, Kim, Maloney, and others advocate is through design, and more specifically, for colleges and universities to build design functions as a core capacity. As Kim and Maloney note, "learning innovation is as much about leading organizational change as it is about pedagogy and technology." We think they understate the case: it is all about how to recognize and facilitate organizational change. The key shift, which the Hub was explicitly designed to address, is the move from the individual to the collective, from the classroom to the

institution. This move is inclusive of the experiences of specific classrooms and individual teachers and students, but, as Kim and Maloney also note, it relocates "the unit of analysis of the conditions that support or inhibit student learning from that of the individual student to the scale of the institution and everywhere in between." (7)

As I have demonstrated throughout this book, I am especially interested in looking at that "in between," at what individuals (instructors, GTAs, students) experience in our writing programs (especially in and around teacher development) and how their experiences are brought into conversation with others and with writing program values. Articulation of these values (for teacher development, for teaching writing) and recognition of these experiences are the conditions under which change—at the programmatic level—can begin and can be sustained. And I look at this in between in the talk that happens in and around the practicum and the texts used to convey the purpose and activity of the practicum course, because of its initiating and central location in GTAs' writing program experience.

I have used the studies in this book to focus on the discursive, conversational work that needs to happen between understanding a local context and crafting interventions—work that considers or undertakes or looks at or brings to the foreground program values and teachers' experiences enacting these values. In engaging this talk around, in, and about the composition teaching practicum, I have worked to provide examples of the tensions that may surround program values, the conditions in which values-driven work may (or may not) manifest productively, and strategies for stronger articulation and presence of these values, specifically values for teacher development. In these final pages, I look at strategies for structuring the composition teaching practicum with this attention. Like the notes from the fall 2018 focus group conducted with GTAs in my home program alert, "If the course does not have a structure, [then] a structure organically evolves." For that group, the structure became "a therapy group," because of their need to "vent a lot." If the practicum is going to be attentive to supporting GTAs with confident decision-making (and is part of a larger sphere of teacher development in the program that does the same), then it must be intentionally structured to do so.

Structuring Sustainable Micro-Level Change Work in Teacher Development

The practicum is central to the experience new GTAs have, as they learn the field and/or learn their role in the workplace of an English department. As

Dobrin (2005) describes, its content is a point of contention (2). The differences between practicum structures in the programs of the WPAs I interviewed showed many differences, if seemingly minor, in the ways new GTAs are professionalized through this course (e.g., whether and how mentor teachers are involved in this professionalization, whether GTAs develop their own lessons and materials or use a common syllabus). The years since the publication of Dobrin's collection have only reinforced the contextual, local nature of teaching writing even as the scholarly concerns of the field become ever expansive. Wardle and Downs (2018) cite "localism" as one of the major values of the field: "What works *here* may not work *there*" they comment, summarizing the field's acknowledgment of the situated nature of pedagogy (and, I will add, therefore of teacher development) (127). And change within the local is, as pointed out earlier, an iterative entity. The constant responsive revisions of my own program's practicum over the last decade, many recounted across this book, affirm that.

Practicum courses, like Michelle's, described in chapter 2, often include opportunities for GTAs to design projects and unit plans for their composition courses with the support of practicum instructor feedback. However, not all GTAs may have the accompanying preparation to meaningfully assess or enact these (idiosyncratic) curricula, particularly if the practicum has been their primary or sole preparation in teaching writing, and even if the practicum includes the perfect balance of theory, practice, reflection, and planning. GTAs will face countless decisions in the day-to-day work of carrying out these personally designed curricula that they will also need to be prepared to work through. More than being ready to tackle macro-level curricular redesigns, that is, GTAs need practice in the micro-level, problem-solving work of teaching writing, and they need the opportunity to share the results of that practice with other program actors. I think this work can be more intentional, better coordinated. Indeed, even as evidenced in examples from chapter 2, while we are often focused on helping teachers learn how to make big changes (i.e., letting GTAs structure their own FYW syllabi for future semesters), the concerns and challenges that have emerged across this book are more about micro-level problems and choices: whether teaching circles should be held during or after the practicum; how to visually present a reading to students in an online course; how to sequence, by weeks, assigned readings in a practicum to capture the widest range of voices, and many others.

It is a historical reality in my program that we have often first tried out new initiatives—small pilots—with GTAs, including in winter 2021, when I asked students in that class to engage in an attentive conferencing model and to track their contact with IC students who were struggling in the course. In other instances, GTAs in our Practicum II course have been the first to work with the university's new course LMS (winter 2018) and to try out open-access resources with FYW students (fall 2019). These pilots—and others—worked because GTAs had the support of a knowledgeable instructor who was invested in the projects and who listened to their experiences to revise work in action. But without that practicum instructor's access to institutional knowledge and experiential evidence, these efforts might not have gone so well. For example, I admit to a challenge I faced in fall 2021, when I taught the practicum during a semester where I was not also teaching FYW. In previous semesters, I had organized the practicum around my own course LMS shell, so I had intimate insight into how the course was structured; in that semester, I used a course LMS shell provided by another instructor in the department, who had been paid to create the shell over the summer. This might sound like an easy-peasy solution to not having to take on the labor of designing my own FYW LMS structure; the problem, however, was that I did not understand the design behind the provided course—neither the pacing nor the organization of materials. This was not a pilot, but it was an utter instructional failure, for me and for GTAs. We can call it a lesson learned, but it remains that new GTAs were left floundering with a resource that was new to them and that none of us understood very well. It was not only GTAs who were not positioned well in this instance—in deciding to use a resource that I did not have insight on and could not manipulate or redesign for the whole group along the way, I did not position myself effectively as an agent of micro-level change in the course. And GTAs in the class—because they were new to the program, to teaching the course, and to the LMS—were not positioned, yet, to suggest changes to the design. They did not yet have the relational status or the practical knowledge to effectively speak up, and I had not structured the course to obtain that specific feedback from them.

The need for attention to micro-level decisions came to my eyes and ears equally loudly and desperately in other studies I conducted during the pandemic. In an account of a group interview I conducted with instructors assigned to serve as "instructional response team" for colleagues at the abrupt start of remote learning in March 2020, Nicole Guinot Varty and I describe how that interview conversation demonstrates the problem of response team members guiding instructors on these kinds of micro-level decisions when team members themselves were not beholden to a core charge beyond "provide support" (Jankens and Guinot Varty 2025, 143). While response team members shared an implicit set of values about their responsivity and mission, their distinctly different approaches to talking with instructors about teaching online meant that instructors' long-held dispositions toward teaching online were maintained rather than brought in line with a program vision during that time (Jankens and Guinot Varty 2025). Earlier in *this* book (chapter 4), I reflected on the echoes of a graduate student, Hunter's, question about whether *our teaching was really going to be different from now on*, whether some of the instructional decisions teachers made during "pandemic semesters" would have any impact on teaching in our program in the long term. This is where an understanding and articulation of program values become especially important.

Here, I explore three strategies for foregrounding program values and structuring the practicum as a site for sustainable program change and supporting GTAs (and the instructors who work with them in various sites of teacher development) as change makers: (1) regularly discuss and revisit program values for teacher development with program personnel, including new teachers; (2) foreground learning encounters in practicum discussions; and (3) use written reflection as a means of assessing and reporting on GTAs' learning encounters and on the refraction of program values in GTAs' teaching and learning experiences. Each of these strategies emerges from the discussions of previous chapters and have also been put into practice in my most recent practicum course (fall 2023). What you will notice as you read these strategies is that while I draw from potentially familiar examples of them in action, what I work to do is explicitly bring the activities of the course in line with program values for teacher development. In doing so, I draw on the strength of pedagogical knowledge in the field to deepen GTAs' connection to what it means to engage in teacher development (ala Stenberg 2005) and in teaching in a particular program. Their attunement to the program's values and to their own reflection as teachers, then, supports their work with the myriad micro-level decisions they make as teachers. In turn, their reflection—as experiential evidence—is structured to contribute as a key node of knowledge circulation in programmatic decision-making and change efforts.

REGULARLY DISCUSS AND REVISIT PROGRAM VALUES FOR TEACHER DEVELOPMENT WITH PROGRAM PERSONNEL, INCLUDING NEW TEACHERS

Program values are an important conversational touchstone. They are not inflexible—they may change over time, and some may be higher priorities than others—however, that they are *articulated* is what is most significant for a writing program that wants to support the development of change makers as it makes its moves forward. This tactic is therefore important for the curricular decisions that function as part of this programmatic change.

It's not enough to only talk about these values at the very introduction of GTAs' time in the practicum. Values are not said-and-done—this is evident in the historical documents related to my program's practicum (and the programmatic attention or inattention paid to them) in the early chapters of this book. Values are living constructs, carried out by action or in need of reexamination and revision. So how does this conversation look across a semester? How can talk about program values in the practicum function as grounded in GTAs' daily teaching and learning experiences, not as more conceptual weight taking attention away from the day-to-day?

My analysis of a brief history of teacher development helped me identify five emergent values for this work in my program—values that seem relatively supported in the small collection of practicum syllabi from across the field that I compiled during the pandemic. Because of this testing of these values as I looked across practicum sites, I felt confident including these—as explicit statements and as structuring principles—as I planned for my fall 2023 new GTA orientation and Practicum I syllabus, previewing for new GTAs how they would be engaging in teacher development across their time in the program, beginning with the pre-semester orientation. One core problematic for the semester made this articulation and discussion of values more pressing to me: I had been tasked with working with this new GTA cohort on using a version of labor-based grading contracts in FYW, with the promise that our entire instructional cohort would soon be moving in that direction. For me, this specific goal required that everyone understand the means we would use to support and assess our efforts. The values already in tacit circulation in our program could explicitly circulate as these intentional means—I could articulate them and use that articulation to incite action.

As I planned for the fall 2023 orientation, I used these articulated values to introduce the activities of the week. Pairing each value with a specific orientation activity helped me ensure I was explicitly addressing and activating these values in the orientation sessions. The values served as a structuring activity that tied new GTAs to learning what it would mean to teach FYW at our university, specifically.

In Practicum I, these values were explicitly presented on the first pages of the syllabus and on the landing page of the LMS, a second point of contact for new GTAs in their early weeks in the program and a framing mechanism for how the course would be structured, how we would spend our time together each week, and the assignments GTAs would work through. Each assignment in the course tied to one or more of these values. This articulation of values, then, also provided me with a touchstone for assessing these two sites of teacher development in our program. Formatively, we could have conversations in orientation and practicum, broadly answering the question, Why do we do things the way that we do? For summative assessment, I would be able to triangulate new GTAs' written reflections (see more in the subsection on reflection), evaluations of the course, and other artifacts with these articulated values to understand how and to what effects these values were being engaged in the activity of teacher development. Though this is outside of what I am looking at in this book, other sites of teacher development in our program would also benefit from a review through the lens of these values: Teaching observations of new and experienced GTAs and part-time faculty, teaching workshops required for all instructors, and even teaching circles could be assessed and potentially revised through our articulated values for teacher development.

These discussions are grounded in the material work of teaching writing; as our values for teacher development are explicitly articulated in the practicum syllabus and then exercised throughout the course, we also consider how other program values—like values for teaching FYW—are enacted through our teaching. Practicing these discussions in the practicum engages peer-to-peer learning and written reflection, two of our central values for teacher development.

FOREGROUND LEARNING ENCOUNTERS IN PRACTICUM DISCUSSIONS

As my reading of curriculum committee and practicum conversations in chapters 3 and 4 highlighted, these conversations include potentially productive moments for digging into the experiential evidence raised by new GTAs alongside deeper consultation of the writing program's local context and history. Learning from this, I considered how to structure these conversational examinations into practicum discussions, finding one possibility in an assignment I usually used at the end of the course.

In the practicum, our work is often oriented on planning ahead or reflecting on what is past; Our discussions of "business matters" (what we need quick answers to today) are often seen as something to get through before we get to the real "stuff" of the day's lessons: the theory, the presentations. Except, as voiced by GTAs and instructors showcased throughout this book, the real stuff is often the human interactions and impacts surrounding these business matters: how to deal with late work, helping a student get access to resources, figuring out what to do when an assignment provided by the program is incomprehensible to a group of students. These seeming one-off questions and experiences sometimes snowball in meaning; I think about how Hunter's question about changing structures for grading has stuck with me for several semesters since he said it. These interactions have functioned for me as what Stenberg (2005) calls "learning encounters." Stenberg explains that for teacher development to function as a reciprocal enterprise, new and experienced teachers need to engage in mutual reflection and growth, a disruption of hierarchical roles that allows for their critical engagement (136). Opportunities for this "critical colleagueship," a term that Stenberg borrows from Brian Lord, not only are found in formal sites of teacher development but may also be found at any point or location in a teacher's institutional life (139). Stenberg presents three examples of these interactions—reflections from other instructors—as demonstrations of teaching being made "public for reflection and revision" (135). Attention to these learning encounters takes already happening activity and positions it to have an impact (as knowledge making) on the field (146).

I have often positioned GTAs' discussions and presentations of significant learning encounters with students or other university personnel at the end of the practicum semester. For a constructive reflection assignment, GTAs have reviewed their teaching notes and journals, reflected on what has been sticking with them, and described several learning encounters, eliciting a teacherly theme. I have emphasized that these encounters may happen in their classrooms; online; anywhere on campus; and with students, peers, or in other institutional dialogues. In a multimodal classroom presentation in the last class session, GTAs talk through selected learning encounters with their classmates; then, as the semester closes, they revise and submit a reflective essay to me.

Reviewing my own encounters with the studies in this book, however, motivated me to invert this reflective assignment, bring the learning encounters into the center of the practicum course, and therefore also bring students' voices (undergraduate and graduate) to the center. In revising this assignment to happen across the semester, and more publicly than privately, I work to get at three outcomes: the depth of and circulation of experiential knowledge I argued for in chapter 3; an enactment of program values for teacher development centered on reflective writing, peer-to-peer learning, and collaborative knowledge making; and a reshaping of how reflection plays out in the practicum, such that it is not always, as GTAs reported in focus groups, "too late." To center these learning encounters, I created an in-class reflection activity that would serve as initial practice with identifying, describing, and reflecting on a learning encounter. In the exercise, a member of the class takes the floor, from whichever location in the classroom they are most comfortable. They describe a learning encounter they have recently had that has helped them think differently about their teaching. In response, the rest of the class may ask them questions to better draw out their experience and reflection. It is their learning encounter that is reinforced in this discussion; other class members may not shift the conversational energy to their own experiences unless the presenter asks them a question in return. Our intention is to deliberately center individual GTAs' experiential evidence and to allow that experience's meaning to take shape through the individual's reflection. In one of the first weeks of the course, I demonstrate my own learning encounter reflection, taking a seat at the front of the room while the class practices asking questions; each subsequent week, another member of the class shares a recent learning encounter. It does not matter whether instructors share "big" events—the learning encounters they share may very well be the kinds of micro-level classroom moments that spur on bigger questions about classroom procedures, policies, relationships, and instructional concepts.

Also significant is the way that Stenberg positions this description of learning encounters in a chapter in which she argues for teacher development to be understood as an experience not only for GTAs but also for experienced teachers in a program (2005, 131). I would hope we consider these learning encounters not as one-off conversational offerings in a program's formal and informal sites of knowledge making (the practicum, committee work, and others) but as experiential evidence worth examining, collaboratively. An additional benefit of centering these learning encounters is the opportunity for formative assessment doing so provides to both GTAs and practicum instructors. As GTAs describe the influences on their teacherly decision-making (students, scholarship, peers, administrators, economics, etc.), practicum instructors can attend to the weight of this influential distribution, and work to understand how to further bolster productive support. The (simple) follow-up questioning I advocated for in chapter 3 makes way for collaborative, inquiry-based learning.

USE WRITTEN REFLECTION AS A MEANS OF ASSESSING AND REPORTING ON GTAS' LEARNING ENCOUNTERS AND ON THE REFRACTION OF PROGRAM VALUES IN GTAS' TEACHING AND LEARNING EXPERIENCES

In chapter 1, I describe the small, administratively housed archive of historical program artifacts I could access to look at the practicum: formal white papers, notes from focus groups with GTAs, and syllabi from our Practicum I and Practicum II courses. While students' voices are represented in the focus group notes, these notes provide only a snapshot of their experiences, taken during a late-semester conversation. As a comment from the end of the winter 2018 session notes indicates, this snapshot is not comprehensive enough to permit a whole assessment: "There are many positive things—we just needed to get out the negative things." These notes leave me—reading as a practicum instructor—needing to know so much more. I echo Restaino's (2012) assertion of "the importance of facilitating opportunities for graduate students' teaching experiences to foster knowledge-making" (117). Restaino leaves the means of this knowledge making for scholars (and practicum instructors) to come; in my role as one such teacher-scholar, I see written reflection as a perhaps simple but underutilized answer. GTAs' experiences can be more regularly captured, sustainably archived, and thoughtfully integrated into program assessment through reflective writing. As indicated by the studies in this book and by scholarship on the teaching practicum, using written reflection to support GTAs' teacher development is nothing new. If teaching is a reflective practice (Schön 1983; Yancey 1998; Bamberg 2002; Burnham and Jackson 2002) and when writing programs value written reflection as an outcome (either at the undergraduate or graduate level, or both), then not only should reflective practice and written reflection be integrated into class sessions, but they should also be utilized as a means for both GTAs and other program personnel to consider what is happening in teacher development.

Theoretically framed reflective assignments are a practical and sustainable way for programs to support GTAs' enculturation into the individual program and into the field at large. Reflective practice in the practicum cannot only be improvisational; consistency in the reflective genres of the practicum—and in how this written reflection is treated—can signify the value of teacher reflection as well as serve as a useful form of assessment. The practicum is only one site of teacher development, only one place that reflection can happen, but "for a culture of reflective practice to exist, it must first be built into the TAs' initial preparation and then sustained through programmatic structures and practices that occur after the practicum" (Bamberg 2002, 150). Betty Bamberg (2002) advocates for a "highly structured day-by-day course outline" to promote GTAs' experience with and induction into a culture of reflective practice (151). In this model, mentors work with TAs to dialogue through teaching problems and planning solutions and next steps (151). The learning encounters assignment I described activates this work in conversation, and it can be capitalized on in writing.

Integrating regular reflection into the practicum comes with some ready admonitions, however. First, as Bamberg points out, the kinds of depth of reflective practice employed in research are "time- and labor-intensive" and not replicable in the weekly work of a practicum course (150). Certainly, as illustrated in chapter 1 via focus group notes and chapter 4 via my description of our winter 2021 Practicum II class, the practicum in our local program is stressed with the burden of too much reflection and too little time. Second, as Lesley Erin Bartlett (2022) emphasizes, the implicit and explicit expectations of "compelled reflective writing" mean that what students put into written reflection may be more reflective of what they expect teachers (or institutions) want to see than of their actual experiences; Bartlett therefore urges instructors to critically reflect on their integration of reflection and reflective writing and students' experiences with these (214). In response to these admonitions, I find two models of reflection are especially worth describing for application in the practicum. These models are both individual and communal; engage a predictable, and thus manageable, pattern; ask all teacher-learners to be reflective writers; and work to help administrators and practicum instructors close feedback loops with program values in mind. Most important, they are contextually viable models—models I can enact in the local circumstances of my pedagogical practica and that meet with program values for teacher development.

For several years, I have been a member of the Documentarian team for the annual CCCC meeting. The *preflective* and reflective practices designed by Julie Lindquist, Bree Straayer, and Bump Halbritter (2023) for this documentarian work have, for me, transcended that exercise and made their way into the research and writing I do daily, including into the responsive IE work I do in this book. I set out expectations for my days, record my processes, and mindfully reflect on the outcomes of my work as well as on the ways that work changes through what I encounter. Bump Halbritter and Julie Lindquist's (2018) experiential learning documentary (ELD) model—from which the documentarian work is drawn—offers core strategies to engage GTAs in the practicum in regular reflective practice that helps them look not only at their teaching but also at their experiences as program actors. Core to the ELD model is students' reflection on both past experiences and present learning (318). Halbritter and Lindquist explain, "The pedagogical approach we describe is one of *projection, collection*, and *recollection*: It assumes that the greatest value for learning is in the reflective (or as we will show, 'forensic') moment" (318). Halbritter and Lindquist describe the "nimble" disposition required for documentary filmmaking (318); this readiness to anticipate what may be important (in collecting data) and to also attend to what happens and ultimately emerges as important (in recollection) makes for reflective composing that centers on students' experiences, that is truly student driven, and that focuses on students' development as learners (see also Lindquist and Halbritter 2019). This model, adapted for the practicum, is a way to deepen experiential evidence both for the individual GTA and for the peers with whom this GTA engages in collaborative knowledge-making. While not culminating in literacy narratives proper, as they do in Lindquist and Halbritter's FYW classrooms, in the practicum GTAs' reflections—often captured as story—accumulate as resources for the teaching stories they will tell themselves and others (2019, 414), shaping individual and communal teacher development. In one way, we work in the practicum to capture and deepen experiential learning as described earlier, in our learning encounters discussions across the semester. We also work to capture and deepen this learning via regular reflective writing.

A second model, described by Elizabeth G. Allan and Dana Driscoll (2014), demonstrates how reflective writing can be useful both in the writing classroom and in larger program contexts. The authors describe their design of an assessment that took up FYW students' reflective writing alongside instructor's course materials and students' research writing (41). Triangulation of these artifacts in assessment not only provided Allan and Driscoll's faculty cohort with more comprehensive evidence of student learning but also allowed for the identification of needed faculty development in teaching reflection (49). I am not digging into the depth of Allan and Driscoll's assessment process as I consider how their work speaks to my concerns in this book, but I turn to their description here because it includes a consequential feedback loop that is often left uncompleted in the hustle and bustle of program assessment: not just what is learned from an assessment but also what we do with our assessment knowledge once we have it. And it positions student reflection as key in this feedback loop. In another article, Allan, Dana Lynn Driscoll, D. R. Hammontree, Marshall Kitchens, and Lori Ostergaard (2015) describe this assessment process as a first step in "creat[ing] a culture of writing program research," a part of a set of program practices that improved department ethos and demonstrated program values in action:

> What we have learned from creating an inclusive model for research and professional development is that many of our contingent faculty members are eager for participation in program development and pedagogical research. They are also more willing to buy-in to program development if they feel invested in the work they are doing and are offered opportunities to engage

in meaningful research that contributes to our writing program's policies and curriculum and that helps all of us to improve our own classroom practices. This strengthens our program and encourages all of us to use more evidence-supported practices in our classrooms and curricular decision-making. By shifting our department culture from "I think" to "we know," we are also modeling the values we seek to instill in our students: sustained inquiry, active collaboration, critical analysis, and a rhetorical approach to writing. (Allan et al. 2015)

The overall design of this assessment process, as part of an overall departmental emphasis on research- and evidence-based teaching, brings both program values and teachers' (and students') voices into programmatic conversation and development (Allan et al. 2015).

Together, these two models, integrated into the practicum and then expanded to the program level, deepen the ways that individual instructors' experiential evidence is brought from one site of teacher development (like the practicum, or a teaching observation, or a teaching circle, or a committee meeting) into program talk and action, ideally creating "a synergy that infuse[s] reflective practice throughout the program" (Bamberg 2002, 153). Coordination of these two models resists the "compelled reflective writing" models Bartlett describes by structuring GTAs' collection of the data of their teacher-learning such that their collection and recollection, in both regular reflections and in final deliverables, serve not only individual teacher development but also program *change*.

In the coordinated model I first employed in fall 2023, GTAs write at least twice weekly in a personal teaching journal and twice weekly in a shared teaching journal, where we accumulate data for public teaching reflection with the entire instructional cohort as a potential audience. Concerned about ensuring the labor of this reflective writing is made both reasonable in the constraints of the two-credit practicum and meaningful in response to program initiatives, I structure these reflective writing moments in small chunks of time (approximately fifteen minutes each) across the week. In GTAs' personal journals, they both respond to prompted questions during class or for homework and write reflections whenever these feel necessary (a habit I describe and demonstrate in class). In the shared journal, GTAs submit anonymous responses to prompted questions in Google-based surveys at the beginning and end of the teaching week. In fall 2023, GTAs' writing in the shared journal provided individual GTAs with an opportunity to regularly reflect on their teaching and integration of labor-based grading practices, supporting their own work and our cohort's, on the micro-level, weekly decision-making required to engage in labor-based grading. In the subsequent semester, GTAs were invited to paid participation in a collaborative assessment activity examining their anonymous shared journal entries. This reflective writing was used to assess our program's integration of labor-based grading in nine sections of FYW (see also Jankens 2024). The experiential evidence provided by GTAs' reflections and in collaborative assessment sessions drove our approach to professional development for the entire instructor cohort prior to the program-wide rollout of labor-based grading. The outcome of GTAs' reflective practice in this design is a collective and recollective body of experiential evidence that serves individual and programmatic development.

The reflection and assessment practices described in this section are not new, but they are not always taken up either, and I see them as critical to engaging GTAs' experiences in larger program discussions. Reflection in the practicum is often used as a means to short-term ends: assessing the success of teaching activities or even assessing whether GTAs have met the learning goals of that course. Sometimes it is used even more narrowly: for individual teachers to reflect privately about their teaching challenges and successes. But if a program values written reflection as integral to teacher development across the teaching cohort, then written reflection in the practicum needs to have more meaningful, tangible stakes than just earning points for passing the class. It should validate micro-level decision-making as part of the reflective practice of teaching and it should provide GTAs with a consistent mechanism for contributing their experiential knowledge about this decision making, and their teaching generally, to the program machine.

Implications

As the examples of practicum structures at various sites showcased through interviews and my own classroom study demonstrate, the conditions for teacher development—and for writing program work generally—vary across institutions. And as working in writing programs in this pandemic and "post-" pandemic period has shown us, these conditions may change within writing programs rapidly. Intentional, values-driven change work, then, also often emerges out of necessity, urgency, and a need for responsive action. Cole and Hassel (2021) acknowledge, "Change work can be initiated locally, or it can be thrust upon us, but it cannot be avoided" (4). The interviews I conducted for chapter 2 suggest that what does seem to be an emergent value in practicum work is an emphasis on new GTAs' work with scholarship and instructional practice that matches the social-justice-oriented energies of the field. The practicum instructors I interviewed for the study in chapter 2 demonstrate both the often-individual nature of making change in the practicum and the strong potential for the energy originated in that course to instigate programmatic change. To that end, the narratives and analyses I have presented in this book present strategies and examples that while circulating around my local program's values for teacher development also suggest ways of articulating program values or engaging values-based discussions in other sites.

Teacher development in composition and writing studies is always responsive as much as it looks to the future. To do both, it must be anchored by an understanding of shared values. This understanding of shared values bolsters collaborative work and gives agency to new teachers—including teachers who may not see themselves as part of writing studies—inviting them into the work of enacting program values. When the practicum, specifically, is based in this collaborative *working-through*—this negotiation of experiential evidence, program values, and teaching practices, rather than through an inculcation of theories and methods—it positions teachers (new GTAs specifically) as do-ers in a writing program, as collaborative agents of (institutional) change. This structure also has the potential to subvert what Inoue (2021) calls the habits of white language—namely, hyperindividualism, the guise of objectivity, and emphasis on control—by emphasizing community impact, positionality, and interconnectedness (22–28); it may help us shape intersectional approaches to GTA training (see Shelton 2019, 30) that do not take instructional outcomes and experiences for granted. Thus, as the location wherein "new" GTAs are introduced to both the program and the discipline, the practicum can support teachers in engaging these practices in their own classrooms, graduate courses, administrative work, and service, and it can just as well learn from them.

While I have briefly discussed in this and earlier chapters attention to labor conditions and examples of approaches to antiracist writing instruction, I have not yet addressed in this chapter many other program values like those articulated by practicum instructors in chapter 2. Like I note in the end of that chapter, talking through the syllabi of a program's core courses—talking about values and then identifying whether and how they manifest in the program's written documents—is a worthwhile, forward-working, and collaborative activity for writing program personnel. Because program values may be tied to specific sites—like the values for teacher development explored across this book—selection of the artifacts that will serve as central to those discussions should be done in a contextual way. These discussions not only should consider the broader disciplinary context and scholarly movements of the time but must also take into account the very local conditions for teaching writing in which our individual writing programs work. Values are enacted in actual contexts and in the midst of material, institutional, and interpersonal tensions. So, to examine and reexamine and even revise them locally, is imperative.

In one quotation early in this chapter, I quote Asao B. Inoue (Lerner 2018, 116), commenting on the need to change the structures of our teaching work such that they match our values and beliefs, "our hearts and our intentions." It is no small load of work to begin by changing these structures such that in the material artifacts and classroom experiences students and new teachers will encounter, they will also find a means of enacting program values; it requires a depth of discussion and reflection and dialogue and question-asking and confidence. But we can shape the practicum classroom—and our committee work, and our curriculum development, and our other program sites—to include and to practice this values-focused, experience-focused conversation.

Summary of the Book

In writing through the studies of this book, I have sought the sometimes-elusive middle space between identifying a need for change and working, as a program, to move forward. Looking at this balance especially in light of teacher development, a primary area in which I spend my daily work life, has helped me, personally, to identify a means of enacting values-based work in my classroom instruction. I hope my examples of inquiry have been illustrative for readers who sense that while the big ideas have been established, we may need strategies for ways forward with attention to all aspects of our writing program ecologies. I further hope that my methodological stance, one that brings together frameworks of institutional ethnography, teacher development, and strategic contemplation in its employment of qualitative methods, has been experienced as intuitive and action oriented.

A significant part of this project has been to pin down, articulate, and enact *values for teacher development* through a series of qualitative methods and pedagogical interventions. I can see from talking with WPAs/practicum instructors and examining practicum syllabi that across programs we share several values for teacher development and how it is enacted. But it will take more work to gauge the manifestation of the broad disciplinary values cited by Wardle and Downs (2018), or the more specific values articulated by participants in this study, across programs. Writing program personnel bring with them a variety of individual values that may or may not be reconciled with each other (Jankens and Torok 2023, 67). So, while I have spoken with WPAs who teach the practicum, who else do we talk to in a program to gather a more comprehensive assessment of program values (and the ways these values manifest in teacher development)? What artifacts do we invite those personnel to consider in assessing their own program values? How do we name distinct potential values for quantification when their concerns may overlap? The five emergent values for teacher development explored through the various studies of this book are most certainly not all encompassing when we see iterative programmatic change in action. There are multiple questions we might continue to ask about values for teacher development: For example, if our programs value attention to linguistic diversity, and standard language ideologies are systemic, then shouldn't teacher development in composition be explicitly grounded in examination of language ideologies (see Bacon 2020; Baker-Bell 2020)? Continuing these inquiries with the responsive orientation I have taken in the studies of this book can just as well be effected in the day-to-day work (and programmatic design and revision) of teacher development.

In earlier chapters of this book, I worked to demonstrate how looking at teacher development in my home program more closely and with different questions illuminates possibilities for bringing the processes of and around teacher development in alignment with program values. While this examination often highlights cracks, shining a light on teacher development and poking around for program values has helped me identify structural possibilities for engaging programmatic change through sites of teacher development.

In chapter 1, this search for structural possibilities is demonstrated through the identification of emergent values for teacher development via the reading of a set of historical program artifacts tied to the composition teaching practicum. Rather than examining a distant history, I looked at artifacts created during the time I worked as part of the instructional cohort for the practicum, aiming to step outside of my own experiences to identify the values driving this work. This reading showed me both that there were evidently shared values for teacher development at work in the program, though these values were/are also tied up with tensions.

In chapter 2, I shifted from reading closely inside of my program to reading outside, specifically through conducting interviews with four WPAs who also taught their program's practicum courses and talking with them about the presence of program values in practicum syllabi. Our conversations and my analysis of practicum syllabi helped me see ways that not only are our efforts toward teacher development coordinated by shared values but also that across writing programs; the practicum functions as a site wherein practicum instructors and WPAs engage efforts toward programmatic change.

Reading and listening both inside and outside of my home program also prepared me to examine curriculum committee documents, as presented in the work of chapter 3. In that chapter, I read transcripts of the committee's meetings—held before the abrupt, pandemic-induced campus closure in March 2020—to understand how they are working through making recommendations about a common syllabus for the Practicum I course. While, as I note in that chapter, my position as a practicum instructor had me initially dismayed by some of the ultimate recommendations, rereading the transcripts with an eye toward the different knowledges at play allowed me to make recommendations about the roles of experiential knowledge in committee discussions. Identifying and working through the tensions evident in programmatic history and the experiential evidence offered in these discussions are part of the integral discursive and dialogic work that must happen within teacher development and alongside change work.

In chapter 4, these discussions happen in the context of my winter 2021 Practicum II course, a course in which we (GTAs and I) negotiated teaching online, teaching during the pandemic, teaching a new curriculum, and teaching with attention to critical language awareness and linguistic diversity. The sometimes aligned and sometimes conflicting demands of these teaching pressures coalesce in GTAs' offerings in classroom discussions to demonstrate the ways that teachers may work to integrate values-based program initiatives while they also express significant concerns about their power and position in doing so.

This final chapter's proposal for attention to micro-level changes thus positions sustainable, values-driven programmatic change within the purview of sites of teacher development, like the practicum. Supporting teachers in making the decisions that will impact their day-to-day program work is supporting change-makers who feel they understand program values. And change makers are both responsive to present conditions and looking toward the future. While teacher development efforts in our writing programs are, in part, engaged to initiate new teachers into the local work of teaching writing and into the conversations and emphases of the field, they are also significant coordinates in writing programs' steps toward administrative, curricular, and, most important, as we consider why we do what we do, social change.

APPENDIX
Semi-Structured Interview Protocol (excerpt)

Interviews with WPAs and Practicum Instructors
1. How is your semester going so far? What classes are you teaching or projects are you managing?
2. Because a primary goal of this study is to understand how WPAs articulate the values of their writing programs, I want to start there before we look at anything. **I'm defining values as the principles that guide your decision-making as a program or represent your standards for the work of your program.** What would you say are the core values of your writing program?
    a. [ask follow-up questions as needed for elaboration]
3. Thank you again for sharing your syllabus with me. I spent some time reading it to understand the outcomes of the course and the learning strategies built into it. Something I am noticing as very important in the way students spend time in the course is ... [insert a specific observation] ... Talk to me about why you structure assignments or projects in that way.
4. [insert questions specific to this instructor's syllabus]
5. How are the learning outcomes for this course similar to or different from the learning outcomes of other graduate level courses in your program?

6. What is similar between the ways you teach this course (or see this course being taught, as evident in this syllabus) and the ways you teach other graduate courses in writing studies? What is different?
7. In looking at the syllabus today, how do you see your program's values emphasized in this document?
    b. Are there ways you think program values manifest in the activities of the course, even though they are not evident in the document?
    c. When you think about what is important to the field of writing studies as a discipline—to our research practices, scholarly agendas, teacher development, and other work—do you see any of those values represented in this document?
8. What do you think GTAs walk out of this class understanding best about the work of our field?
9. Is there anything else you would like to say about the document(s) or about the values of your writing program?
10. Is there anything else you'd like to say in general, or to ask me?

Notes

Introduction

1. I will use *writing studies* as a broad term for the discipline in this book.
2. Espedal et al.'s (2022) *Researching Values: Methodological Approaches for Understanding Values Work in Organisations and Leadership* is exactly the book I would have loved to have at the beginning of my research in 2020!
3. Simon Sinek, "How Great Leaders Inspire Action," *TED*, September 2009, https://www.ted.com/talks/simon_sinek_how_great_leaders_inspire_action.

Chapter 1: Looking Back (and) to the Future

1. Since that year, GTAs have taught a 1/2 load their first year and a 2/1 load each subsequent year.

Chapter 2: Finding Values in the Practicum Syllabus in Interviews with WPAs and Practicum Instructors

1. This study was approved by my university's Institutional Review Board (IRB-20-12-3065).
2. Asao B. Inoue's blog post on this forthcoming statement, posted a few months before my interview with Stephanie, may be found here: http://asaobinoue.blogspot.com/2021/06/first-year-composition-goals-statement.html.

216 : NOTES

Chapter 3: Getting to Slow Agency via Slowing Conversation in Curricular Committee Work

1. This study (IRB-20-01-1674) was reviewed and approved by my university's Institutional Review Board.
2. In the year following data collection for this study, full-time, NTT lecturers at my university were appropriately and necessarily retitled (assistant or associate) professors of teaching as a result of union negotiations. I retain the title *lecturers* in this chapter as a matter of historical detail. Similarly, we elected to revise our doctoral program title from rhetoric and composition, to rhetoric and writing studies (RWS) to better capture the ways that our actual coursework prepared students for work in the field. However, during data collection for this study, we were still a *rhet/comp* program, and that term is present in the committee's discussion. As of the writing of this chapter, over a year into being *RWS*, we have managed some uptake of the new title among program insiders but across the department are still often referred to as "rhet/comp" or in meeting notes "RC."
3. We have published some descriptions of this committee work (e.g., Risse et al. 2012; Wallis and Jankens 2017; Jankens and Torok 2023; and others).
4. At the point of final manuscript preparation, the link in the committee's documents does not lead to an article with this title.

Chapter 4: "But Here We Are!" Still Learning How to Teach About Language

Epigraph: While the author's Twitter account has been deleted since September 2021, I received email permission from the author to include this tweet.

1. This study was approved by my university's Institutional Review Board: IRB-20-12-3027.
2. In AY 2023–2024, we further revised this curriculum, developing a schedule with lessons on language and voice in scholarly literature reviews and literature reviews designed for a range of audiences.
3. One analytical impulse I did not follow in my work for this study was to analyze the speaking time of each participant in Practicum II for each recorded class session. Salinas et al.'s (2021) demonstration of this kind of study uses "automated analysis of speech data" to look at a much larger sample of undergraduate students. The authors report the value of equitable speaking time (during coherent discussions) for collaborative activities. This remains interesting to me for assessing group discussion in online classes, but the phenomenon was really outside of the purview of my study.

Chapter 5: Between Mission and Action

1. The book I found online is Stefan Kühl's (2018) *Developing Mission Statements: A Very Brief Introduction*, from Organizational Dialogue Press. I do not present more on Kühl's work in this chapter, because I veer away from attention to statements into attention to action, and do not study the mission statements of writing programs or their processes of developing these. A point Kühl makes about the audience of mission statements, including both those external to the organization and internal to it, does factor into the work I am doing in this chapter: "Staff have only a limited interest in an attractive front because their everyday work grants them views and glimpses of the organization's backstage life. From this perspective, mission statements often have an off-putting effect on an organization's own employees because it presents to them an airbrushed front that is meant for external audiences and has little to do with the backstage that they know is closer to reality" (57). In this chapter, I look more at how we can work effectively "backstage" in the stage play of teacher development to activate writing program missions.

References

Addison, Joanne. 2005. "The Teaching Practicum as a Site of Inquiry and Action." In *Don't Call It That: The Composition Practicum*, edited by Sidney I. Dobrin, 256–265. Urbana, IL: NCTE.

Adler-Kassner, Linda. 2016. "What Is Principle?" In *A Rhetoric for Writing Program Administrators*, edited by Rita Malenczyk, 460–472. 2nd ed. Anderson: Parlor Press, 2016.

Adler-Kassner, Linda, and Elizabeth Wardle, eds. 2015. *Naming What We Know: Threshold Concepts of Writing Studies*. Logan: Utah State University Press.

Allan, Elizabeth G., and Dana Lynn Driscoll. 2014. "The Three-Fold Benefit of Reflective Writing: Improving Program Assessment, Student Learning, and Faculty Professional Development." *Assessing Writing* 21: 37–55.

Allan, Elizabeth G., Dana Lynn Driscoll, D. R. Hammontree, Marshall Kitchens, and Lori Ostergaard. 2015. "The Source of Our Ethos: Using Evidence-Based Practices to Affect a Program-Wide Shift from 'I Think' to 'We Know.'" *Composition Forum* 32 (Fall). https://compositionforum.com/issue/32/oakland.php.

Amador, José A., and Helen Mederer. 2013. "Migrating Successful Student Engagement Strategies Online: Opportunities and Challenges Using Jigsaw Groups and Problem-Based Learning." *Journal of Online Teaching and Learning* 9 (1): 89–105.

Anson, Chris M., and Robert L. Brown Jr. 1999. "Subject to Interpretation: Researching the Textual Representation of Writing Programs and Its Effects on the Politics of Administration." In *The Writing Program Administrator as Researcher: Inquiry in*

Action and Reflection, edited by Shirley K. Rose and Irwin Weiser, 141–152. Portsmouth, NH: Heinemann/Boynton-Cook.

Antiracist Language and Literacy Practices Research Team. 2022. "Research Team Values and Practices Draft." Unpublished document.

Association of College and Research Libraries. 2016. "Framework for Information Literacy for Higher Education." American Library Association. Accessed January 18, 2025. https://www.ala.org/sites/default/files/acrl/content/issues/infolit/Framework_ILHE.pdf.

Bacon, Chris K. 2020. "'It's Not Really My Job': A Mixed Methods Framework for Language Ideologies, Monolingualism, and Teaching Emergent Bilingual Learners." *Journal of Teacher Education* 71 (2): 172–187.

Baker-Bell, April. 2020. *Linguistic Justice: Black Language, Literacy, Identity, and Pedagogy*. New York: NCTE-Routledge.

Ball, Cheryl, and Drew M. Loewe, eds. 2017. *Bad Ideas About Writing*. Morgantown: West Virginia University Libraries. https://textbooks.lib.wvu.edu/badideas/badideasaboutwriting-book.pdf.

Bamberg, Betty. 2002. "Creating a Culture of Reflective Practice." In *Preparing College Teachers of Writing: Histories, Theories, Programs, Practices*, edited by Betty P. Pytlik and Sarah Liggett, 147–158. Oxford: Oxford University Press.

Bartlett, Lesley Erin. 2022. "Performing Reflection in Institutional Contexts: A Genre Approach to Compelled Reflective Writing." In *Writing the Classroom: Pedagogical Documents as Rhetorical Genres*, edited by Stephen E. Neaderhiser, 212–228. Logan: Utah State University Press.

Beaufort, Anne. 2007. *College Writing and Beyond: A New Framework for University Writing Instruction*. Logan: Utah State University Press.

Beavers, Melvin. 2021. "Reimagining the Possibilities: A Narrative Account of a Journey Toward Anti-Racist Administration." *WPA: Writing Program Administration* 44 (3): 155–157.

Belanger, Kelly, and Sibylle Gruber. 2005. "Unraveling Generative Tensions in the Composition Practicum." In *Don't Call It That: The Composition Practicum*, edited by Sidney I. Dobrin, 113–140. Urbana, IL: NCTE.

Berchini, Christina. 2015. "Why Are All the Teachers White?" *Education Week*, April 28. https://www.edweek.org/leadership/opinion-why-are-all-the-teachers-white/2015/04.

Black, Laurel, and Mary Ann Cessna. 2003. "Teaching Circles: Making Inquiry Safe for Faculty." *Essays on Teaching Excellence: Toward the Best in the Academy* 14 (3). https://digitalcommons.unl.edu/cgi/viewcontent.cgi?article=1122&context=podarchives.

Blakeslee, Ann, and Cathy Fleischer. 2019. *Becoming a Writing Researcher*. 2nd ed. New York: Routledge.

Borgman, Jesse, and Casey McArdle. 2019. *Personal, Accessible, Responsive, and Strategic: Resources and Strategies for Online Writing Instructors*. Fort Collins, CO: WAC Clearinghouse and University Press of Colorado.

Boudreau Smith, Nicole. 2017. "A Principled Revolution in the Teaching of Writing." *English Journal* 106 (5): 70–75.

Branson, Tyler S., and James Chase Sanchez. 2021. "Programmatic Approaches to Antiracist Writing Program Policy." *WPA: Writing Program Administration* 44 (3): 71–76.

Brent, Douglass. 2013. "The Research Paper and Why We Should Still Care." *WPA: Writing Program Administration* 37 (1): 33–53.

Brereton, John. 1981. "The Doctorate in Composition at Wayne State University." *Journal of Basic Writing* 3 (2): 14–22.

Brewer, Meaghan. 2020a. *Conceptions of Literacy: Graduate Instructors and the Teaching of First-Year Composition*. Logan: Utah State University Press.

Brewer, Meaghan. 2020b. "The Limits of Neutrality: How New Graduate Instructors Negotiate Politics, Race, and Ideology in the Composition Classroom." In *On Teacher Neutrality: Politics, Praxis, and Performativity*, edited by Daniel P. Richards, 27–40. Logan: Utah State University Press.

Burnham, Chris, and Rebecca Jackson. 2002. "Experience and Reflection in Multiple Contexts: Preparing TAs for the Artistry of Professional Practice." In *Preparing College Teachers of Writing: Histories, Theories, Programs, Practices*, edited by Betty P. Pytlik and Sarah Liggett, 159–170. Oxford: Oxford University Press.

Carillo, Ellen C. 2021. *The Hidden Inequities in Labor-Based Contract Grading*. Logan: Utah State University Press.

Carroll, Laura Bolin. 2010. "Backpacks vs. Briefcases: Steps Toward Rhetorical Analysis." In *Writing Spaces: Readings on Writing*. Vol. 1. Fort Collins, CO: WAC Clearinghouse; West Lafayette, IN: Parlor Press. https://wac.colostate.edu/docs/books/writingspaces1/carroll--backpacks-vs-briefcases.pdf.

Carter-Tod, Sheila. 2021. "Why So Few of US: Addressing Larger Issues of Systemic Exclusions That Limit the Numbers of Black Writing Program Administrators." *WPA: Writing Program Administration* 44 (3): 49–55.

Cicchino, Amy. 2020. "A Broader View: How Doctoral Programs in Rhetoric and Composition Prepare Their Graduate Students to Teach Composition." *WPA: Writing Program Administration* 44 (1): 86–106.

Cole, Kirsti, and Holly Hassel. 2021. "Introduction: Transformations in a Changing Landscape." In *Transformations: Change Work Across Writing Programs, Pedagogies, and Practices*, edited by Holly Hassel and Kirsti Cole, 3–16. Utah State University Press.

Collopy, Trisha. 2020. "Pivoting in a Pandemic: Online Writing Strategies to Help Us All 'Do It Better.'" *Council Chronicle* 30 (2): 22–25.

Comer, Denise K. 2011. "Bending the Gaze: Transparency, Reciprocity, and Supervisory Classroom Visits." *Pedagogy* 1 (3): 517–537.

Condon, Frankie, and Vershawn Ashanti Young. 2017. "Introduction." In *Performing Antiracist Pedagogy in Rhetoric, Writing, and Communication*, edited by Frankie Condon and Vershawn Ashanti Young, 3–16. Fort Collins, CO: WAC Clearinghouse and University Press of Colorado.

Conference on College Composition and Communication. 1974. "Students' Right to Their Own Language." https://cccc.ncte.org/cccc/resources/positions/srtolsummary.

Conference on College Composition and Communication. 2015. "CCCC Statement on Preparing Teachers of College Writing." https://cccc.ncte.org/cccc/resources/positions/statementonprep.

Conference on College Composition and Communication. 2020. "This Ain't Another Statement! This Is a DEMAND for Black Linguistic Justice!" https://cccc.ncte.org/cccc/demand-for-black-linguistic-justice.

Conference on College Composition and Communication. 2021a. "CCCC Statement on Recent Violent Crimes Against Asians, Asian Americans, and Pacific Islanders." https://cccc.ncte.org/cccc/recent-violent-crimes-against-asians-asian-americans-and-pacific-islanders/.

Conference on College Composition and Communication. 2021b. "CCCC Statement on White Language Supremacy." https://cccc.ncte.org/cccc/white-language-supremacy.

Conners, Patricia E. 1990. "The History of Intuition and Its Role in the Composing Process." *Rhetoric Society Quarterly* 20 (1): 71–78.

Costello, Kristi Murray, and Jacob Babb. 2020. "Introduction: Emotional Labor, Writing Studies, and Writing Program Administration." In *The Things We Carry: Strategies for Recognizing and Negotiating Emotional Labor in Writing Program Administration*, edited by Courtney Adams Wooten, Jacob Babb, Kristi Murray Costello, and Kate Navickas, 3–16. Logan: Utah State University Press.

Council of Writing Program Administrators. 2014. "WPA Outcomes Statement for First-Year Composition (v3.0)." https://wpacouncil.org/aws/CWPA/pt/sd/news_article/243055/_PARENT/layout_details/false.

Council of Writing Program Administrators, National Council of Teachers of English, and the National Writing Project. 2011. *Framework for Success in Postsecondary Writing*. https://wpacouncil.org/aws/CWPA/asset_manager/get_file/350201?ver=7548.

Courtney, Jabari. 2018. "The Aging of the N-Word." *VOXATL*, December 5.

Creswell, John W., and J. David Creswell. 2018. *Research Design: Qualitative, Quantitative, and Mixed Methods Approaches*. 5th ed. Los Angeles: Sage Publications, Inc.

Dardello, Andrea. 2019. "Breaking the Silence of Racism and Bullying in Academia: Leaning in to a Hard Truth." In *Defining, Locating, and Addressing Bullying in the WPA Workplace*, edited by Cristyn L. Elder and Bethany Davila, 102–123. Logan: Utah State University Press.

Davies, Laura J. 2013. "Taking the Long View: Investigating the History of a Writing Program's Teacher Evaluation System." *WPA: Writing Program Administration* 37 (1): 81–111.

Diab, Rasha, Thomas Ferrel, Beth Godbee, and Neil Simpkins. 2017. "Making Commitments to Racial Justice Actionable." In *Performing Antiracist Pedagogy in Rhetoric, Writing, and Communication*, edited by Frankie Condon and Vershawn Ashanti Young, 19–40. Fort Collins, CO: WAC Clearinghouse and University Press of Colorado.

Diab, Rasha, Beth Godbee, Cedric Burrows, and Thomas Ferrel. 2019. "Rhetorical and Pedagogical Interventions for Countering Microaggressions." *Pedagogy* 19 (3): 455–481.

Dobrin, Sidney I. 2005. *Don't Call It That: The Composition Practicum*. Urbana, IL: NCTE.
Donahue, Christiane. 2016. "What Is WPA Research?" In *A Rhetoric for Writing Program Administrators*, edited by Rita Malenczyk, 447–459. 2nd ed. Anderson, SC: Parlor Press.
Dong, Yu Ren. 2008. "Productive Tensions: Student Teachers' Handling of Sociocognitive Conflicts During the Classroom Discussion." *English Education* 40 (3): 231–255.
Driscoll, Dana Lynn. 2011. "Introduction to Primary Research: Observations, Surveys, and Interviews." In *Writing Spaces: Readings on Writing*. Vol. 2, edited by Charles Lowe and Pavel Zemliansky, 153–174. Anderson, SC: Parlor Press.
Driscoll, Dana Lynn, S. Rebecca Leigh, and Nadia Francine Zamin. 2020. "Self-Care as Professionalization: A Case for Ethical Doctoral Education in Composition Studies." *College Composition and Communication* 71 (3): 453–480.
Dryer, Dylan B. 2012. "At a Mirror Darkly: The Imagined Undergraduate Writers of Ten Novice Composition Instructors." *College Composition and Communication* 63 (3): 420–452.
Dunbar, Mitra, and W. Douglas Baker. 2014. "Teaching as Emotional Labor: Preparing to Interact with All Students." *Language Arts Journal of Michigan* 30 (1): 32–40.
Ebest, Sally Barr. 2002. "When Graduate Students Resist." *WPA: Writing Program Administration* 26 (1/2): 27–43.
Ebest, Sally Barr. 2005. *Changing the Way We Teach: Writing and Resistance in the Training of Teaching Assistants*. Carbondale: Southern Illinois University Press.
Elbow, Peter. 1973. *Writing Without Teachers*. Oxford: Oxford University Press.
Emerson, Robert M., Rachel I. Fretz, and Linda L. Shaw. 2011. *Writing Ethnographic Field Notes*. 2nd ed. Chicago: University of Chicago Press.
Espedal, Gry, Beate Jelstad Løvaas, Stephen Sirris, and Arild Wærass. 2022. *Researching Values: Methodological Approaches for Understanding Values Work in Organisations and Leadership*. Cham, Switzerland: Palgrave MacMillan.
Fedukovich, Casie J., Susan Miller-Cochran, Brent Simoneaux, and Robin Snead. 2017. "A State of Permanent Contingency: Writing Programs, Hiring Practices, and a Persistent Breach of Ethics." In *Labored: The State(ment) and Future of Work in Composition*, edited by Randall McClure, Dayna V. Goldstein, and Michael A. Pemberton, 126–146. Anderson, SC: Parlor Press.
Fleischer, Cathy. 1995. *Composing Teacher-Research: A Prosaic History*. Albany: State University of New York Press.
Fleischer, Cathy. 2004. "Professional Development for Teacher-Writers." *Educational Leadership* 62 (2): 24.
Foley-Schramm, Ashton, Bridget Fullerton, Eileen M. James, and Jenna Morton-Aiken. 2018. "Preparing Graduate Students for the Field: A Graduate Student Praxis Heuristic for WPA Professionalization and Institutional Politics." *WPA: Writing Program Administration* 21 (2): 89–103.
Formo, Dawn, and Kimberly Robinson Nealy. 2020. "Threshold Concepts and FYW Writing Prompts: Helping Students Discover Composition's Common Knowledge with(in) Assignment Sheets." *Teaching English in the Two-Year College* 47 (4): 335–354.

Freeman, Donald, and Steve Cornwell, eds. 1993. *New Ways in Teacher Education*. Alexandria, VA: Teachers of English to Speakers of Other Languages.

Germano, William, and Kit Nicholls. 2020. *Syllabus: The Remarkable, Unremarkable Document That Changes Everything*. Princeton, NJ: Princeton University Press.

Glenn, Cheryl. 2018. "At the Intersection of Feminism, Rhetoric, and Writing Program Administration." In *Academic and Professional Writing in an Age of Accountability*, edited by Shirley Wilson Logan and Wayne H. Slater, 108–127. Carbondale: Southern Illinois University Press.

Goleman, Judith. 2002. "Educating Literacy Instructors: Practice Versus Expression." In *Preparing College Teachers of Writing: Histories, Theories, Programs, Practices*, edited by Betty P. Pytlik and Sarah Liggett, 86–96. Oxford: Oxford University Press.

Gorzelsky, Gwen. 2013. "Experiential Knowledge: How Literacy Practices Seek to Mediate Personal and Systemic Change." *College English* 75 (4): 398–419.

Grabill, Jeffrey T., Sarah Gretter, and Erik Skogsberg. 2022. *Design for Change in Higher Education*. Baltimore: Johns Hopkins University Press.

Grant, Adam. 2016. *Originals: How Non-Conformists Move the World*. New York: Penguin.

Gray, Lisa M., Gina Wong-Wylie, Gwen R. Rempel, and Karen Cook. 2020. "Expanding Qualitative Research Interviewing Strategies: Zoom Video Communications." *Qualitative Report* 25 (5): 1292–1301.

Grouling, Jennifer. 2015. "Resistance and Identity Formation: The Journey of the Graduate Student-Teacher." *Composition Forum* 32. https://compositionforum.com/issue/32/resistance.php.

Grouling, Jennifer. 2018. "Training Writing Teachers: An Assignment in Mapping Writing Program Values." *Prompt* 2 (1): 5–16.

Guerra, Juan C., and Anis Bawarshi. 2005. "Managing Transitions: Reorienting Perceptions in a Practicum Course." In *Don't Call It That: The Composition Practicum*, edited by Sidney I. Dobrin, 43–66. Urbana, IL: NCTE.

Halbritter, Bump, and Julie Lindquist. 2018. "It's Never About What It's About: Audio-Visual Writing, Experiential-Learning Documentary, and the Forensic Art of Assessment." In *The Routledge Book of Digital Writing and Rhetoric*, edited by Jonathan Alexander and Jacqueline Rhodes, 317–327. New York: Routledge.

Hansen, Kristine. 2018. "Discipline and Profession: Can the Field of Rhetoric and Writing Be Both?" In *Composition, Rhetoric, and Disciplinarity*, edited by Rita Malenczyk, Susan Miller-Cochran, Elizabeth Wardle, and Kathleen Blake Yancey, 134–158. Logan: Utah State University Press.

Hesse, Douglas. 2012. "Writing Program Research: Three Analytic Axes." In *Writing Studies Research in Practice: Methods and Methodologies*, edited by Lee Nickoson and Mary P. Sheridan, 140–157. Carbondale: Southern Illinois University Press.

Hewett, Beth L. 2015a. *The Online Writing Conference: A Guide for Teachers and Tutors*. Boston: Bedford/St. Martin's.

Hewett, Beth L. 2015b. *Reading to Learn and Writing to Teach: Literacy Strategies for Online Writing Instruction*. Boston: Bedford/St. Martin's.

Hsieh, Hsiu-Fang, and Sarah E. Shannon. 2005. "Three Approaches to Qualitative Content Analysis." *Qualitative Health Research* 15 (9): 1277–1288.

Huntley, Lu Ellen. 2005. "Finding Myself Lost in the Composition Practicum Course." In *Don't Call It That: The Composition Practicum*, edited by Sidney I. Dobrin, 284–300. Urbana, IL: NCTE.

Inman, Joyce Olewski, and Rebecca A. Powell. 2018. "In the Absence of Grades: Dissonance and Desire in Course-Contract Classrooms." *College Composition and Communication* 70 (1): 30–56.

Inoue, Asao B. 2015. *Antiracist Writing Ecologies: Teaching and Assessing Writing for a Socially Just Future*. Anderson, SC: Parlor Press and WAC Clearinghouse.

Inoue, Asao B. 2019a. "2019 CCCC Chair's Address: How Do We Language So People Stop Killing Each Other, or What Do We Do About White Language Supremacy?" *College Composition and Communication* 71 (2): 352–369.

Inoue, Asao B. 2019b. "Afterword: Who Is Served, and Gets Served, in WPA Work?" In *Black Perspectives in Writing Program Administration*, edited by Staci M. Perryman-Clark and Collin Lamont Craig, 141–153. N.p.: CCCC/NCTE.

Inoue, Asao B. 2019c. "Classroom Writing Assessment as an Antiracist Practice: Confronting White Supremacy in the Judgments of Language." *Pedagogy* 19 (3): 373–404.

Inoue, Asao B. 2021. *Above the Well: An Antiracist Literacy Argument from a Boy of Color*. Fort Collins, CO: WAC Clearinghouse and University Press of Colorado.

Jackson, Austin, and Geneva Smitherman. 2002. "'Black People Tend to Talk Eubonics': Race and Curricular Diversity in Higher Education." In *Strategies for Teaching First-Year Composition*, edited by Duane Roen, Lauren Yena, Veronica Pantoja, Eric Waggoner, and Susan K. Miller, 46–51. Urbana, IL: NCTE.

Jankens, Adrienne. 2013. "ENG 1020 website discussion." YouTube video, July 14. https://youtu.be/DiFE6JHRL08.

Jankens, Adrienne. 2024. "Writing the Story of Labor-Based Grading at an Urban Research University." *CCCC 2024 Convention Companion Publication*. N.p.: NCTE/CCCC.

Jankens, Adrienne, and Nicole Guinot Varty. 2025. "Navigating 'A More Tense Area': A Response Team's Approaches to Conversations About Online Teaching During the Shift to Remote Instruction." In *WPAing in a Pandemic and Beyond: Revision, Innovation, and Advocacy*, edited by Todd Ruecker and Sheila Carter-Tod, 138–151. Logan: Utah State University Press.

Jankens, Adrienne, and Joe Torok. 2023. "Structuration and Genre: Revising Teaching Observations to Reflect Program Values." *Composition Studies* 51 (1): 65–90.

Jay, David, Sarah Etchells, and Stephanie Dimond-Bayir. 2021. "Pedagogical Literacies: A Hidden Benefit of the Jigsaw Technique." *Innovative Practice in Higher Education* 4 (2): 104–132. https://journals.staffs.ac.uk/index.php/ipihe/article/view/34.

Jones, Natasha, Laura Gonzales, and Angela M. Haas. 2021. "So You Think You're Ready to Build New Social Justice Initiatives? Intentional and Coalitional Pro-Black Programmatic and Organizational Leadership in Writing Studies." *WPA: Writing Program Administration* 44 (3): 29–34.

Kinloch, Valerie. 2020. "Not a Conclusion: Keeping Focused on Race, Justice, and Activism in Literacy Instruction." In *Race, Justice, and Activism in Literacy Instruction*, edited by Valerie Kinloch, Tanja Burkhard, and Carlotta Penn, 203–204. New York: Teachers College Press.

Kleinfeld, Elizabeth. 2019. "Reimagining Multimodality Through UDL: Inclusivity and Accessibility." In *Bridging the Multimodal Gap: From Theory to Practice*, edited by Santosh Khadka and J. C. Lee, 30–42. Logan: Utah State University Press.

Kynard, Carmen. 2019. "Administering While Black: Black Women's Labor in the Academy and the 'Position of the Unthought.'" In *Black Perspectives in Writing Program Administration*, edited by Staci M. Perryman-Clark and Collin Lamont Craig, 28–50. N.p.: CCCC/NCTE.

LaFrance, Michelle. 2019. *Institutional Ethnography: A Theory of Practice for Writing Studies Researchers*. Logan: Utah State University Press.

LaFrance, Michelle, and Elizabeth Wardle, eds. 2019. "Building a Twenty-First-Century Feminist Ethos: Three Dialogues for WPAs." *WPA: Writing Program Administration* 42 (2): 3–36.

Lamos, Steve. 2012. "Institutional Critique in Composition Studies: Methodological and Ethical Considerations for Researchers." In *Writing Studies Research in Practice: Methods and Methodologies*, edited by Lee Nickoson and Mary P. Sheridan, 158–170. Carbondale: Southern Illinois University Press.

Latterell, Catherine G. 1996. "Training the Workforce: An Overview of GTA Education Curricula." *WPA: Writing Program Administration* 19 (3): 7–23.

Lerner, Neal. 2018. "*WAC Journal* Interview of Asao B. Inoue." *WAC Journal* 29 (1): 112–118.

Lerner, Neal. 2019. *Reformers, Teachers, Writers: Curricular and Pedagogical Inquiries*. Logan: Utah State University Press.

Lebaron, John, and Diane Miller. 2005. "The Potential of Jigsaw Role Playing to Promote the Social Construction of Knowledge in an Online Graduate Education Course." *Teachers College Record*. https://doi.org/10.1111/j.1467-9620.2005.00537.x.

Lindquist, Julie, and Bump Halbritter. 2019. "Documenting and Discovering Learning: Reimagining the Work of the Literacy Narrative." *College Composition and Communication* 70 (3): 413–445.

Lindquist, Julie, Bree Straayer, and Bump Halbritter. 2023. *Recollections from an Uncommon Time: 4C20 Documentarian Tales*. N.p.: CCCC/NCTE; Fort Collins, CO: WAC Clearinghouse.

Macaulay, William J., Jr. 2021. "Introduction: Rhetoric and Composition TA Observed, Observing, Observer." In *Standing at the Threshold: Working Through Liminality in the Composition and Rhetoric TAship*, edited by William J. Macauley Jr., Leslie R. Anglesey, Brady Edwards, Kathryn M. Lambrecht, and Phillip Lovas, 3–11. Logan: Utah State University Press.

Macauley, William J., Jr., Leslie R. Anglesey, Brady Edwards, Kathryn M. Lambrecht, and Phillip Lovas, eds. 2021. *Standing at the Threshold: Working Through Liminality in the Composition and Rhetoric TAship*. Logan: Utah State University Press.

Malenczyk, Rita. 2016. "Introduction, with Some Rhetorical Terms." In *A Rhetoric for Writing Program Administrators*, edited by Rita Malenczyk, 3–8. 2nd ed. New York: Parlor Press.

Malenczyk, Rita, Susan Miller-Cochran, Elizabeth Wardle, and Kathleen Blake Yancey, eds. 2018. *Composition, Rhetoric, and Disciplinarity*. Logan: Utah State University Press.

Mapes, Aimee C., and Susan Miller-Cochran. 2019. "Framing Graduate Teaching Assistant Preparation Around Threshold Concepts of Writing Studies." In *(Re)Considering What We Know: Learning Thresholds in Writing, Composition, Rhetoric, and Literacy*, edited by Linda Adler-Kassner and Elizabeth Wardle, 208–226. Logan: Utah State University Press.

Marback, Richard. 1995. "Wayne State University, ENG 704: The Teaching of Writing." *Composition Studies* 23 (2): 98–103.

Martin, Wanda, and Charles Paine. 2002. "Mentors, Models, and Agents of Change: Veteran TAs Preparing Teachers of Writing." In *Preparing College Teachers of Writing: Histories, Theories, Programs, Practices*, edited by Betty P. Pytlik and Sarah Liggett, 222–232. Oxford: Oxford University Press.

Martinez, Aja Y. 2018. "The Responsibility of Privilege: A Critical Race Counterstory Conversation." *Peitho* 21 (1): 212–233.

Martinez, Aja Y. 2019. *Counterstory: The Rhetoric and Writing of Critical Race Theory*. Champaign, IL: CCCC/NCTE.

McBeth, Mark, and Tim McCormack. 2017. "An Apologia and a Way Forward: In Defense of the Lecturer Line in Writing Programs." In *Contingency, Exploitation, and Solidarity: Labor and Action in English Composition*, edited by Seth Kahn, William B. Lalicker, and Amy Lynch-Biniek, 41–55. Fort Collins, CO: WAC Clearinghouse and University Press of Colorado.

McMurtrie, Beth. 2018. "The Future of Learning and How It Could Change Your Classroom." *Chronicle of Higher Education*, May 17. https://www.chronicle.com/newsletter/teaching/2018-05-17.

McWhorter, John. 2019. "The Idea That Whites Can't Refer to the N-Word." *Atlantic*, August 27.

Merriam, Sharan B. 2009. *Qualitative Research: A Guide to Design and Implementation*. San Francisco: Jossey-Bass.

Meyer, Jan, and Ray Land. 2006. *Overcoming Barriers to Student Understanding: Threshold Concepts and Troublesome Knowledge*. New York: Routledge.

Micciche, Laura R. 2007. *Doing Emotion: Rhetoric, Writing, Teaching*. Portsmouth, NH: Boynton/Cook.

Micciche, Laura. 2011. "For Slow Agency." *WPA: Writing Program Administration* 35 (1): 73–90.

Miller, Susan Kay, Rochelle Rodrigo, Veronica Pantoja, and Duane Roen. 2005. "The Composition Practicum as Professional Development." In *Don't Call It That: The Composition Practicum*, edited by Sidney I. Dobrin, 82–97. Urbana, IL: NCTE.

Mitchell, Koritha. 2015. "I'm a Professor. My Colleagues Who Let Their Students Dictate What They Teach Are Cowards." *Vox*, June 10.

Mitchell, Koritha. 2018. "Teaching and the N-word: Questions to Consider." *Koritha Mitchell*. http://www.korithamitchell.com/teaching-and-the-n-word/.

Monroe, Stephen. 2021. "White Supremacists and Urgent Agency: Memories from a Writing Program Administrator." *WPA: Writing Program Administration* 44 (3): 68–70.

Norgaard, Rolf. 2017. "The Uncertain Future of Past Success: Memory, Narrative, and the Dynamics of Institutional Change." In *Contingency, Exploitation, and Solidarity: Labor and Action in English Composition*, edited by Seth Kahn, William B. Lalicker, and Amy Lynch-Biniek, 133–149. Fort Collins, CO: WAC Clearinghouse and University Press of Colorado.

Obermark, Lauren, Elizabeth Brewer, and Kay Halasek. 2015. "Moving from the One and Done to a Culture of Collaboration: Revising Professional Development for TAs." *WPA: Writing Program Administration* 39 (1): 32–53.

Odom, Mary Lou, Michael Bernard-Donals, and Stephanie L. Kerschbaum. 2005. "Enacting Theory: The Practicum as the Site of Invention." In *Don't Call It That: The Composition Practicum*, edited by Sidney I. Dobrin, 214–237. Urbana, IL: NCTE.

Osorio, Ruth, Jaclyn Fiscus-Cannaday, and Allison Hutchison. 2021. "Braiding Stories, Taking Action: A Narrative of Graduate Worker-Led Change Work." In *Transformations: Change Work Across Writing Programs, Pedagogies, and Practices*, edited by Holly Hassel and Kirsti Cole, 19–36. Logan: Utah State University Press.

Perryman-Clark, Staci M. 2016. "Who We Are(n't) Assessing: Racializing Language and Writing Assessment in Writing Program Administration." *College English* 79 (2): 206–211.

Perryman-Clark, Staci M. 2018. "Creating a United Front: A Writing Program Administrator's Institutional Investment in Language Rights for Composition Students." In *Academic and Professional Writing in an Age of Accountability*, edited by Shirley Wilson Logan and Wayne H. Slater, 168–184. Carbondale: Southern Illinois University Press.

Perryman-Clark, Staci M. 2019. "Race, Teaching Assistants, and Workplace Bullying: Confessions from an African-American Pre-Tenured WPA." In *Defining, Locating, and Addressing Bullying in the WPA Workplace*, edited by Cristyn L. Elder and Bethany Davila, 124–137. Logan: Utah State University Press.

Perryman-Clark, Staci M., and Collin Lamont Craig. 2019. "Introduction: Black Matters: Writing Program Administration in Twenty-First Century Higher Education." In *Black Perspectives in Writing Program Administration*, edited by Staci M. Perryman-Clark and Collin Lamont Craig, 1–27. N.p.: CCCC/NCTE, 2019.

Pimentel, Octavio, Charise Pimentel, and John Dean. 2017. "The Myth of the Colorblind Writing Classroom: White Instructors Confront White Privilege in Their Classrooms." In *Performing Antiracist Pedagogy in Rhetoric, Writing, and Communication*, edited by Frankie Condon and Vershawn Ashanti Young, 109–122. Fort Collins. CO: WAC Clearinghouse and University Press of Colorado.

Pinkert, Laurie A., and Kristen R. Moore. 2021. "Programmatic Mapping as a Problem-Solving Tool for WPAs." *WPA: Writing Program Administration* 44 (2): 58–79.

Poblete, Patti. 2014. "Battlegrounds and Common Grounds: First-Year Composition and Institutional Values." *Composition Forum* 30 (Fall). https://compositionforum.com/issue/30/battlegrounds.php.

Poe, Mya. 2017. "Reframing Race in Teaching Writing Across the Curriculum." In *Performing Antiracist Pedagogy in Rhetoric, Writing, and Communication*, edited by Frankie Condon and Vershawn Ashanti Young, 87–105. Fort Collins, CO: WAC Clearinghouse and University Press of Colorado.

Pruchnic, Jeff, and Chris Susak. 2015a. "White Paper on Composition Curricula (January 2015)." White Paper. Wayne State University, Detroit, MI.

Pruchnic, Jeff, and Chris Susak. 2015b. "White Paper on GTA Composition Practica (February 2015)." White Paper. Wayne State University, Detroit, MI.

Pruchnic, Jeff, and Chris Susak. 2015c. "White Paper on GTA Training (February 2015)." White Paper. Wayne State University, Detroit, MI.

Pytlik, Betty P., and Sarah Liggett. 2002. "Preface." In *Preparing College Teachers of Writing*, edited by Betty P. Pytlik and Sarah Liggett, xv–xxii. Oxford: Oxford University Press.

Ratcliffe, Krista. 2005. *Rhetorical Listening*. Carbondale: Southern Illinois University Press.

Ray, Ruth. 1992. "Composition from the Teacher-Researcher Point of View." In *Methods and Methodology in Composition Research*, edited by Gesa E. Kirsch and Patricia A. Sullivan, 172–189. Carbondale: Southern Illinois University Press.

Ray, Ruth. 1993. *The Practice of Theory: Teacher Research in Composition*. Urbana, IL: NCTE.

Ray, Ruth. 1996. "Afterword: Ethics and Representation in Teacher Research." In *Ethics and Representation in Qualitative Studies of Literacy*, edited by Peter Mortensen and Gesa E. Kirsch, 287–300. Urbana: NCTE.

Reid, E. Shelley. 2017. "On Learning to Teach: Letter to a New TA." *WPA: Writing Program Administration* 40 (2): 129–145.

Reid, E. Shelley, Heidi Estrem, and Marcia Belchier. 2012. "The Effects of Writing Pedagogy Education on Graduate Teaching Assistants' Approaches to Teaching Composition." *WPA: Writing Program Administration* 36 (1): 32–73.

Restaino, Jessica. 2012. *First Semester: Graduate Students, Teaching Writing, and the Challenge of Middle Ground*. Carbondale: Southern Illinois University Press.

Rice, Jeff. 2005. "The New Media Instructor: Cultural Capital and Writing Instruction." In *Don't Call It That: The Composition Practicum*, edited by Sidney I. Dobrin, 266–283. Urbana: NCTE.

Risse, Derek, Jeff Pruchnic, Joseph Paszek, David MacKinder, Adrienne Jankens, Jared Grogan, and Gwen Gorzelsky. 2012. "Introducing WAW: Grounding Negotiation in Assessment." *Writing About Writing Newsletter* 1 (1): 2–12.

Ritter, Kelly. 2018. "Undergraduate Rhetoric at UIUC: Revising a Curriculum, Rethinking a Program." In *Academic and Professional Writing in an Age of Accountability*, edited by Shirley Wilson Logan and Wayne H. Slater, 47–64. Carbondale: Southern Illinois University Press.

Rose, Shirley K. 1999. "Preserving Our Histories of Institutional Change: Enabling Research in the Writing Program Archives." In *The Writing Program Administrator as Researcher: Inquiry in Action and Reflection*, edited by Shirley K. Rose and Irwin Weiser, 107–118. Portsmouth, NC: Boynton/Cook.

Rose, Shirley K. 2016. "What Is a Writing Program History?" In *A Rhetoric for Writing Program Administrators*, edited by Rita Malenczyk, 287–299. 2nd ed. Anderson, SC: Parlor Press.

Royster, Jacqueline Jones, and Gesa E. Kirsch. 2012. *Feminist Rhetorical Practices: New Horizons for Rhetoric, Composition, and Literacy Studies*. Carbondale: Southern Illinois University Press.

Russell, Clare Jennifer. 2020. *Curricular Inquiry: A Survey of Writing Pedagogy Practicum Instructors*. Doctoral dissertation, Wayne State University, Detroit, MI. https://digitalcommons.wayne.edu/oa_dissertations/2425.

Saidy, Christina, and Thomas Sura. 2020. "When Everything Changes Overnight: What We Learned from Teaching the Writing Practicum in the Era of Covid-19." *Teaching/Writing: The Journal of Writing Teacher Education* 9 (1). https://scholarworks.wmich.edu/wte/vol9/iss1/21.

Saldaña, Johnny. 2016. *The Coding Manual for Qualitative Researchers*. 3rd ed. Los Angeles: Sage.

Salinas, Omar, Diego Monsalves, Fabián Riquelme, Roberto Muñoz, Cristian Cechinel, and Roberto Martinez-Maldonado. 2021. "Can Analytics of Speaking Time Serve as Indicators of Effective Team Communication and Collaboration?" *CLIHC 2021: X Latin American Conference on Human Computer Interaction*. https://dl.acm.org/doi/10.1145/3488392.3488404.

Sandy, Kirsti A. 2002. "After Preparing TAs for the Classroom, What Then? Three Decades of Conversation About Preparing TAs for the Job Market." In *Preparing College Teachers of Writing: Histories, Theories, Programs, Practices*, edited by Betty P. Pytlik and Sarah Liggett, 28–39. Oxford: Oxford University Press.

Schön, Donald A. 1983. *The Reflective Practitioner*. New York: Basic Books.

Schwaller, Emily Jo. 2022. "Rethinking Graduate Student Instructors' Resistance as Acts of Well-Being." *Composition Studies* 50 (2): 112–131.

Shelton, Cecilia. 2019. "Shifting Out of Neutral: Centering Difference, Bias, and Social Justice in a Business Writing Course." *Technical Communication Quarterly* 29 (1): 18–32.

Slinkard, Jennifer, and Jeroen Gevers. 2020. "Confronting Internalized Language Ideologies in the Writing Classroom: Three Pedagogical Examples." *Composition Forum* 44. https://compositionforum.org/issue/44/language-ideologies.php.

Smagorinsky, Peter, and Michael W. Smith. 1992. "The Nature of Knowledge in Composition and Literacy Understanding: The Question of Specificity." *Review of Educational Research* 62 (2): 279–305.

Smitherman, Geneva. 1977. *Talkin and Testifyin: The Language of Black America*. Detroit: Wayne State University Press.

Stenberg, Shari. 2005. *Professing and Pedagogy: Learning the Teaching of English*. Urbana, IL: NCTE.

Stenberg, Shari, and Amy Lee. 2002. "Developing Pedagogies: Learning the Teaching of English." *College English* 64 (3): 326–347.

Stevenson, Paulette. 2021. "Circulating NTTF Stories to Effect Change: The Case of ASU against 5/5." In *Transformations: Change Work Across Writing Programs, Pedagogies, and Practices*, edited by Holly Hassel and Kirsti Cole, 37–52. Logan: Utah State University Press.

Strickland, Donna. 2011. *The Managerial Unconscious in the History of Composition Studies*. Carbondale: Southern Illinois University Press.

Trubek, Anne. 2005. "Chickens, Eggs, and the Composition Practicum." In *Don't Call It That: The Composition Practicum*, edited by Sidney I. Dobrin, 160–182. Urbana, IL: NCTE.

University Center for Excellence in Teaching. 2025. "Transparency in Learning and Teaching (TILT)." Indiana University. Accessed January 12. https://iu.instructure.com/courses/1540449/pages/transparency-in-learning-and-teaching-tilt.

Vieira, Kate, Lauren Heap, Sandra Descourtis, Jonathan Isaac, Samitha Senanayake, Brenna Swift, Chris Castillo, Ann Meejung Kim, Kassia Krzus-Shaw, Maggie Black, Olá Oládipò, Xiaopei Yang, Patricia Ratanapraphart, Nikhil M. Tiwari, Lisa Velarde, and Gordon Blaine West. 2019. "Literacy Is a Sociohistoric Phenomenon with the Potential to Liberate and Oppress." In *(Re)Considering What We Know: Learning Thresholds in Writing, Composition, Rhetoric, and Literacy*, edited by Linda Adler-Kassner and Elizabeth Wardle, 36–55. Logan: Utah State University Press.

Wallis, Jule, and Adrienne Jankens. 2017. "Collaborative Development: Reflective Mentoring for GTAs." In *Writing Program and Writing Center Collaborations: Transcending Boundaries*, edited by Alice Myatt and Lynee Gaillet, 161–178. New York: Palgrave MacMillan.

Wardle, Elizabeth, and Doug Downs. 2018. "Understanding the Nature of Disciplinarity in Terms of Composition's Values." In *Composition, Rhetoric, and Disciplinarity*, edited by Rita Malenczyk, Susan Miller-Cochran, Elizabeth Wardle, and Kathleen Blake Yancey, 111–133. Logan: Utah State University Press.

Wayne State University Composition Program. 2018. "White Paper on GTA Course Assignments and Cross-Course Training." White Paper. Wayne State University, Detroit, MI.

Weiser, Irwin. 2002. "When Teaching Assistants Teach Teaching Assistants to Teach: A Historical View of a Teacher Preparation Program." In *Preparing College Teachers of Writing: Histories, Theories, Programs, Practices*, edited by Betty P. Pytlik and Sarah Liggett, 40–49. Oxford: Oxford University Press.

Wenger, Etienne. 1998. *Communities of Practice: Learning, Meaning, and Identity*. Cambridge: Cambridge University Press.

Wenger, Etienne, Richard McDermott, and William M. Snyder. 2002. *Cultivating Communities of Practice: A Guide to Managing Knowledge*. Boston: Harvard Business Review Press.

Wible, Scott. 2019. "Forfeiting Privilege for the Cause of Social Justice: Listening to Black WPAs and WPAs of Color Define the Work of White Allyship." In *Black Perspectives in Writing Program Administration: From the Margins to the Center*, edited by Staci M. Perryman-Clark and Collin Lamont Craig, 74–100. N.p.: CCCC/NCTE.

Winslow, Rosemary. 2005. "The GTA Writing Portfolio: An Impact Study of Learning by Writing." In *Don't Call It That: The Composition Practicum*, edited by Sidney I. Dobrin, 315–336. Urbana, IL: NCTE, 2005.

Wood, Shane. 2020. "Engaging in Resistant Genres as Antiracist Teacher Response." *Journal of Writing Assessment* 13 (2). https://escholarship.org/uc/item/2c45c0gf.

Wooten, Courtney Adams. 2020. "How to Be a Bad WPA." In *The Things We Carry: Strategies for Recognizing and Negotiating Emotional Labor in Writing Program Administration*, edited by Courtney Adams Wooten, Jacob Babb, Kristi Murray Costello, and Kate Navickas, 270–284. Logan: Utah State University Press.

Yancey, Kathleen Blake. 1998. *Reflection in the Writing Classroom*. Logan: Utah State University Press.

Yancey, Kathleen Blake. 2002. "The Professionalization of TA Development Programs: A Heuristic for Curriculum Design." In *Preparing College Teachers of Writing: Histories, Theories, Programs, Practices*, edited by Betty P. Pytlik and Sarah Liggett, 63–74. Oxford: Oxford University Press.

Yancey, Kathleen Blake. 2015. "Introduction: Coming to Terms: Composition/Rhetoric, Threshold Concepts, and a Disciplinary Core." In *Naming What We Know: Threshold Concepts of Writing Studies*, edited by Linda Adler-Kassner and Elizabeth Wardle, xvii–xxxi. Logan: Utah State University Press.

Young, Vershawn Ashanti. 2010. "Should Writers Use They Own English?" *Iowa Journal of Cultural Studies* 12 (1): 110–118. https://doi.org/10.17077/2168-569X.1095.

Young, Vershawn Ashanti. 2021. "CCCC 2020 Chair's Address: Say They Name in Black English: George Floyd, Breonna Taylor, Atatiana Jefferson, Aura Rosser, Trayvon Martin, and the Need to Move Away from Writing to Literacies in CCCC and Rhetoric and Composition." *College Composition and Communication* 72 (4): 623–639.

Zemeckis, Robert, dir. 1985. *Back to the Future*. Universal Pictures, 1 hour, 56 minutes.

Index

Above the Well, 12, 116
absence policies, 75, 80
accessibility: disciplinarity, 7, 64; institutional knowledge, 17, 107, 109, 198; multimodal composing, 152; program values, 64, 100, 106; research data, 47, 49, 82, 98, 110, 147–48; syllabi reading lists, 87, 123, 125; teaching writing, 92
accountability, Black graduate teaching assistants (GTAs), 156–57
action research projects, 191
action-oriented instruction, 180–81, 188
ad hoc committees, 106, 109
adjunct positions, 76, 77, 85, 86, 156, 189
Adler-Kassner, Linda, 7, 10, 48, 63, 132
administration labor: communities of practice, 97; composition studies instructors, 189; graduate teaching assistants (GTAs), 201–2; institutional change, 93; on-the-job training, 86; orientation, 24, 119–20, 130; portfolio evaluations, 35; program values, 25, 36, 38, 91; structures, 33; subjectivity, 134; syllabus language, 66; teacher development, 62; white papers, 36, 54
agency: change-making, 10; graduate teaching assistants (GTAs), 139, 177–78, 191, 209;

impact, 137; languaging, 167; mentoring relationships, 53; practicum instructors, 84; problem-solving, 100; rhetorical listening, 171, 175
agenda-driven curriculum, 40, 66, 95, 98, 137, 155–57, 179
Allan, Elizabeth G., 206–7
allyship, 143, 188, 194
analytic research framework, 21, 23
annual revisions to practicum courses, 26, 94
anonymity, research participants, 71–72, 111
Antiracist Writing Assessment Ecologies, 139
antiracist teaching: curricular revisions, 188, 195; emergent values, 166–69; inclusivity, 82; intermediate composition (IC), 140, 165; language practices, 14, 187; local commitment, 139; practicum courses, 26–27, 29, 84, 138, 150; program values, 13, 73, 74, 76, 91, 140–46, 194–95; reading assignments, 143, 153; white talk, 144; writing programs, 22, 25, 30–31, 165–66, 173, 175, 209
Arizona, University of, 16
articulation of values. *See* writing studies programs
assessment practices: antiracist teaching, 14, 139, 142, 144, 195; classroom writing, 152,

188; curriculum development, 189–90; faculty, 38; flexibility, 81; intersectional training, 143; local programs, 106; peer feedback, 12; problem-solving, 109; professionalization, 135; program values, 91; reflective writing, 68, 119, 127, 130–31, 203–8; revision, 188; teaching experiences, 199; white standards, 166–67
assignments: classroom practices, 51; development, 9; feedback, 175–77; grading, 12, 80, 158, 176; implicit values, 96; practicum courses, 49–50, 138–40, 200–201; reflection, 202; sharing, 13; teaching portfolios, 74
asynchronous learning, 33, 44, 79, 98, 111, 124, 150, 153, 158, 160, 163, 174
audience, 216n2 (chap. 4)
audio recordings, 109–11
author positioning, 152
authority, 19, 29, 53, 77, 78, 111, 140, 151, 168, 173, 177–78

Back to the Future, 32
Bad Ideas About Writing, 83
Baker-Bell, April, 145, 153, 154, 163, 164, 168
Baker, Nicki Litherland, 49
Baker, W. Douglas, 124
Ball, Cheryl, 48
Bamberg, Betty, 204–5
Bartholomae, David, 48, 125
Bartlett, Lesley Erin, 205, 207
Barton, Ellen, 40
basic writing courses, 39, 138
Bawarshi, Anis, 28, 35–36, 108
Beaufort, Anne, 105–7
Becker, Alton L., 103
behaviorism learning theory, 125
Belanger, Kelly, 185
Bergmann, Linda S., 48
Berlin, James, 125
Black faculty, 63, 143, 145, 155–57, 192, 194
Black Language, 76, 145, 153
Black Lives Matter, 93
Black, Laurel, 45
Borgman, Jessie, 52
boundary setting, 16, 26, 81, 101, 140, 151, 173–77
Branson, Tyler S., 195
Brent, Douglass, 124
Brewer, Elisabeth, 44
Brewer, Meghan, 141, 143, 145, 149, 180
Broad, Bob, 9
Brookfield, Stephen D., 48
bullying, 11, 117–18, 143
burnout, 26, 32, 47, 174

Cambourne, Brian, 3, 48, 58
care program value, 73, 74
Carillo, Ellen C., 80
Carroll, Laura Bolin, 48, 124
Carter-Tod, Sheila, 192
CCCC (Conference on College Composition and Communication), 63, 83, 93, 165–66, 169, 205
Cessna, Mary Ann, 45
challenges: cultural, 78; grading, 98; idiosyncrasy, 99, 133; mentor/mentees, 54; online teaching, 173, 181; positionality, 111; practicum scholarship, 16, 81; productive programmatic action, 11–12, 74; race work, 63; teaching topics, 33, 50–51, 166–68; writing program administration, 32
change-making. *See* programmatic change
Chickering, Arthur W., 125
Cicchino, Amy, 17, 67, 68, 87, 89–90, 146
classroom assessment ecology, 12, 80, 152, 188
classroom environment: antiracist teaching, 91, 139, 166; conflict, 126, 143, 179; discussion topics, 27, 143–44, 166–68; diversity/equity, 14, 141–42, 145; feedback loops, 162; marginalized theory, 51; minorities, 170–71; negotiation, 18, 21; observation, 77; online teaching, 18, 19, 30, 38, 78–81, 140, 180–82; programmatic changes, 5; relationship-building, 160; teacher talk, 178–79; teaching circles, 46–47; white privilege, 116, 144
co-construct knowledge, 57–58, 88, 89
coaching approach, 11
code-meshing, 152
coding, data collection and analysis, 9, 42, 70, 88, 89, 112
cognitive constructivism, 125
cohorts, 109, 190
Cole, Kirsti, 24, 64, 83, 192–93, 208–9
collaborative practices: assessment sessions, 208; coding, 70; cohorts, 109; criteria mapping, 9; curriculum design, 100–101, 106; equitable speaking time, 216n3 (chap. 4); institutional change, 195, 209; knowledge-making, 16, 202, 206; language ideologies, 51; practicum revision, 35–36; problem-solving, 78; professional development, 44; programmatic change, 195; reflective writing, 127, 130–31, 194; sharing materials, 57–58, 89, 124; teacher development, 15, 44, 89; teaching circles, 45–47; teaching, 190; textual analysis, 69
collective goals, 194
colorblind teaching practice, 144

Comer, Denise K., 6
committee work. *See* curriculum committees
common practices, institutional knowledge, 106–8, 112
common syllabus, 12, 21, 27–28, 34, 40–45, 56, 60, 98, 108–10, 121–25
communities of practice, 7, 97, 101–3, 154
community-engaged learning, 73, 74, 174–75, 189
community-specific knowledge, 105–6
compassion program value, 73, 74, 79, 80, 161, 172, 176, 180
complete/incomplete grading practice, 12, 80
composition studies: disciplinarity, 7; emergent values, 54–61, 88, 89, 127, 128–31; local programs, 36–37; pedagogy, 3, 39, 79; professionalization, 91–92; reading lists, 12, 48–49, 82; teaching circles, 45
composition teaching practicum. *See* practicum courses
composition theory, 47–50, 58, 67, 113
Composition, Rhetoric, and Disciplinarity, 7
Condon, Frankie, 141
Conference on College Composition and Communication (CCCC), 63, 83, 93, 165–66, 169, 205
conferencing model, 173–74, 198
Conners, Patricia, 103–4
contextual influences, 18–19
contract grading, 84, 158, 161–62, 175–76, 200
core instructional assignments, 190
core values, writing programs, 25–26, 73–74, 105
Counterstory, 145
Courtney, Jabari, 165, 166
COVID-19 pandemic, 212; curriculum committee, 101; first-year students, 38; grading practices, 80; intermediate composition (IC), 157–63; online teaching, 18, 19, 30, 38, 79–81, 140, 180–82; pandemic semester, 70; practicum curriculum, 139; research work, 198–99; teaching practices, 41, 79–81, 161–62, 173
Craig, Collin, 48
creative writing, 36, 118
credit hours, 39, 40, 60
criteria mapping, 9
critical colleagueship, 202
critical language awareness, 146, 191–92
critical reading program value, 73, 74
cross-disciplinarity, 15, 114
cross-institutional teacher training, 44–45
cultural context, 33, 76, 144
curricular intervention, 139

curricular resistance, 154
curricular structure perspective, 161
curricular tokenism, 50–51
curriculum committees: agendas, 110, 156–57; antiracist initiatives, 38, 142, 144, 188, 195; committee work, 216n3 (chap. 3), 216n4 (chap. 3); communities of practice, 97, 101, 102; decision-making process, 98–99; faculty, 109; feedback, 102; first-year writing (FYW), 10, 108–9, 118, 134, 189; institutional change, 93; intermediate composition (IC), 100–101, 140, 149–50, 151–55, 166–67, 181; knowledge domains, 17, 28, 99–100, 105, 111–18, 121–23, 133–36; language, 216n2 (chap. 4); local programs, 26–27, 105, 106, 127, 128, 134; mission statements, 194; origins, 33; program-prescribed, 157; question-asking and response, 134–35; reading lists, 123–25, 139–40; revision process, 24; shared program values, 27, 28; teacher development, 28, 108–9, 133, 186, 197, 212; vision statements, 194; voice, 216n2 (chap. 4); writing pedagogy (WPE), 146

daily work, 56, 108, 186
Dardello, Andrea, 11–12
data collection and analysis: classroom studies, 208; coding, 88, 89, 112; collaborative textual analysis, 69; course texts, 148; curricular committee, 26–28, 99; group discussions, 27; historical program documents, 21, 23, 41, 42, 50–54, 98, 203–4, 211; institutional ethnographers (IE), 21; interviews, 19, 28, 68, 72, 95–96, 213–14; note-taking, 147–48; observation, 98–99, 109–10; practicum syllabi, 87–88, 95–96; research participants, 29, 69, 71, 216n3 (chap. 4); recordings, 109–11, 147–48; strategic contemplation, 22–23; students' writing, 148; syllabus language, 19, 68; teaching journals, 131, 207–8; themes, 42–43; transcripts, 19, 21, 28–29, 49, 70, 77, 90, 95, 98, 103, 107, 110–12, 126, 134, 148, 165; writing pedagogy education (WPE), 67
Davies, Laura J., 35
day-to-day program work, 212
Dean, John, 144
decision-making process, 98–99, 108, 172, 208
deep listening, 27
defective language view, 164
democratic methods, programmatic change, 192, 193
demographics, research participants, 149
department administration, 11–12, 18, 190

design-based problem-solving, 195
Design for Change in Higher Education, 195
Developing Mission Statements: A Very Brief Introduction, 216n1 (chap. 5)
Dewey, John, 125
dialectical teacher development model, 143
dialogical teacher development model, 143
digital archives, 106
digital literacy, 39, 52, 174, 179
Dinan, John, 3
disciplinary frameworks: claiming, 187–88; curriculum, 132–33; emergent values, 58; graduate teaching assistants (GTAs), 16, 55, 58–59; intermediary roles, 95; knowledge, 16–17, 105; pedagogy, 3; position statements, 10, 58–59, 63, 83, 93, 127, 132; reading assignments, 49, 151; scholarly writing process, 149; scholarship, 4, 99, 108; shared values, 7, 64, 87; teacher development, 6, 70, 88, 89–90; teaching practices, 58; textual production, 7; writing programs, 7, 26, 33
discourse communities, 106, 143, 149, 156, 164, 176, 193
discussion boards, student engagement, 174
disregard, institutional knowledge, 23–24
disruption of power structures, 12, 184, 185
dissertation completion, 54
divergent values, 45–47, 62, 115
diversity and inclusion, 13–14, 64, 72, 82–83, 115–16, 141, 188, 193–94
Dobrin, Sidney I., 4, 17, 39, 87, 108, 197
doctoral programs, 36–37
domain of knowledge, 102
dominant English, 166–67
Don't Call It That, 39, 108
Dong, Yu Ren, 143, 179
Downs, Doug, 7, 10, 64, 92, 197, 210–11
Driscoll, Dana Lynn, 206–7
Dryer, Dylan B., 115
Duffy, Will, 138
Dunbar, Mitra, 124
dynamic criteria mapping, 9

Ebest, Sally Barr, 114
educational theory, 99, 124–25, 134
Elbow, Peter, 48, 167
emergent values: antiracist teaching, 166–69; curricular planning, 27, 28; guest presentations, 57; historical program documents, 55; local curriculum, 55, 56, 128; mentors/mentees, 89, 128; misalignment, 153; position statements, 10, 58–59, 63, 83, 93, 132; practicum courses, 63, 64, 87, 89, 140, 208–9;

program values, 11, 13; reflective writing, 59, 89, 119, 130–31; research participants, 88, 89; ruling relations, 13, 133; sharing materials, 57–58, 89, 130; teacher development, 27, 34, 42, 54, 62, 70, 88, 127, 211; writing program administrators (WPAs), 63
emotional labor, 33, 63
English departments, 36–37, 95
epistemological exclusion, 192
equity program value, 14, 73, 74, 216n3 (chap. 4)
Espedal, Gry, 215n2 (Introduction)
evaluation systems, 35
evidence-based programs, 63, 207
exigent arguments, 8
expansion of definition of writing program value, 73, 74
expectations section in syllabus, 80–81, 158
experienced graduate teaching assistants (GTAs), 57, 200, 201, 203
experiential knowledge: coding, 112; curricular committees, 28, 99–100, 105, 107–8, 114–15, 121, 122, 134–36; graduate teaching assistants (GTAs), 65, 206–8; group discussions, 104; identification, 107; literacy scholarship, 104–5; lived experiences, 188, 193; negotiation, 209; practicum instructors, 198; programmatic change, 103, 186; reading assignments, 50; reflective writing, 119, 127, 130–31, 202; slow agency, 135; teaching practices, 172–73
experiential learning documentary (ELD) model, 205
experiential value research methodology, 18
explicit values, 11, 12–13, 73–75, 96, 136, 140, 193
Exploring Composition Studies, 48

faculty, 36, 37, 193; composition, 95; diversity, 188; professional development, 85; staffing issues, 190; teaching observation, 6; white privilege, 192; workload, 77
fatigue, 26, 47, 174
feedback; grading practices, 161–62; language differences, 167; loops, 159–60, 162, 205, 206; online teaching, 158; peer-to-peer, 89; practicum course, 40, 79, 138, 181, 197; professionalization, 78; student assignments, 175–77; teaching writing, 86; video-based teaching, 158
first semester teachers, 170
first-semester practicum course, 87
first-year writing (FYW) course: antiracist teaching, 142, 195; articulated values, 90–91; course assessment, 189; curriculum devel-

opment, 10, 65, 108, 189; enrollment, 39; feedback, 12–13; goals, 215n2 (chap. 2); institutional position, 4; labor-based grading system, 200, 208; languaging, 167, 170; nonwhite authors, 195; open-access resources, 198; pedagogy, 10; practicum revision, 35–36; programmatic teaching evaluations, 87, 124; reflective writing, 8–9, 206; syllabus revision, 12–13, 41, 43, 56, 188; teacher development, 21, 90–91, 106; teaching writing, 48–49, 118; textbooks, 74
Fiscus-Cannady, Jaclyn, 193
Fleischer, Cathy, 48, 58
flexibility, graduate teaching assistants (GTAs), 81, 176
focus group notes, 21, 41, 42, 47, 49, 50–54, 59–61, 204
Foley-Schramm, Ashton, 135–36
foregrounding, 199
formal training, 39
form revision, 6
Framework for Success in Postsecondary Writing, 10, 49, 50, 58
Freire, Paolo, 15, 48, 125
From Inquiry to Academic Writing, 48
Fullerton, Bridget, 135

Gamson, Zelda F., 125
general education composition courses, 8–9, 37, 170
genre knowledge program value, 73, 74, 77, 151
Germano, William, 66, 67, 69–70, 128
Gevers, Jeroen, 142, 152
Giroux, Henry, 125
Glenn, Cheryl, 23, 85–86, 94–95
goals and objectives, 30, 67, 215n2 (chap. 2)
Goleman, Judith, 143
Gonzales, Laura, 195
Good, Tina Lavonne, 48
Gorzelsky, Gwen, 104, 105
Grabill, Jeffrey T., 195
grading practices: assignments, 176; complete/incomplete, 12, 80; contract grading, 84, 161, 162; labor-based, 207–8; online teaching, 80, 158; practicum courses, 87, 202
Graduate Student Praxis Heuristic, 135
Graduate Students Teaching Writing: The Challenge of Middle Ground, 114
graduate teaching assistants (GTAs): administrative labor, 201–2; authority, 78, 170–71, 177–78; boundary setting, 81, 174–77; change-making, 83, 140, 156, 188–91, 193; collaboration, 206, 208; commitment, 92;

critical work, 180; curriculum design, 109, 135, 197; daily work, 186; decision-making, 178–80, 193, 197; disciplinary frameworks, 16–17, 58–59; disruption, 185; emergent values, 55, 127; experience, 65, 102, 172, 193, 199, 204, 206–8; first-semester teachers, 170; focus groups, 47, 49; interconnectedness, 209; intersectional training, 143; intuition, 114–15, 119–21; isolation, 140, 173–75; job requirements, 80–81; knowledge-making, 204; learning management systems (LMS), 52; marginalized/minoritized, 116, 192, 194; mentor/mentee relationships, 45, 53–54, 57, 65, 128–30; negotiation, 136; observation, 5–6; orientation and practicum sequence, 28, 43–45; position statements, 10, 58–59, 63, 83, 93, 132; positionality, 25, 143, 156–57, 180–81, 209; problem-solving, 154; professionalization, 76–79, 136, 138–39; program values, 141, 189, 199; reflective writing, 59, 130–31, 172, 199, 203–8; scholarship work, 28, 126; small pilot initiatives, 197–98; support, 53, 186, 191; teaching circles, 45–47; white allyship, 143; workload, 39, 41, 43, 77, 93, 141–42, 193, 209, 215n1
graduate-level practicum courses, 8–9
grant funding, 70
Grant, Adam, 184, 185, 186
Greene, Stuart, 48
Gretter, Sarah, 195
Grouling, Jennifer, 9, 68, 128, 191
group discussion: deep listening, 27; equitable speaking time, 216n3 (chap. 4); experiential knowledge, 104; home programs, 23–24; pedagogy readings, 139; practicum curriculum, 60, 140; program values, 126, 199–200, 209–10; teacher development, 199; writing process, 8
Gruber, Sibylle, 185
Guerra, Juan C., 28, 35–36, 108
guest speakers, 57, 91
guided meditations, 104–5
Guinot Varty, Nicole, 12, 26, 33, 38, 172, 198

Haas, Angela M., 195
Hairston, Maxine, 103
Halasek, Kay, 44
Halbritter, Bump, 205–6
Hammontree, D. R., 206–7
Hanlon, Aaron R., 48
Hansen, Kristine, 15–17
Hassel, Holly, 24, 64, 83, 192–93, 208–9
Hierarchy of Needs, 125

heuristic, teacher development, 92, 134–36
Hewett, Beth, 49, 52, 124, 159–60
hiring practices, 16, 76, 192
historical program documents, 21–24, 38–39, 41–43, 50–55, 60–61, 106, 203–4, 211
Hollander, Edwin, 185
home programs: curriculum, 11; disciplinary frameworks, 93; emergent shared values, 27, 88; historical program documents, 23–24, 90; marginalized/minoritized students, 188; practicum courses, 21; problem-solving, 109; project teams, 98; shared values, 20, 42; teacher development, 18, 20, 28, 29, 61, 211; values, 11, 126
hooks, bell, 48, 125
Hub (Michigan State University), 195
Huntley, Lu Ellen, 26
Hutchison, Allison, 193

IC. See intermediate composition (IC) course
identification, 10, 107
ideological goals, 154
idiosyncrasies, values, 11, 12, 34, 40, 49, 55, 62, 91, 101, 132–33, 185, 186
Illinois Urbana-Champaign (UIUC), University of, 8
implicit program values, 7, 11, 12, 74–75, 96
imposter syndrome, 115
In Our Own Voice: Graduate Students Teaching Writing, 48
inclusion, 7, 64, 73, 74, 185, 206–7
Indigenous scholars, 83
individual values, 40: antiracist teaching, 91; curricular choices, 12; experiential knowledge, 107, 114–15; institutional structures, 105; motivation, 50; practicum, 209; program values, 73, 74, 85, 91, 94–95; project teams, 105, 116; reflection, 22–23, 203; teacher development, 21–22, 93–94; textbooks, 91; writing programs, 196
inference, 103–4
informal writing program records, 34–35
inherent racism, 139
initiative-building tools, 100
innovation, power structures, 184, 185
Inoue, Asao B., 12, 116, 139, 142, 152, 165–66, 169–70, 187, 192, 209–10, 215n2 (chap. 2)
inquiry-based research program value, 73, 74
insight, writing process, 103
Institute of Race, Rhetoric, and Literacy, 84
institutional ethnographer (IE), 20, 21, 24
institutional knowledge: administration, 93; antiracist teaching, 141–46, 181–82, 194–95;

change-making efforts, 10, 25, 103, 189, 209, 210; coding, 112; collaborative workspace, 195; common practices, 105–7; curricular committees, 17, 28, 105, 107–8, 111–12, 117–18, 134–36; disregard, 23–24; diversity, 141; first-year writing (FYW), 4; historical program documents, 34, 61; labor conditions, 122, 189; language diversity, 141–46; memory, 106; practicum courses, 66, 198; problem-solving, 195; program values, 63, 64, 93–95; race, 141; slow agency, 135; social responsibility, 181–82; standard language ideologies, 164; writing programs, 7, 208
Institutional Review Board (IRB), 98, 140, 215n2 (chap. 1), 216n3 (chap. 1), 216n4 (chap. 1)
instructional videos, 78, 80
instructor autonomy, 73, 74, 93, 181, 192
instructor program values, 35, 55, 73, 74, 142, 154, 189
Intellipedia, 184
interaction program value, 7, 64
interconnectedness, 209
intermediary roles, 95
intermediate composition (IC) course: antiracist teaching, 140, 143, 153, 165–67, 181; asynchronous, 158; conferencing model, 198; critical language awareness, 191–92; curriculum design, 100–101, 140, 149–50, 166–67, 181; enrollment, 39; feedback loops, 159–60; genre analysis, 151; grading contracts, 161; in-class workshopping, 149; instructor positionality, 154; language differences, 153, 166–67; linguistic diversity, 163, 181, 191–92; online teaching, 157–63; programmatic change, 156; reading assignments, 143, 145, 151–55, 160–61, 169–70; students' needs, 175–77; syllabi, 149–50; teaching demands, 29; teaching practices, 141
international students, 142
intersectional training, 55, 143, 209
interviews, research participants, 19, 28, 68–70, 71, 72–76, 95–96, 112, 213–14
intuition: coding, 112; curricular committees, 28, 99–100, 107–8, 111–12, 119–21, 134–35; graduate teaching assistants (GTAs), 178; knowledge-making, 103–4; problem-solving, 107; programmatic change, 103, 114–15; slow agency, 135; writing process, 103–4
IRB (Institutional Review Board), 98, 140, 215n1 (chap. 2), 216n1 (chap. 3), 216n1 (chap. 4)
isolation, teaching experience, 140, 172–73

Jackson, Austin, 156
James, Eileen M., 135
jigsaw discussions, 82, 143–44, 150–52, 154, 156, 162, 165–67, 179
job insecurity, 193
John Jay College, 189
Johnson, Nan, 86
Jones, Natasha, 195
justice-oriented curriculum change, 157, 180–81

kairos, 189
Kirsch, Gesa E., 19, 23
Kitchens, Marshall, 206–7
Kleinfeld, Elizabeth, 152
knowledge domains. *See* experiential knowledge; institutional knowledge; intuition
knowledge-making, 102–4, 202, 204, 206
knowledge transfer, 8–9, 137
Koshnick, Damian, 48
Kühl, Stefan, 216n1 (chap. 5)

labor-based grading contracts, 161, 162, 200, 207–8
labor conditions, 44, 76, 91, 122, 188–91, 193, 208, 209
LaFrance, Michelle, 13, 18, 20–21, 31, 50, 65–66, 102, 109, 115, 132
language differences program value, 73, 74, 84, 141–46, 152–54, 165–67, 216n2 (chap. 4)
language of literature review, 181
language practices, 14, 164, 176, 187
languaging, 167–71
Latterell, Catherine, 4, 28
Lauer, Janice M., 103
Learner, Neal, 187
learning encounters, 87, 199, 201–3
learning management systems (LMS), 47, 52, 87, 175, 200–201
learning outcomes, 9, 92, 117, 213
Lee, Amy, 64, 65
Lerner, Neal, 10
Lessner, Steven, 48
Lidinsky, April, 48
life cycles of programmatic change, 97–98
Lindquist, Julie, 48, 205–6
linguistic diversity, 76, 140, 141, 145, 166–69, 181, 191–92, 194, 211
linguistic double-consciousness, 154
linguistic justice, 9, 26–27, 93, 142, 143, 145, 150, 163, 173, 175
Linguistic Justice: Black Language, Literacy, Identity, and Pedagogy, 145, 153, 154, 163

linguistic resources, 188
listening pedagogy, 79
literacy practices, 14, 140, 143
literacy scholarship, 104–5
literature review essay, 153
literature, culture, and media studies, 36
lived experiences. *See* experiential knowledge
LMS. *See* learning management systems (LMS)
local programs: antiracist teaching, 139; curricular development, 26–27, 105, 106; disciplinary values, 7, 10, 93; diversity, 141; idiosyncrasies, 34; individual values, 85; institutional knowledge, 106–7, 117–18; practicum courses, 87, 127, 128; professionalism, 91–93; ruling relations, 13, 133; scholarship work, 139; teaching observation process, 6; teaching writing, 56, 197; values-based program change, 27, 34, 62, 64, 76, 83, 85–86, 126, 132; writing pedagogy education (WPE), 146; writing studies, 33, 63
Loewe, Drew M., 48
Lord, Brian, 200

Macrorie, Ken, 48
Majewski, John, 48
Malenczyk, Rita, 7, 94, 187
Mapes, Aimee, 16
mapping program values, 9–10
marginalized authors, 148
marginalized theory, 51
Martin, Wanda, 52–53
Martinez, Aja Y., 145, 168
materials design, 89
Mazlow, Abraham, 125
McArdle, Casey, 52
McBeth, Mark, 189, 190
McCormick, Tim, 189, 190
McDermott, Richard, 98
McKeachie, Wilbert J., 48
McKinney Maddalena, Kate, 48
McWhorter, John, 164, 166
Medina, Carmen, 184, 185
mentor/mentee relationships: authority, 53; Black students, 194; graduate teaching assistants (GTAs), 52–54, 55, 57, 65; materials assessments, 9; non-tenure track (NTT) faculty, 109; research participants, 77; teacher development, 15, 45, 88, 89, 127, 128–30
Merriam, Sharan B., 110
Micciche, Laura, 24, 28, 35, 94, 95, 100, 101, 135
Michigan State University, 195

micro-level decision-making, 178–80, 186–87, 197–99, 208, 212
microaggressions, 142
Miller-Cochran, Susan, 7, 16
Miller, James E., 103
Miller, Susan K., 91–92
minority students, 142, 170–71
mission statements, 84, 91, 184, 194, 216n1 (chap. 5)
Mitchell, Koritha, 154, 164
Monroe, Stephen, 24, 28, 94
Moore, Kristen R., 9–10
Morris, Kristi, 70
Morton-Aiken, Jenna, 135
multi-genre projects, 3
multilingual students, 142
multimodality program value, 9, 52, 56, 73, 74, 152

Naming What We Know, 7, 48, 83, 132
negotiation: graduate students, 136; knowledge domains, 135, 209; positionality, 18; program values, 85; reading assignments, 158
New Ways in Teacher Education, 130–31
Nhat Hanh, Thich, 104
Nicholls, Kit, 66, 67, 69–70, 128
non-tenure track (NTT) faculty: assessments, 38, 109; challenges, 33; guest presentations, 57; mentoring, 109, 127, 128–30; practicum instructor role, 41; programmatic change work, 83; rhetoric, composition, and writing studies, 37; scholarship work, 28; teacher development, 38, 189–90; teaching circles, 45; union negotiations, 216n2 (chap. 3)
nonwhite authors, 195
Norgaard, Rolf, 35, 106
note-taking, 147–48

Obermark, Lauren, 44
objectivity, 11, 61, 109–10, 209
observation research method, 98–99
Oljenik, Mandy, 192
on-the-job training, 86
one-on-one conferences, 8
online teaching: classroom relationships, 160; COVID-19 pandemic, 18, 19, 38, 79–81, 140, 180–81; decision-making, 198–99; equitable speaking time, 216n3 (chap. 4); feedback, 158; feedback loops, 159–60; grading practices, 80, 158; intermediate composition (IC), 157–63; peer review, 159; practicum courses, 27, 149–50, 158–59; student engagement, 159, 174; synchronous, 159; teacher development, 33; technology, 52; time management, 149; writing instruction, 161–63
The Online Writing Conference: A Guide for Teachers and Tutors, 159–60
open-access resources, 198
open coding, 42, 70, 112
oppression, systems of, 142, 190
O'Reilly, Mary Rose, 48
orientation, 28, 35–36, 43, 44, 45, 53, 54, 60, 119–20, 130
Originals: How Non-Conformists Move the World, 184
Osorio, Ruth, 193
Ostergaard, Lori, 206–7
Otter.ai, 70, 148

Paine, Charles, 52–53
Palmer, Parker J., 48
pandemic semester, 70
Pantoja, Veronica, 91–92
paradigm shifts, 161–62
pass rates, students, 190
pedagogy: antiracist teaching, 82, 141–47, 165–66; disciplines, 3, 39; first-year writing (FYW), 10, 48–49; group discussion, 139; individual motivation, 50; linguistic justice, 154, 171; programmatic change, 24–26, 83–86, 142, 192–93; reading lists, 50; reflective writing, 131; research, 56, 126; tacit values, 11, 126; teacher development, 14–17, 67, 82, 195; theory and practice, 47, 64, 92, 139, 160; writing as a process, 3, 10. See also teaching writing
peer feedback, 8, 12–15, 58, 74, 89, 159, 174, 201–2
Performing Antiracist Pedagogy in Rhetoric, Writing, and Communication, 141
Perryman-Clark, Staci M., 117–18, 142, 143, 192
Pike, Kenneth L., 103
Pimental, Charise, 144
Pimental, Octavio, 144
Pinkert, Laurie A., 9–10
Poe, Mya, 141, 145
pop-out quotes, 152
portfolio evaluation system, 35, 80
position statements, 10, 58–59, 63, 83, 93, 127, 132
positionality: graduate teaching assistants (GTAs), 25, 143, 156–57, 180–81, 209; negotiation, 18; practicum instructors, 134; reflection, 160–61; researchers, 19, 111; white privilege, 194; writing instructors, 154
Postman, Neil, 48

Index : 239

power structures, 170–71, 184, 185
PowerPoint presentations, 158
practicum courses: assessment process, 189, 207; change-making, 186; course sequence, 43, 98, 118, 139–40; credit hours, 40, 60, 82, 119, 125, 150; curricular tokenism, 50–51; equity, 14; focus, 25; foregrounding, 199; genre knowledge, 77; grading structures, 202; historical program documents, 21, 27, 38–39, 41, 42, 50, 53–54, 59–61, 106, 117–18, 188; learning outcomes, 66, 117; limitations, 93–94; linguistic diversity, 140, 145, 173, 175; reading lists, 47–50, 58, 72, 114–15, 123–25, 133, 148; structure, 196; tacit values, 11, 126, 140; ungrading, 138
Practicum I, 18, 26, 29, 36, 37, 41, 47, 42, 48–49, 55, 56, 58–60, 122–25, 133, 158, 200–201
Practicum II, 18, 36, 37, 42, 46, 47, 49, 52, 56, 59–60, 122, 124, 137–40, 146–52, 154, 158, 172–78
practicum instructors, 41, 62, 63, 71, 95–96, 134, 146, 147, 197, 198, 213–14
practicum syllabi: antiracist teaching, 26–27, 84; curricular committee, 20, 27, 28, 108–9, 111–12, 134–36; diversity, 72, 82–83; educational theory, 99; expectations section, 80–81; feedback structure, 79; first-year writing (FYW), 12–13, 41, 43, 56; impact, 66; instructional videos, 80; language, 49–50, 65–70, 84, 200–201; learning management systems (LMS), 87; learning outcomes, 92, 117; position statements, 10, 58–59, 63, 83, 93, 127, 132; program values, 25, 28, 63, 64, 74–75, 83, 87, 88, 89, 209, 211–12, 128; reading lists, 81–83, 113, 123–25; research data, 19, 72, 87–88, 95–96; scholarship work, 126, 146; shared values, 62–63; slow agency, 135; teacher development, 113; values-driven, 65
pre-semester orientation, 38, 43, 44, 45, 54, 57, 60, 119–20, 138
problem-solving tools, 100, 107, 154
problematics, 21
procedural knowledge, 104–5, 112
productive programmatic action, 11–12
Professing and Pedagogy: Learning the Teaching of English, 14–15, 131
professional development, 4, 84, 85, 109, 138–39, 206–7
professionalization: assessment, 135; collaborative problem-solving, 78; composition teaching practicum, 91–92; graduate teaching assistants (GTAs), 76–77, 135, 136; heuristic, 135–36; local programs, 91–93; teaching observation, 77–79

program archives management, 34–35, 96, 98, 99
program values. *See* writing studies programs
programmatic change: administrative actions, 11–12; antiracist teaching, 76, 91, 140–46, 181, 194, 195; daily work, 108, 212; decision-making, 193–94; democratic methods, 192, 193; institutional reform, 10, 210; justice-oriented, 157; knowledge domains, 16, 93–95, 103, 111–16, 119–21, 207, 209; labor conditions, 122, 188–91; language diversity, 141–46; life cycles, 97–98; linguistic justice, 93, 140, 166–69, 181, 194, 211; mapping, 9; micro-level, 186–87, 212; negotiation, 85; non-tenure track (NTT) faculty, 83; power structures, 151–55, 184, 185; practicum syllabi, 28, 33–34, 88, 140, 209, 212; problem-solving, 195; shared knowing, 34; slow agency, 100; teaching evaluations, 87; tensions, 114–15, 126, 196; values-driven, 24–25, 28, 62, 64, 87, 153, 187, 208–9; writing program administrators (WPAs), 25, 64–65, 86, 94–95. *See also* teacher development
project teams, 98, 105, 116, 135
projection, collection, and recollection approach, 205–6
public research universities, 71

qualifications for teaching writing, 16–17
qualitative research. *See* data collection and analysis
qualitative viewpoints, 26
quantification of codes, 88, 89
question-asking and response, 134–35

race work, 63, 156, 185
racial justice program value. *See* antiracist teaching
Ranciere, Jacques, 138
Ratcliffe, Krista, 167
Ray, Ruth, 147
reading assignments: antiracist teaching, 143, 147, 153; classroom writing assessment, 152; composition pedagogy, 47; disciplinary, 151; experiential knowledge, 50, 122; first-year writing (FYW), 49; intermediate composition (IC), 161, 169–70; jigsaw discussions, 82; language knowledge, 152, 153; learning management systems (LMS), 47; linguistic justice, 143, 145; multimodality, 56, 152; online teaching, 158–59; practicum courses, 48–49, 50, 58, 60, 72, 81–83, 123–25, 137, 139–40, 148, 150, 156–57; scholarly writing,

151, 152; subject matter, 160–61; time limitations, 82–83
reading outside, 183, 211–12
Reading to Learn and Writing to Teach: Literacy Strategies for Online Writing Instruction, 49, 52, 124
reciprocal engagement/learning, 6, 57, 194, 200
reflection model, 143
reflection program value, 8–9, 20, 22–24, 45, 74, 147, 151, 160–61, 170, 202–7
reflective writing: assessment process, 206–7; decision-making, 172, 208; first-year writing (FYW), 8–9, 206; graduate teaching assistants (GTAs), 59, 119, 199, 203–8; knowledge transfer, 8–9; slow agency, 94; teacher development, 15, 127, 130–31, 201, 202; teaching observation, 6, 194; teaching writing, 88, 89
Reformers, Teachers, Writers: Curricular and Pedagogical Inquiries, 10
Reid, E. Shelley, 114
relationship-building, 69, 172–75
remote teaching and learning. *See* online teaching
research methodology, 18, 21
research methods. *See* data collection and analysis
research participants: anonymity, 71–72, 111; contextual influences, 18–19; curricular subcommittee, 26–27, 98–99; data collection and analysis, 29, 216n3 (chap. 4); demographic, 149; emergent values, 89; graduate teaching assistants (GTAs), 29; interviews, 28, 70, 72–76; mentor teachers, 77; observation, 109–10; positionality, 111; practicum courses, 148; professional goals, 86; program values, 72–73; proposals, 8, 98; relationship-building, 69; work, 18, 22–25, 67, 91, 144, 205–6; writing program administrators (WPAs), 68–69, 71, 95–97
research program value, 73, 74
research-based teaching practices, 207
Researching Values: Methodological Approaches for Understanding Values Work in Organisations and Leadership, 215n2 (Introduction)
Restaino, Jessica, 114, 141, 180, 186, 204
retention rates, students, 38, 190
revision process of writing program values, 22, 24, 73, 74, 140, 188, 193–94, 200, 214
A Rhetoric for Writing Program Administrators, 94
rhetoric, composition, and writing studies, 7, 8, 36, 37, 48–49, 55, 64, 67–69, 71, 89, 110, 113, 216n2 (chap. 3)
rhetorical flexibility, 73, 74, 81, 83

rhetorical listening, 167–69, 171
rhetorical nature, 161
Rice, Jeff, 39
Ritter, Kelly, 8, 30, 35, 48, 142, 187
Rodrigo, Rochelle, 91–92
Roen, Duane, 91–92
Rose, Shirley K., 33–35
Royster, Jacqueline Jones, 19, 23
ruling relations, workplaces, 13, 132, 133
Russell, Clare, 50, 51, 145–46

Saldaña, Johnny, 42
Salinas, Omar, 216n3 (chap. 4)
Sanchez, James Chase, 195
scaffolding, 58, 77, 81, 129, 131, 185
scholarship work: antiracist teaching, 82, 145, 169; artifacts, 19; composition teaching practicum, 141; critical language awareness, 146; discourse communities, 149; graduate teaching assistants (GTAs), 28, 36; grant funding, 70; Institutional Review Board (IRB), 215n1 (chap. 2), 216n1 (chap. 3), 216n1 (chap. 4); knowledge domains, 100, 103, 104; local programs, 17, 34, 139; non-tenure track (NTT) faculty, 28; practicum course, 16, 19, 25, 28, 109, 141, 146, 149; social justice issues, 140, 146; teacher development, 34, 54, 62, 67, 81, 90, 139–40; values-based action, 26; writing programs, 29, 63, 81, 86, 98–99, 125, 145, 151, 165, 189, 216n2 (chap. 4)
Schwaller, Emily Jo, 36
Seitz, David, 48
self-training, writing program administrators (WPAs), 94
semi-structured interviews, 19, 28, 68–70, 71, 72–76, 95–96, 112, 213–14
senior graduate teaching assistants (GTAs), 52–54, 57
sexism, 116, 156
shared program values. *See* teacher development; writing studies programs
sharing of materials, 88, 89, 127, 130
Shelton, Cecelia, 154, 155
Shipka, Jody, 48, 56
Shor, Ira, 48, 125
siloing, 174
Sinek, Simon, 215n3 (Introduction)
The Skillful Teacher, 48
Skogsberg, Erik, 195
Slinkard, Jennifer, 142, 152
SLOs (student learning objectives), 8
slow agency: curriculum design, 100–101; decision-making, 35; knowledge domains, 111–15, 119–21; reflective practice, 24, 94;

teacher development, 28; writing program administrators (WPAs), 35, 99, 100, 135
Smagorinsky, Peter, 105–6
small pilot initiatives, 197–98
Smith, Michael W., 105–6
Smith, Nicole Boudreau, 145
Smitherman, Geneva, 145, 156
Snyder, William M., 98
social constructivism, 125
social-justice teaching, 26–27, 142–47, 150, 153, 173, 175, 181–82
staffing issues, 189, 190
standard language ideologies, 153, 163–66, 211
Stenberg, Shari J., 5, 14–15, 22, 48, 65, 131, 200, 203
Straayer, Bree, 205
strategic contemplation, 20, 22–23
Strickland, Donna, 92, 95
student learning objectives (SLOs), 8
students: agency, 167–68; authority tension, 177–78; colorblind teaching practice, 144; data collection and analysis, 148; diversity, 141, 142, 188; engagement, 159, 170–75; expectations, 158; feedback, 86, 206; goals, 64; language practices, 176; learning experiences, 205; minoritized, 170–71; one-on-one conferences, 8; practicum syllabi, 87; reflective writing, 205; retention rates, 38, 190; success initiative, 39
subject matter, 145, 160–61
subjectivity, 18, 19, 23–24, 134–35, 143
support for graduate teaching assistants (GTAs), 53, 191
Susak, Chris, 149
sustainability of program values, 4–5, 8, 25, 29, 31, 34–35, 60, 63, 64, 101, 137, 145, 187–88, 193, 212
syllabus design. *See* practicum syllabi
synchronous learning, 44, 52, 98, 110, 150, 152, 159, 163
Syracuse University, 35

tacit values, 11, 12, 126, 136, 140
The Talk and Texts of Teacher Development: Values, the Practicum, and Programmatic Change in Writing Studies, 25
task-oriented learning perspective, 117, 161
teacher development: collaboration, 15, 44, 58, 201, 202, 209; disciplinary frameworks, 4, 5, 14–15, 50, 99, 149; emergent values, 27, 28, 34, 42, 54, 55, 62, 70, 88, 127, 140, 208–9, 211; experience, 65, 69–70, 102, 172–73, 179–80, 199, 204; formal training, 39; group discussions, 140, 199; individual values, 21–22, 91,
93–94; intersectional training, 143; learning encounters, 201–3; lifelong process, 14–15; mentors/mentees, 15, 40, 45, 128–30; mission statements, 184; non-tenure track (NTT) faculty, 38, 189–90; portfolios, 74; position statements, 10, 58–59, 63, 83, 93, 132; program values, 5, 6, 16, 28, 31, 33–34, 140, 196, 199; reading outside, 183; reflective writing, 15, 22–23, 119, 130–31, 201, 204; shared values, 27, 30, 36, 64, 89–91, 93–94, 209–11; social justice issues, 145–47, 173, 175, 181–82, 212; teaching circles, 45–47, 57, 60; teaching observation forms, 5–9, 18, 30, 38, 77–79, 193–94; time limitations, 146, 205; workshops, 32, 44, 149
teacher disposition, 145
teacher research study, 140, 141, 147
teacher-learner roles, 177–79, 181
teaching assistants (TAs). *See* graduate teaching assistants (GTAs)
teaching practicum courses. *See* practicum courses
Teaching Tips, 48
teaching writing: accessibility, 92; antiracist teaching, 138, 140, 145–47, 175; belonging, 4; challenging topics, 50–51; composition pedagogy, 36, 48–49; COVID-19 pandemic, 41, 79–81, 161–62; feedback, 12–13, 86, 206; knowledge domains, 115–18, 121, 122, 123, 172; local programs, 20, 26, 28, 56–57, 106, 128, 197; negotiation, 209; online teaching, 30, 33, 180–81; paradigm shifts, 161–62; professional development, 3, 91–92; qualifications, 16–17; reflective writing, 88, 89, 119, 127, 130–31; relationship-building, 173–75; rhetorical listening, 171; scaffolding, 58, 77, 81, 129, 131, 185; scholarship, 81, 126; support, 212; teaching labor, 92, 93, 188; teaching practices, 11, 144; technology, 51–52; variability, 36; "Wayne way," 55, 56, 58, 106, 128, 133
technical and professional writing, 36, 39, 44, 67, 138
technological teaching tools, 51–52, 78, 79, 80, 195
tenure-line faculty, 37, 38, 41, 108, 188
textbooks, 74, 87, 91
theoretical concepts, 7, 16, 47, 152
"This Ain't Another Statement! This Is a DEMAND for Black Linguistic Justice!," 76, 93
threshold concepts, 7, 10, 11, 16, 48
time management, 63, 82–83, 98, 101, 146, 149–50, 172, 205

Tobin, Lad, 48
Torok, Joe, 5, 8, 30, 57, 193–94
transcripts, research data, 19, 21, 28–29, 49, 70, 77, 90, 95, 98, 103, 107, 110–12, 126, 134, 148, 165
Transformations: Change Work Across Writing Programs, Pedagogies, and Practices, 24, 83, 192
transparency, 80, 95, 125, 157, 162, 171
trauma-informed pedagogy, 82, 84

undergraduate programs, 8, 36–37, 39, 185
Understanding Rhetoric, 49
union negotiations, 216n2 (chap. 3)
unit plans, 56, 127, 197
universities: administration, 100; diversity, 38, 96, 122, 123, 164, 166, 188; equity, 14; financial demands, 189; local values, 8, 20; orientation policies, 43–44, 119–20, 130; student retention rate, 190; urgent agency, 24, 28, 94
use value, threshold concepts, 7

values and practices document, 13–14
values-driven change work, 7–11, 25, 65, 72–76, 86, 87, 93, 108, 184, 187, 188, 208–9
video recordings of research participants, 147–48
video-based teaching demonstrations, 158
Vieira, Kate, 145, 152
voice, curriculum, 216n2 (chap. 4)

Wallis, Jule, 45
Wardle, Elizabeth, 7, 10, 48, 64, 92, 132, 197, 210–11
Warshauer, Leanne B., 48
Wayne State University, 43, 108, 123, 127, 170
"Wayne way," 55, 56, 58, 106, 128, 133
Weingartner, Charles, 48
Weiser, Irwin, 53
Wenger, Etienne, 97, 98, 101, 102
What the Best College Teachers Do, 48
white allyship, 143, 188, 194
white papers, 21, 36, 41–46, 52, 54, 56, 60–61, 203–4
white privilege, 116, 144, 192, 194, 195
white supremacist literacy standards, 14, 30, 93, 115–16, 142–45, 149, 166–67, 188, 209
White, Edward M., 48
Wible, Scott, 194
working conditions program value, 73, 74, 77, 93, 142
working through, 21, 42, 59, 129, 154, 169, 179, 209, 212

workload, 32, 39, 41, 63, 77, 92, 93, 141, 175–77, 189, 190, 215n1 (chap. 1)
workshops, 32, 38, 44, 45, 53, 67, 92, 149–50, 185
WPAing in a Pandemic and Beyond: Revision, Innovation, and Advocacy, 26
WPAs. *See* writing program administrators (WPAs)
writing instructors. *See* teaching writing
writing pedagogy education (WPE), 67–68, 146
writing process, 8, 73, 74, 103–4, 149
writing program administrators (WPAs): administration labor, 62, 95, 186; bullying, 117–18, 143; challenges, 32; decision-making, 193; expectations, 96; faculty of color, 63, 192; group discussions, 27; knowledge domains, 10, 111–12, 114–15, 119–21, 135; labor conditions, 76, 86, 188–89; learning outcomes, 117, 213; mentorships, 89; program values, 27, 64–65, 94–95, 211–14; reflective practice, 24; research participants, 68–70, 71, 83, 95–96; slow/urgent agency, 35, 94, 100; workload, 63, 77
writing studies programs research, 5–7, 29, 68–69, 72–73, 86, 185, 188, 206–7
writing studies programs: core values, 20, 25–26, 73–74; definition, 215n1 (Introduction); digital literacy, 39; discourse, 193; diversity, 142, 194; frameworks, 63–64; group discussions, 199–200, 209–10; individual values, 40, 74, 85, 91, 94–95, 196; informal records, 34–35; institutional knowledge, 7, 117–18, 122–23, 208; intersection, 55; labor conditions, 91, 189; lived experience, 188; local programs, 27, 34, 62, 76, 85, 127, 128; mapping, 9–10; mission statements, 84, 216n1 (chap. 5); policies, 33; priorities, 96; professionalization, 76–79; project teams, 98, 116; reading outside, 211–12; recommendations, 137; ruling relations, 13, 133; values, articulation of, 11, 12–14, 30, 36, 60, 61, 64, 73, 74–75, 108, 126, 156, 193–94, 207. *See also* emergent values; programmatic change
writing-about-writing program value, 10, 73, 74
written reflection. *See* reflective writing

Yancey, Kathleen Blake, 7, 48, 56, 92
Young, Richard E., 103, 169–70
Young, Vershawn Ashanti, 141

Zepernick, Janet, 48
Zoom, 47, 69, 71, 72, 140, 147–50, 152, 156, 158, 163, 172

About the Author

Adrienne Jankens is assistant professor of rhetoric and writing studies in the English Department at Wayne State University, where she has been awarded the President's Award for Excellence in Teaching (2020), the General Education Teaching Award (2021), and the College of Liberal Arts and Sciences Excellence in Teaching Award (2024).